34

3400 WORLD'S WORST JOKES RIDDLES & PUNS

3 VOLUMES IN ONE

EDITED BY

HELEN HOKE & JOSEPH LEEMING

Bell Publishing Company • New York

This 1982 edition is published by Bell Publishing Company, distributed by Crown Publishers, Inc., by arrangement with Franklin Watts, Inc.

Manufactured in the United States of America

Library of Congress Cataloging in Publication Data
Jokes, riddles, puns.
 3400 world's worst jokes, riddles, and puns.

 Reprint. Originally published: Jokes, riddles, puns. New York : Watts, [1959]
 Contains three previously published works: Joke, jokes, jokes, and Puns, puns, puns, selected by Helen Hoke, and Riddles, riddles, riddles, selected by Joseph Leeming.
 1. American wit and humor. 2. Puns and punning. 3. Riddles. I. Hoke, Helen, 1903- II. Leeming, Joseph, 1897-1968.   III. Title. IV. Title: Thirty four hundred world's worst jokes, riddles, and puns.
PN6162.J63 1982   808.88′2   82-9483
                                  AACR2
ISBN: 0-517-38695X
h g f e d c b a

CONTENTS

JOKES, JOKES, JOKES

PUNS, PUNS, PUNS

RIDDLES, RIDDLES, RIDDLES

Jokes, Jokes, Jokes

Edited by HELEN HOKE

Illustrated by

RICHARD ERDOES

Absent-Minded Antics

ABSENT-MINDED PROFESSOR: "Lady, what are you doing in my bed?"

LADY: "Well, I like this bed, I like this neighborhood, I like this house, and I like this room. And anyway, I'm your wife!"

A farmer who was on his way home from market had the feeling that he had forgotten something; but what it was he couldn't figure out.

As he neared home this conviction increased to such a degree that he stopped his horses two or three times, scratched his head in perplexity, and tried to recall what he had forgotten, but in vain.

At last he reached home and was met by his daughter, who looked at him in surprise and cried, "Why Father, what have you done with Mother?"

•

Did you hear about the absent-minded professor who:

Returned from lunch and saw a sign on his door, "Back in 30 minutes," and sat down to wait for himself?

Slammed his wife and kissed the door?

Got up and struck a match to see if he had blown out the candle?

•

The absent-minded professor had been married only a short time. One evening upon arriving home at his usual time, he found his wife acting cool toward him.

"What is the matter, dear?" he asked worriedly.

"Well George, you didn't kiss me when you left this morning," she said.

"Oh, darling," he said in wonderment. "Then who *was* it that I kissed?"

Did you hear about the absent-minded professor who held an egg in his hand and boiled his watch?

●

"Where is the car?" demanded Mrs. Stevenson, as her husband came up the front steps.

"Dear me!" exclaimed Professor Stevenson. "Did I take the car out?"

"You certainly did. You drove it to town."

"How odd! I remember now that after I got out I turned around to thank the gentleman who gave me the lift and wondered where he had gone."

●

Two absent-minded professors were driving home in an automobile.

"Say," one said, "be sure to turn out for that bridge that's coming down the road toward us."

"What do you mean, *me* turn out?" the other said, surprised. "I thought *you* were driving."

●

The absent-minded professor staggered from a train, his complexion very white.

"Riding backwards for ten hours," he explained. "I never could stand that."

"Why," his wife inquired, "didn't you ask the person sitting opposite to change seats with you?"

"I couldn't do that," said the professor. "There wasn't anybody there."

5

Did you hear about the absent-minded professor who fell overboard and forgot he could swim?

●

The phone rang about 2 A.M. and the absent-minded professor answered it. "Hello," he said.

THE VOICE: "Is this Dexter eleven eleven?"

PROFESSOR: "No, this is Dexter one one one one."

THE VOICE: "Oh—I am sorry to have bothered you!"

PROFESSOR: "It's quite all right. I had to get up to answer the phone anyhow."

G. I. Jibes

The farmer watched the paratroop maneuvers with evident interest. Finally, one of the paratroopers landed in a tree near by. The farmer watched the soldier as he cut himself away from his harness and scrambled down.

"Boy," said the G.I., "that was something."

"Sure was," drawled the farmer. "First time I ever did see a man climb down a tree without climbing up first."

SUPPLY OFFICER: "Does the new uniform fit you?"
RECRUIT: "The jacket isn't bad, sir, but the trousers are a little loose around the armpits."

●

SOLDIER SAM: "Don't bother me. I am writing to my girl."
SOLDIER DAN: "But why are you writing so slowly?"
SOLDIER SAM: "She can't read very fast."

●

GUARD: "Halt! You can't go in there."
PRIVATE: "Why not?"
GUARD: "Because it's the General's tent."
PRIVATE: "Then what's it doing with that big sign 'PRIVATE' on the door?"

●

ADMITTING OFFICER (examining recruit): "Have you any scars on you?"
RECRUIT: "No, sir, but I can give you a cigarette."

●

The soldier was a mess. His trousers were covered with mud and stains. As he was walking along the company street with a pail, an officer stopped him.

> "Just where do you think *you're* going, soldier?"
> "To get some water," was the reply.
> "In those trousers?"
> "Don't be silly, sergeant," replied the G.I. "In the pail."

Young Tom told his father that when he grew up, he wanted to drive a big army tank.

"Well, Son," said his dad, "if that's what you want to do, I certainly won't stand in your way."

•

"Without a doubt, you're the stupidest guy in the service," roared the officer.

"Can't help it," replied the recruit. "I was born that way."

"All right, just answer me two simple questions," continued the officer. "First—what would happen if one of your ears were shot off?"

"That's easy, sir," replied the G.I. "I wouldn't be able to hear."

"Okay," said the irritated officer. "Next—then what would happen if *both* your ears were shot off?"

"Then I couldn't *see*," answered the recruit promptly.

"What do you mean, you couldn't *see*?" the officer yelled.

"Well, sir," explained the G.I., "if my ears was both shot off, my helmet would slide down over my eyes."

•

GENERAL, on inspection tour: "Why do you keep scratching yourself?"

PRIVATE: "I'm the only one who knows where it itches, sir."

RECRUIT: "Shall I mark time with my feet, sir?"
SERGEANT, sarcastically: "My good man, did you
ever hear of marking time with your hands?"
RECRUIT: "Yes, sir! Clocks do it."

●

BOASTFUL SOLDIER, at a party: "The bullet struck
my head and went careening into space."
BORED FRIEND: "You're being honest about it, anyway."

●

HANK: "They tell me when I'm in the saddle I'm a
part of the horse."
YANK: "Yes, but did they tell you what part?"

●

What did the drum say to the drummer boy?

If you beat me, I'll call out the troops.

School
Daze

BIG BROTHER: "Well, Joe, how do you like school?"
JOE: "Closed!"

•

TEACHER: "You can be sure that if Moses were alive today, he'd be considered a remarkable man."
LENNY: "He sure ought to be, he'd be more than 2,500 years old."

A small boy went to a school picnic, but it hardly met his expectations. He was stung by a bee; he fell into a creek; a little girl pulled his hair; he got badly sunburned. As he arrived home, limping and with torn and muddy clothes, his mother greeted him and asked, "Well, Son, what kind of time did you have at the picnic?"

"Mom," Sonny replied slowly, "I'm so glad I'm back, I'm glad I went."

•

TEACHER: "Yes, Sammy, what is it?"

SAMMY: "I don't want to scare you, but Pop said if I didn't get better grades, someone is due for a licking."

•

"What's the difference between a freshman and a senior?"

"Well, a freshman knows what he wants, and a senior knows he can't have it."

•

VISITOR: "What's your boy going to be when he finishes his education?"

DISCOURAGED PARENT: "An octogenarian, I think."

•

TEACHER: "How many sexes are there?"

SAMMY: "Three."

TEACHER: "Three! Can you name them?"

SAMMY: "Male sex, female sex, and insex!"

12

The teacher was trying to impress upon her students the advantages of peace. "How many of you young people object to war?" she asked. Up went several hands.

"Sammy, will you tell the class why you object to war?"

"Because wars make history," replied Sammy promptly.

•

TEACHER, to tardy student: "Why are you late?"

BARRY: "Well, a sign down the street said—"

TEACHER, interrupting: "Now what can a *sign* possibly have to do with it?"

BARRY: "The sign said: 'School ahead; go slow.'"

•

TEACHER: "Paul, can you tell me the name of an animal that travels great distances?"

PAUL: "Yes. A goldfish. It travels around the globe."

TEACHER: "Name five things that contain milk."
BARRY: "Butter, cheese, ice cream, and—and—two cows."

●

TEACHER, brightly: "As we walk out-of-doors on a cold winter's morning and look about us, what do we see on every hand?"
SECOND-GRADERS, in unison: "Gloves!"

●

GEORGIE: "Teacher, would you scold anybody for something they didn't do?"
TEACHER: "Of course not. But why, Georgie?"
GEORGIE: "Well, I didn't do my arithmetic!"

●

TEACHER: "That's a comet."
LITTLE EDDIE: "A what?"
TEACHER: "A comet. *You* know what a comet is?"
LITTLE EDDIE: "No."
TEACHER: "Don't you know what they call a star with a tail?"
LITTLE EDDIE: "Sure—Mickey Mouse."

●

TEACHER: "What are the people of New York noted for?"
CHARLIE: "For their stupidity."
TEACHER: "Where ever did you get *that* idea?"
CHARLIE: "It says here in this book that the population of New York is very dense."

Little Betty was crying bitterly. Teacher asked what was the matter.

BETTY: "Oooh! My new shoes *hurt* me!"

"Well, no wonder," explained Teacher, "you have them on the wrong feet."

But Betty kept right on crying. "I *haven't* any other feet!" she cried.

●

TEACHER: "Jasper, I can scarcely read your handwriting. You *must* learn to write more clearly."

KID: "Aw, what's the use? If I wrote any better, you'd start complaining about my spelling!"

●

TEACHER: "Name three collective nouns."

HORACE: "Fly-paper, waste-basket, and vacuumcleaner."

One rainy day poor Miss Kindergarten Teacher spent over a half hour pulling galoshes onto wet little feet, getting the children ready to go home. When she came to little Johnny, his galoshes took several minutes to struggle him into. Finally they were on.

"Thank you, Teacher," said Johnny. "You know, Teacher, these galoshes aren't mine."
Poor teacher groaned, sat Johnny down again, and pulled and pulled until his galoshes came off again. "Now then," she asked patiently, "whom *do* these belong to?"

"My brother," explained Johnny. "But my mother makes me wear them anyhow."

•

"Are your mother and father in?" asked the visiting teacher of young Billy, who opened the door.

"They *was* in," he explained, "but they is out just now."

"They *was* in. They *is* out. Shame on you! Where's your grammar?"

"She's gone to the store," explained Billy, "for some cat meat."

•

TEACHER (answering the phone): "You say George Gage has a bad cold and can't come to school? Who is this speaking?"
VOICE (with assumed hoarseness): "This is my father."

ARITHMETIC TEACHER: "If I gave you two apples and told you to give one to your brother, would you give him the little one or the big one?"

GEORGIE: "Do you mean my *little* brother, or my *big* brother?"

•

FRESHMAN: "But I don't think I deserve a zero on this paper."

PROFESSOR: "Neither do I, but it's the lowest mark I can give you."

•

SAMMY: "Do you think anyone can predict the future with cards?"

DANNY: "My mother can. She takes one look at my report cards, then tells me exactly what will happen when my dad gets home."

•

BIGGER BOY: "What are you doing with a pencil and paper?"

LITTLE BOY: "I'm writing a letter to my brother."

BIGGER BOY: "Who're you kidding? You know you don't know how to write."

LITTLE BOY: "Sure, but my brother doesn't know how to read, either."

•

TEACHER (teaching the alphabet): "What comes after *O*?"

DOPEY: "Yeah!"

How many books can you put into an empty school bag?

> *One, because after that is in, the bag won't be empty.*

●

TEACHER: "Tell me the truth now, who really did your homework?"

JOHNNIE: "My father."

TEACHER: "All alone?"

JOHNNIE: "No, I helped him with it!"

●

BOASTFUL COLLEGE COUSIN: "I'm taking three courses in college: French, Spanish, and algebra."

HIGH SCHOOL COUSIN: "Okay—let me hear you say good evening in algebra."

●

TEACHER: "What do hippopotamuses have that no other animals have?"

JACKIE: "Little hippopotamuses."

GEORGIE: "What part of the body is the fray?"

TEACHER: "What part of the body is the fray? What are you talking about?"

GEORGIE: "Well, right here in the history book it says—the general was shot in the thick of the fray."

●

"I guess I've lost another pupil," said the professor as his glass eye rolled down the kitchen sink.

●

TEACHER: "This composition on 'Our Cat' is, word for word, the same as your brother's."

TOMMY: "Yes, ma'am, it's the same cat."

●

GEORGE: "I want to buy a pencil."

CLERK: "Hard or soft?"

GEORGE: "Hard. It's for a stiff exam."

●

The teacher had been reading to her class about the rhinoceros family. "Now name some things," she said, "that are very dangerous to get near to, and that have horns."

"Automobiles," promptly answered Lenny.

TEACHER: "If we breathe oxygen in the daytime, what do we breathe at night?"
GRACIE: "Why, nitrogen, of course!"

•

TEACHER: "Explain the manners and customs of the natives of Borneo."
PUPIL: "They ain't got no manners and they don't wear no customs."

•

Exam question: "What's the best way to prevent infection caused by biting insects?"
DOPEY's answer: "Don't bite any."

•

A tutor who tooted a flute
Tried to teach two young tooters to toot.
    Said the two to the tutor,
    "Is it harder to toot, or
To tutor two tooters to toot?"

TEACHER: "Why are you late, George?"

GEORGE: "Sorry, Teacher. It was late when I started from home."

TEACHER: "Then why didn't you start early?"

GEORGE: "But Teacher—by that time it was too late to start early."

●

PAUL, about the new boy in the class: "His name is George, but we call him Flannel."

SAUL: "His name is George, but you call him Flannel? I suppose you call him Flannel for short?"

PAUL: "No, because he shrinks from washing."

●

TEACHER: "Kitty, what would you do if a man-eating tiger were chasing you?"

KITTY: "Nothing—'cause I'm a girl!"

●

TEACHER: "If you have ten potatoes and must divide them equally among seven persons, how would you do it?"

SAMMY: "I'd mash them."

●

Little Peter came home from school and said to his mother,

"Our teacher is really dumb. For four days she has asked us how much is two and two. We told her it was four. But she still doesn't know it; this morning she asked again."

A teacher called for sentences using the word "beans."

"My father grows beans," said the bright boy of the class.

"My mother cooks beans," said another pupil.

Then a third popped up: "We are all human beans."

●

TEACHER: "At your age I could name all the Presidents—and in the proper order."

BOBBY: "Yes, but there were only three or four of them then."

Pun Points

WOMAN (opening door of a refrigerator and finding a rabbit inside): "What are you doing there?"

RABBIT: "This is a Westinghouse, isn't it?"

WOMAN: "Yes."

RABBIT: "Well, I'm just westing."

LAWYER: "When they tried him the judge let him go free."

FRIEND: "Why?"

LAWYER: "The robber was deaf."

FRIEND: "What has that got to do with it?"

LAWYER: "Well, don't you know that you can't convict a man without a hearing?"

•

ANDY: "Al is the first person you learn about when you go to school."

SANDY: "Al who?"

ANDY: "Alphabet."

•

Mama Gnu was waiting for Papa Gnu as he came home for dinner one evening. "Our little boy was very bad today," she declared. "I want you to punish him."

"Oh, no," said Papa Gnu. "I won't punish him. You'll have to learn to paddle your own gnu."

•

"There's a hair in my coke," complained the teenager.

"That's quite possible," retorted the soda jerk. "I just finished shaving the ice."

•

If you put three ducks into a crate, what would you have?

A box of quackers.

The Eskimo was telling a story while sitting on a cake of ice. He finished. "Well, my tale is told," he lisped, as he stood up with his back to the fire.

•

HUGHIE: "Gee, I'd like to meet that swell-looking girl over there. Who is she, anyway?"
LOUIE: "Oh, she belongs to the Nodding Club."
HUGHIE: "What's that?"
LOUIE: "Nodding doing."

•

BABY EAR OF CORN: "Mamma, where did I come from?"
MAMMA EAR OF CORN: "Hush, darling, the stalk brought you."

•

TEACHER: "Give me a sentence with the word 'vermin' in it."
DOPEY: "Before I go fishin' I go vermin'."

•

LITTLE ROBBIE: "Doctor, I've just been bit by a dog."
DOCTOR: "Well, was he a rabid dog?"
LITTLE ROBBIE: "No sir, doctor. He was just a plain old bird dog."

•

PAUL: "What kind of cake is that?"
MOM: "It's marble cake. Want a piece?"
PAUL: "No, I'll just take it for granite."

25

GARAGE MECHANIC: "The horn on your car must be broken."
MOTORIST: "No, it's just indifferent."
MECHANIC: "What do you mean, indifferent."
MOTORIST: "It just doesn't give a hoot."

•

Sign on a Japanese bakery wagon in Yokohama:

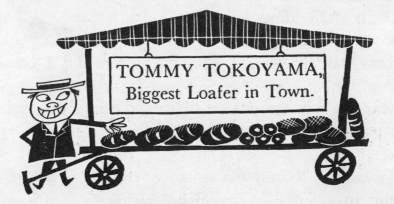

TOMMY TOKOYAMA,
Biggest Loafer in Town.

DOLLY: "What are you doing with your socks on inside out?"
MOLLY: "My feet got too hot, so I turned the hose on them."

•

You tell 'em, Butcher . . . you've got lots of tongue!

•

HABERDASHER'S CLERK: "These are especially strong shirts, madam. They simply laugh at the laundry."
CUSTOMER: "No, thank you! I know that kind; I had some which came back with their sides split."

 26

DOPE: "Do you know who owned the smallest radio in the world?"

DUNCE: "No, who owned the smallest radio in the world?"

DOPE: "Paul Revere—he broadcast from one plug."

•

MEDIEVAL MAMMA: "Hast Sir Knight ast ye for thy hand in wedlock?"

DAUGHTER: "Not yet, Mamma, but the knight is young."

•

FIRST CANNIBAL: "Am I late for chow?"

SECOND CANNIBAL: "Yes, everybody's eaten."

•

Why shouldn't a doctor be seasick?

Because he is accustomed to see sickness.

•

Why does an Indian wear feathers?

To keep his wigwam.

•

RONNIE: "I see in the paper that a guy ate six dozen pancakes."

JOHNNIE: "Oh, how waffle!"

•

HORACE: "What would a cannibal be who ate his mother's sister?"

MORRIS: "I'll bite—what?"

HORACE: "An aunt-eater, of course."

27 😊

TEACHER: "Thomas, construct a sentence using the word 'archaic'."

TOMMY: "We can't have archaic and eat it, too."

●

"I guess your brother was pleased when he found himself the father of twin boys," said one neighbor to another when they met on the bus.

"Was he! He went around grinning from heir to heir."

Pal
Patter

LEADER OF THE GANG: "I'll give you to understand my father is a big man. He's a Lion, a Moose, and an Elk."

ONE OF THE GANG: "Gee—how much does it cost to see him?"

●

BUSTER: "That your dog?"

RUSTY: "Yes, he used to be a pointer but my mother spoiled him."

BUSTER: "How?"

RUSTY: "She taught him it wasn't polite to point."

PAUL: "That cake you're eating looks good."

SAUL: "It *is* good."

PAUL: "It makes my mouth water."

SAUL: "To show you what a good guy I am, here's a blotter."

●

LITTLE HARRY: "I don't like what you said and I'll give you five minutes to take it back!"

BIG BARRY: "Yeah, and what if I *don't* take it back in five minutes?"

LITTLE HARRY: "Well, then I'll give you longer."

●

COLLEGE FRESHMAN: "Had a tough time raising this mustache."

COLLEGE SOPHOMORE: "Well, crops are bad everywhere this year."

●

HUGHIE: "Hey! Why are you wearing my raincoat?"

LOUIE: "You wouldn't want your best suit to get wet, would you?"

●

RANDY: "Did you fill in that blank yet?"

ANDY: "What blank?"

RANDY: "The one between your ears."

●

RANDY: "What would you do if you were in my shoes?"

SANDY: "Polish them!"

30

Farmer Fare

They walked down the lane together,
the sky was covered with stars;
They reached the gate in silence,
he lifted down the bars.
She raised her brown eyes to him,
there's nothing between them now;
For he was just a farmer's boy,
and she—a Jersey cow!

31

FARMER, to deaf hired man: "Abner, where's that mule I told you to take out and have shod?"

NEW HAND: "Did you say 'shod'? *I* thought you said '*shot*'. I've just been buryin' her."

●

A farmer was walking down Main Street when he saw a sign over a plumbing supply store. It said, CAST IRON SINKS.

"By Jiminy!" he said. "Anyone knows that!"

●

A farmer's wife shipped a crate of eggs to a wholesale house in a city, but before doing so she wrote on one of the eggs: "I got 5 cents for this egg. What did you pay for it?"—to which she signed her name and address.

Months later she received a letter from an actor, on very fancy stationery.

"My dear Madam," he wrote, "while playing the lead in a Shakespearean play recently, I received your egg for nothing."

●

Young Philip had just come back from an agricultural college. He was showing off to the neighboring farmer. "Your farming methods are so old-fashioned," he said. "Why, I bet you don't get ten pounds of apples from that tree."

"I daresay you're right," said Farmer Putney. "That there's a pear tree."

Mom and Pop Potter went to the big city. In an antique shop they saw a Swiss cuckoo clock. They stood and watched it for a half hour, while the shop owner turned it back and forth to make it cuckoo. Finally Pop Potter asked the price.

"Fifty-two dollars."

"We'll think it over," Pop told the owner, and thanked him for his kindness.

Several months later, Pop Potter had gathered together enough money to buy the cuckoo clock, and he sent to the city for it, as a surprise present for Mom Potter's birthday.

A big package came—right on the very day of Mom Potter's birthday—and they had the time of their lives with it. Every hour and half-hour, on the minute, they rushed in from their work around the farm, to see and listen to the cuckoo speak.

That night in bed, Pop Potter listened, along with Mom, till two o'clock, then was so sleepy he couldn't stay awake any longer.

At three A.M., suddenly the cuckoo clock made a sort of whirring sound, the cuckoo rushed out and cuckoo'd once, twice, seven times—then, finally, eighteen times!

"Wake up! Wake up!" shouted Mom Potter, as she shook Pop Potter violently. "Wake up and *do* something, Pa! It's later than I ever knowed it to be before!"

A stingy farmer was reproving his hired man for carrying a lantern to go calling on his best girl.

"Why, when I was courtin' I didn't need to carry a lantern," he said.

"Yeah—and look what *you* got," the hired man retorted.

●

The embarrassed city hostess said to her country cousin: "I thought I suggested you come after supper."

"Right," said the country cousin, "that *is* what I came after."

●

FARMER BOY: "My Pop can't decide whether to get a new cow or a tractor for his farm."
CITY BOY: "He'd certainly look silly riding around on a cow."
FARMER BOY: "Yeah, but he would look a lot sillier milking a tractor!"

●

A farmer was trying hard to fill out a railway company claim sheet for a cow that had been killed on the track. He came down to the last item: "DISPOSITION OF THE CARCASS." After puzzling over the question for some time, he wrote: "Kind and gentle."

Catty Quips

JEAN: "Bob didn't blow his brains out when you rejected him, after all. He came right around and proposed to *me*."

JOAN: "Well, he must have gotten rid of them some other way, then."

LITTLE JOAN, at dancing school: "You'd be a fine dancer except for two things."
JOHN: "What?"
JOAN: "Your feet!"

●

POLLY, annoyed at a tale-bearing classmate: "People should call you 'Amazon'."
MOLLY: "Why?"
POLLY: "Because you're so wide at the mouth."

●

The reason a dog has so many friends is that his tail wags instead of his tongue.

●

NELL: "Do you think that Jack would be happy with a girl like me?"
BELLE: "Maybe—if she wasn't *too* much like you."

●

MRS. PRETTY: "Whenever I'm in the dumps, I get a new hat."
MRS. MEAN: "Oh, so *that's* where you get them!"

●

FIRST SORORITY SISTER: "Is Marguerite a good partner in bridge?"
SECOND SORORITY SISTER: "She was awful. You couldn't tell by the expression on her face how she would play."
FIRST SORORITY SISTER: "Poker face?"
SECOND SORORITY SISTER: "No, but I wanted to."

SALLY: "Well, I'm falling in love and I think I should go to a palmist or a mind reader. Which would you suggest?"

HALLIE: "You'd better go to a palmist—you *know* you've got a palm."

•

BABS, about the pretty new neighbor girl: "She must be very musical."

MABS: "How can you tell?"

BABS: "By the cords in her neck."

•

BILL: "Last night I met a girl and fell in love at first sight."

PHIL: "Why don't you invite her to the prom?"

BILL: "I took a second look."

•

PATTY: "Where did he meet her?"

HATTIE: "They met in a revolving door and he's been going around with her ever since."

•

BETTY: "I'm sorry—I quite forgot your party the other evening!"

BETSEY: "Oh, weren't you there?"

•

A boring classmate spoke to the class favorite, Peggy, one bright Monday morning.

"I passed your house yesterday," she said.

"Thanks. We appreciate it," retorted Peggy

37 😀

PAUL: "Last night I told my girl, 'I'm going to kiss you tonight or die in the attempt!' "
SAUL: "Well, did you?"
PAUL: "You didn't see my name in the obituary column this morning, did you?"

●

HARRY: "Please give me a kiss."
CARRIE: "My lips are chapped."
HARRY: "Well, one more chap won't hurt them."

●

POLLY: "Say, Molly, will you loan me a dime. I want to call a friend."
MOLLY: "Here's thirty cents, call *all* your friends."

●

EDYTH: "She said your hair was dyed."
REDYTH: "It's false!"
EDYTH: "That's what *I* told her."

●

MOLLY, showing a picture of her beau: "I hooked him on the pier last Saturday night."
POLLY: "Oh? Well, I think you should have thrown him right back."

Riddle Rumpus

What two letters of the alphabet contain nothing?
> *M. T.*

●

What kind of coat is made without sleeves and put on wet?
> *A coat of paint.*

●

What is the difference between a cloud and a boy who is being spanked?
> *One pours rain; the other roars with pain.*

Why is a snake a careless animal?
>*He loses his skin.*

●

If you lived in a cemetery, with what would you open the gate?
>*With a skeleton key.*

●

What is it that is black and white and red all over?
>*A book.*

●

When should any pig be able to write?
>*When he has been turned into a pen.*

●

What part of a fish weighs the most?
>*The scales.*

●

Which is the strongest day of the week?
>*Sunday, because all the rest are weak days.*

●

When is a hat not a hat?
>*When it becomes a pretty girl.*

●

Why does Uncle Sam wear red-white-and-blue suspenders?
>*To hold his pants up.*

●

Why is the sea restless?
>*Because it has rocks in its bed.*

What did the big hand on the watch say to the little hand?

I'll be around in an hour.

●

What kind of serpents are like babies' toys?

Rattlers.

●

When is a piece of string like a stick of wood?

When it has knots in it.

●

What is it that we have in December that we don't have in any other month?

The letter D.

●

On which side does a chicken have the most feathers?

The outside.

●

Why is a healthy boy like the United States?

Because he has a good constitution.

●

When you lose something why do you always find it in the last place you look?

Because you stop looking when you find it.

●

What is the difference between a prizefighter and a man with a cold?

One knows his blows, and the other blows his nose.

I occur once in every minute, twice in every moment, and yet not once in a billion years. What am I?

The letter M.

●

Why does a dog turn around several times before lying down?

Because one good turn deserves another.

●

When do 2 and 2 make more than 4?

When they make 22.

●

What keeps the moon in place?

Its beams.

●

Why should fish be better educated than bugs?

Because they live in schools.

●

When is a piece of wood like a king?

When it is made into a ruler.

●

What did the big chimney say to the little chimney?

"You're too young to smoke."

●

At what time of day was Adam created?

A little before Eve.

●

Why are pianos like good people?

Because they are upright, grand, and square.

For how long a period of time did Cain hate his brother?

>*As long as he was Abel.*

●

Why is your hand like a hardware store?

>*It has nails.*

●

When does a boat show affection?

>*When it hugs the shore.*

●

What city is a small stone?

>*Little Rock.*

●

Who dares to sit before the Queen of England with his hat on?

>*Her chauffeur.*

What is everybody doing at the same time?
    Growing older.

●

What is it that is always behind time?
    The back of a clock.

●

What is the difference between here and there?
    The letter T.

●

If twelve make a dozen, how many make a million?
    Very few.

●

Why is a dog's tail like the heart of a tree?
    Because it's farthest from the bark.

●

When is the time of the clock like the whistle of a train?
    When it is two to two.

●

What is horse sense?
    Just stable thinking.

●

Why was the giant Goliath very much astonished when David hit him with a stone?
    Because such a thing had never before entered his head.

Gloomy Gertie
and Gloomy Gus

GLOOMY GERTIE: "I've been asked to get married lots of times."

GLOOMY GUS: "Who asked you?"

GLOOMY GERTIE: "My mother and father."

●

GLOOMY GUS: "I've got a brother with three feet."

GLOOMY GERTIE: "What do you mean?"

GLOOMY GUS: "Well, my mother got a letter from my brother who's away at school and he said: 'You would hardly know me—I've grown three feet.'"

GLOOMY GERTIE: "What did you get that little silver medal for?"

GLOOMY GUS: "For singing."

GLOOMY GERTIE: "What did you get that big gold medal for?"

GLOOMY GUS: "For stopping."

●

GLOOMY GUS: "I like George; he's different from the other boys my sister knows."

GLOOMY GERTIE: "Different? How?"

GLOOMY GUS: "Well, he's willing to go out with her."

●

Gloomy Gertie is so modest she pulls down the shade to change her mind.

●

GLOOMY GERTIE: "I'm going home—I expect a phone call."

GLOOMY GUS: "From whom?"

GLOOMY GERTIE: "I don't know."

GLOOMY GUS: "Then how do you know the phone will ring?"

GLOOMY GERTIE: "Because I'm going to take a bath. The phone almost always rings while I'm in the tub."

GLOOMY GUS: "That's right! I've noticed myself how the phone generally rings while I'm taking a shower."

GLOOMY GERTIE: "Yeah, but sometimes I have to take two or three baths to make it ring."

"Gloomy Gertie just has no style," complained a classmate.

"How come?" asked another.

"Well! Did you see those baseball stockings she wore all last week?"

"*Baseball* stockings?"

"Yes! They had four runs in them."

•

Gloomy Gertie finally got tired of all her girl friends saying she was bound to be an old maid.

"Listen! I can marry anyone I please," she said.

"Why *don't* you, then?" said one of the girls.

"I don't please anybody."

•

"Why do you go steady with Eloise?" asked Gloomy Gus's father.

"She's different from other girls," said Gloomy Gus, "*quite* different."

"How so?"

"She's the only girl who will go with me."

•

Gloomy Gus calls his car "Baby," because it never goes without a rattle.

•

As soon as Gloomy Gus found out that little things count, he had to quit swiping from his kid brother's piggy bank.

47

GLOOMY GERTIE, suspiciously: "I think he plans to marry me for my money."

CANDID FRIEND: "Well, if he does, he'll have earned it."

•

Gloomy Gus failed in all his exams this spring.

"What's the meaning of this?" asked his teacher.

"It's not my fault," explained Gloomy Gus. "The guy who usually sits beside me was home sick that day."

•

"I get blamed for everything that goes on around here. Even as a baby, they were always pinning things on me," said Gloomy Gus.

Ah, Women!

Mrs. Gush, lighting the candles: "Have a look at this cake I decorated for my birthday party. Don't you think my sense of design is wonderful?"

Mrs. Meow: "Yes, but your arithmetic is terrible."

"What would be the first thing you'd do if you had hydrophobia?" asked one teacher of another.

"I'd ask for a pencil and some paper."

"To make your last will?"

"No," replied the other wearily. "To make a list of the people I want to bite."

●

A woman visiting the aquarium asked an attendant, "Can you tell me whether I could get a live shark here?"

"A live shark?" said he in surprise. "Whatever could you do with a live shark?"

"A neighbor's cat has been eating my gold-fish, and I want to teach him a lesson."

●

JUNIOR DEVIL: "Heh, heh, heh."

SATAN: "What are you laughing at?"

JUNIOR DEVIL: "I just locked a woman in a room with a thousand hats and no mirror."

●

The toastmistress at a banquet introduced Thomas Alva Edison, mentioning his many inventions and dwelling at length on the talking machine. The aged inventor then rose to his feet, smiled, and said gently: "I thank the lady for her kind remarks, but I must insist upon a correction. God invented the talking machine. I only invented the first one that can be shut off."

Little Percival's mother moved to a small town where there was no private school. She reluctantly took her precious child to attend public school.

On the first day of school, she gave the teacher a long list of instructions. "My Percival is ever so sensitive," she explained. "Don't ever punish *him*. Just slap the boy *next* to him. That will frighten Percival quite enough!"

●

On what day of the year do women talk the least?
                    The shortest day.

●

GRATEFUL MOTHER: "Were you the one who saved my little boy from drowning?"
LIFEGUARD: "Yes."
MOTHER, angrily: "Well, where's his cap?"

●

"What could be more sad," mused the sentimental professor, "than a man without a country?"

"A country without a man," answered the pretty girl.

●

"Now, Johnny," coaxed his mother, "be a good boy and say 'Ah-h-h,' so the nasty doctor can get his finger out of your mouth."

51

A woman got on a bus. "Does this bus go to Parkview Boulevard?" she asked Pat, the driver.

"Yes," replied Pat.

A few minutes passed. "Are you *sure* it goes to Parkview Boulevard?" the lady asked again.

"Yes," replied Pat.

"There's no danger we'll go past Parkview Boulevard, is there?"

"No," said Pat.

Every two minutes she asked him about Parkview Boulevard.

"Will you *tell* me when we're near it?"

"Yes!"

"Just how will I *know* when we get to Parkview Boulevard?"

Pat finally exploded. "By the smile on me face, lady!"

Home, Sweet Home

A very high-pressure vacuum-cleaner salesman was forcing a home demonstration on a prospective customer. He took a large paper bag out of his case, and proceeded to scatter the contents all over Mrs. Whipple's beautiful living-room rug—coffee grounds, lint, gravel, dust, eggshells, and all sorts of dirt. Then he said, "Madam, I'll eat every bit of this stuff that my vacuum cleaner doesn't pick up."

Mrs. Whipple started out of the room.

"Where are you going?" asked the salesman.

"To get you a knife and fork," she said. "You see, we don't have electricity."

The music professor in a small town met Pop Parker on the street, carrying a long music case.

PROFESSOR: "Oh, Mr. Parker, I see you've bought a saxophone."

POP PARKER: "No, I just borrowed it from the man next door."

PROFESSOR: "But why did you want to do that? You can't play it, can you?"

POP PARKER: "No, but neither can the man next door, while I've got it."

●

MOM PARKER, to the new hired girl: "Hannah, have you given the goldfish fresh water today?"

HANNAH: "No, ma'am. They haven't finished the water I gave them yesterday."

●

"I must say these are fine biscuits!" exclaimed the young husband.

His wife's mother looked at him severely. "How can you say they are fine, when you know they are not?" she asked.

"I didn't say they were fine," said the young husband. "I merely said I must say so."

●

MOM PARKER, to the new maid: "Be careful not to drop those china dishes, Maggie."

MAGGIE: "Don't you worry, ma'am. If they did fall they're too light to hurt my feet!"

Two of the little Parker boys had a favor to ask of their mother.

"You ask her," said Paul, ten.

"No, it would be better if you did," answered Peter, six. "You've known her longer than I have."

•

A young bachelor was entertaining a young lady for dinner at his apartment. As his Chinese servant served coffee she asked him: "Ling Lee, how do you make such delicious coffee?"

"Him take plentee boil water and stir in coffee velly, velly slow," explained the servant.

"Yes, but it's always so clear! How do you strain it so cleverly?" questioned the guest.

"Him take master's silk socks . . ." the servant started to say.

"What!" gasped his master. "You take my best silk socks to strain the coffee?"

"Oh, no, master," replied the servant, "him never take master's *clean* socks."

•

"Freddie," said his mother. "I wish you would run down the street and see how old Mrs. Cheever is this morning."

"Okay," Freddie agreed, and soon he returned and reported.

"Mrs. Cheever says it's none of your business how old she is."

On a card in the front window of a suburban house appeared the following notice: "A piano for sale." In the window next door, another card appeared bearing just one word: "HURRAH!"

●

FIRST NEIGHBOR: "What's the idea of the Smiths taking French lessons?"

SECOND NEIGHBOR: "They have adopted a French baby, and want to understand what she says when she begins to talk."

●

A peddler knocked at the door of a housewife.

"I sell all kinds of things for the house. Do you want to buy something?"

"No, I don't want anything," said the housewife firmly.

"Maybe a pan or a pot?"

"No, I don't want anything. Now, get going. I don't want anything."

"Maybe a clothes brush?"

"No, I don't want anything!"

"Maybe a vacuum cleaner?"

"I don't want *anything*. Get going!"

"Maybe a tablecloth? Some hairpins? I've got all kinds of things."

"Now, listen to me. If you don't get going, I'll whistle for a policeman."

"Do you want to buy a whistle?"

"People who say they sleep like a baby," says Pop Parker, "usually never had one."

●

When are houses like books?

When they have stories in them.

●

Why are trees in winter like troublesome visitors?

Because it's a long time before they leave.

●

Mrs. Richmoney's new maid, Norah, had a very bad habit of interrupting her mistress with unimportant household problems, usually just when Mrs. Richmoney was right in the middle of a telephone chat, or serving tea to the Friday Afternoon Club ladies. One day just after Norah had interrupted a particularly important party, Mrs. Richmoney warned her that if she ever did it again, she could pack her things and leave immediately.

The very next day, Mrs. Richmoney was in the midst of a bridge game, and Norah appeared in the doorway, gesturing and about to speak. Mrs. Richmoney waved her back, finished the game, excused herself, and stepped into the kitchen to talk to Norah.

"I'm glad to see you understand that I meant what I said yesterday. Now tell me, what's on your mind?"

"Well, ma'am," said Norah, "I just wanted to tell you that the house is on fire."

RALPH: "I'm homesick."

LOUIS: "But don't you live at home?"

RALPH: "Yes, but I'm sick of it."

•

A man met a friend he hadn't seen for a long time.

"Why, George," he said, "you've changed! What's making you look so old?"

"Trying to keep young," said George.

"Trying to keep young?" queried the man.

"Yes," was the gloomy response, "nine of them."

•

POP PARKER, to a friend at work: "Well, we've managed to furnish three of the rooms in our house with the soap coupons my wife collects."

FRIEND: "Furnished three rooms by collecting soap coupons? Aren't you going to furnish the other three rooms?"

POP PARKER: "No—they're full of soap."

•

Summer is the dreaded season when youngsters, for no earthly reason, will slam, until they almost splinter, the doors they didn't close all winter.

Squelch Squibs

The fresh young fellow in the barber shop kept asking the pretty manicurist for a date. She repeatedly said "No."

Finally, the young man insisted: "Well, *why* won't you go out with me?"

"Because I'm engaged," replied the pretty manicurist.

"What difference does that make?" quipped the eager young smart-aleck. "Ask your fiancé."

"Ask him yourself," the manicurist retorted. "He's shaving you."

The quiet Martin family lived in a city apartment building right next to the noisy Bangs family, who gave very lively parties several nights a week. The Martins suffered the racket quietly for some time, until one day Mr. Martin noticed the air duct which ran through from the Bangs's living room to the Martins' living room. This gave Martin a fine idea about how to get even.

The next night a noisy party was going on next door. Martin quietly removed the grille over his air duct, and, reaching in, scotch-taped the microphone of his home recording machine to the Bangs's air duct. He let it record a good hour's hilarity.

The next night, when he knew the Bangses would be going to bed very early, to make up for staying up so late the night before, he put the loud-speaker of his machine where the microphone had been the night before, turned up the volume, and really let the Bangses have it.

The Martins haven't had any trouble since.

●

The butcher was busy waiting on a customer when a woman rushed in, pushed through the waiting customers to the counter, and demanded: "Give me a pound of cat food, quick!"

Turning to the other customers she said, "I hope you don't mind my getting waited on before you."

"Not if you're *that* hungry," a woman retorted.

BERNIE: "We've got a hen down at our house that lays white eggs."

ERNIE: "What's so wonderful about that?"

BERNIE: "Can *you* do it?"

●

Leonora's new beau was far from modest in relating his exploit.

"I shot this tiger in India," he said, "under terrific odds; it was a case of me or the tiger."

"Well, the tiger certainly makes the better rug," agreed Leonora boredly.

●

The loquacious old gentleman boarded a transport plane and started a conversation with the pilot.

"This plane takes all my courage," he said, "I was almost killed twice in an airplane."

"Once would have been enough," replied the bored pilot.

●

LATE-STAYING GUEST: "Well, good night. I hope I have not kept you up too late."

YAWNING HOST: "Not at all. We would have been getting up soon, anyway."

●

PHOTOGRAPHER, to an extremely disagreeable and fussy customer: "Look pleasant, please. As soon as I snap the picture, you can resume your natural expression."

"This table," said Mrs. Richmoney, "goes back to Louis the Fourteenth."

"You don't have a thing on me," replied her maid. "My dining-room set goes back to Sears Roebuck on the thirteenth."

●

JOHNNY, at breakfast: "Dad, today is Lincoln's birthday. My, he was a great man, wasn't he?"
POP, always eager to teach his young son a lesson: "Yes, Son, indeed he was. And mind you," he added pompously, "when Abraham Lincoln was *your* age, he was out splitting rails."

"Yes, Dad, I know," retorted Johnny. "And when he was *your* age, he was President of the United States."

●

FUSSY LADY in the fish market, haughtily: "I don't like the looks of that codfish."
FISHMONGER, sarcastically: "Well, if it's looks you're after, why don't you buy a goldfish?"

Baby Talk

MOTHER: "Did you thank Mrs. Porter for the lovely party she gave?"

LITTLE DOROTHY: "No, Mommie, I didn't. The girl leaving just before me thanked her and Mrs. Porter said, 'Don't mention it,' so I didn't."

•

One day Johnny's father brought his boss home with him for dinner.

After being served, young Johnny paused, and for a moment studied his plate intently, then asked his mother if the meat on his plate was mutton.

"No, that is roast beef, Johnny," she replied. "Why do you ask?"

"Because Daddy said he was going to bring a muttonhead home for dinner with him this evening."

ANDY: "How's your uncle doing with his farm?"

SANDY: "Not so good. There ain't so much money in milk and eggs any more. So he sits up all night trying to think of something else for the hens and cows to do."

•

TEACHER: "I hear you've got a new baby over at your house, Robert."

ROBERT: "Well," hesitatingly, "I guess he *is* new— but from the way he cries, you'd think he had had a lot of experience!"

•

BARBER: "Well, son, how would you like your hair cut?"

SMALL BOY: "Just like Dad's, and be sure to leave that little round hole on the top where his head comes through."

•

ED: "What goes 999 thump! 999 thump! 999 thump?"

NED: "I dunno. What?"

ED: "A centipede with a wooden leg."

•

LITTLE GIRL: "My big brother has a new invention, and it's very practical, too."

NEIGHBOR: "What is it?"

LITTLE GIRL: "He makes the chickens swim in hot water so they'll lay hard-boiled eggs."

ALEX: "We've got an animal family."

FELIX: "How's that?"

ALEX: "Well, Mother's a dear, Sister's a lamb, I'm a kid, and Dad's the goat."

•

Why does a horse eat the least of all the animals?

> *Because he eats best when there isn't a bit in his mouth.*

•

BILL: "Is it bad luck to have a cat follow you?"

PHIL: "It depends. Are you a man or a mouse?"

TOMMY: "Say, Mom, was our baby sent down from heaven?"

MOTHER: "Yes, son."

TOMMY: "I guess they like to have things quiet up there, huh?"

DOCTOR'S SON: "*My* pop makes his money easy. All he does is look at a person, talk to him, then write something down—and he gets five dollars."

LAWYER'S SON: "*That's* nothing, *my* pop sits in his office. Someone comes in. He tells them he'll look it up in a book, and then he gets fifty dollars."

MINISTER'S SON: "Oh, but after *my* dad gets up to talk it takes six men to bring the money down the aisles!"

•

MOTHER: "Now Eddie, you must not be selfish. You must let your little brother have the sled half the time."

EDDIE: "But Mother, I do. *I* have it going down the hill, and *he* has it coming up."

•

The little city girl was on her first visit to the country. She was quite impressed by the cows, pigs, and chickens. But when she saw the peacock, she was amazed.

"Look," she gasped, "a rooster in full bloom!"

•

Mother was telling stories of the time she was a little girl. Little Reggie listened thoughtfully as she told of having a Shetland pony and a cart, going to a country fair, and wading in the brook on the farm.

Finally he said with a sigh, "Gee! I wish I had met you earlier, Mom."

Daddy was showing Junior the family album and came across the picture of himself and his wife on their wedding day.

"Was that the day Mom came to work for us?" Junior inquired.

•

Little Georgie was given two dimes one Saturday evening. "One of the dimes," said his father, "is for Sunday school tomorrow, and the other is for an ice-cream cone for yourself."
As Georgie ran to the drug store to get his ice-cream cone, he stumbled and one of the dimes rolled into the sewer drain. "Oh dear," said Georgie, "there goes the Lord's dime!"

•

"How is your Aunt Tilly?" a neighbor woman asked little Paul.
"She had her appendix taken out the other day," Paul informed her.
"Did they give her anything for it?"
"No," answered the literal-minded child, "it wasn't worth anything."

•

GRANDMA: "And were you a good little girl at church this morning, Susie?"
SUSIE: "Oh, yes, grammaw! A nice man offered me a big plate full of money, but I said, 'No, thank you, sir.'"

A kind neighbor stopped little Dopey on his way to school and said, "That's an interesting pair of socks you have on—one blue and one yellow."

"Yes," answered Dopey eagerly. "And the funny thing is, I've got another pair just like it at home!"

•

Two little girls were playing on the front porch when one of them ran into her house, was gone a moment, then came back out carrying two big red apples.

"Just look what Grannie gave us!" she cried. The other girl looked puzzled. "Grannie? What's a Grannie?" she asked.

"A Grannie," said the first little girl, "is an old lady who keeps your mother from spanking you."

•

A sturdy little boy ran by a policeman on the block at top speed. Five minutes later he rushed by again as fast as the first time. After this had happened a half-dozen times, the policeman stopped him and asked, "What's the idea, Sonny? What's the rush?" The boy looked up very indignantly and shouted, "I am running away from home!"

"Oh," said the policeman. "But you've gone around this same block at least five times."

"I know it!" shouted the boy over his shoulder as he started running again. "My mom won't let me cross the street."

NEIGHBOR: "Where have you been, Betty?"

BETTY: "To Sunday school."

NEIGHBOR: "What's that paper in your hand?"

BETTY: "Oh, just an ad about heaven."

●

VISITOR: "What was your Mommy's name before she was married?"

LITTLE PAUL: "I think it must have been 'Statler'—that's the name on most of our towels."

●

BIG SISTER: "Bobby, if you eat the rest of that pumpkin pie, you'll burst!"

BOBBY: "Okay. Pass the pie and get outa the way."

●

JONATHON: "Mother, was that policeman over there ever a little baby?"

MOTHER: "Why, certainly. Of course."

JONATHON: "Oh, I would just *love* to see a baby policeman!"

●

Young Tommy greeted his sister's boy friend enthusiastically:

"That mouth organ you gave me for my birthday is absolutely by far the best present I've ever had."

"I'm glad you like it."

"Yes—Mother gives me a quarter a week not to play it."

JAKE: "I et six eggs for breakfast this morning."
TEACHER: "You mean ate, don't you?"
JAKE: "Well, maybe it *was* eight I et."

●

FRIEND OF THE FAMILY: "Well, Charles, how do you like your new little sister?"
CHARLES: "Oh, she's all right, I guess; but there are lots of things we needed worse."

Animal Crackers

The keeper of the zoo found the new employee standing uneasily before the lion's cage.

KEEPER: "Didn't I tell you that when a lion wags his tail he's friendly?"

EMPLOYEE: "Yes, but he was roaring and wagging his tail at the same time."

KEEPER: "Well, what's that got to do with it?"

EMPLOYEE: "I didn't know which end to believe."

71

What is it that has four legs, eats oats, has a tail, and sees equally well from both ends?

A blind mule.

•

What are the two flowers that should decorate the zoo?

A dandelion and a tiger lily.

•

OLD HEN: "Let me give you a piece of good advice."

YOUNG HEN: "What is it?"

OLD HEN: "An egg a day keeps the ax away."

•

Two leopards were having lunch and one sat back and sighed contentedly, "Mmmm, just hit the right spots!"

•

PAPA KANGAROO: "Anabelle, where's the baby?"

MAMA KANGAROO: "My goodness! I've had my pocket picked!"

What animal took the most luggage into the Ark, and what animal took the least?

> *The elephant took his trunk; and the rooster had only a comb.*

•

Why is a watchdog bigger by night than he is by day?

> *Because he is let out at night and taken in in the morning.*

•

The teacher took her class to the zoo. When they passed the lion's cage, she asked, "What's the plural of lion?"

One of the boys answered, "Lions."

"What's the plural of sheep?" she asked.

One of the girls answered, "Sheep."

"Right," said the teacher.

A little farther along they came upon a hippopotamus.

"What's the plural of hippopotamus?" the teacher asked little Johnny.

Johnny shuddered. "*Who* would want two of *those*?"

•

FIRST NEIGHBOR: "What were all your chickens doing out in front of your house early this morning?"

SECOND NEIGHBOR: "They heard some men were going to lay a sidewalk and they wanted to see how it was done."

ADMIRING HORSEWOMAN: "How did your horse happen to win the race?"

JOCKEY: "Well, I just kept whispering in his ear:
'Roses are red, violets are blue—
horses that lose are made into glue!' "

●

A teacher was giving her class a test in natural history.

"Now Johnny," she said, "tell me where the elephant is found."

Johnny thought a minute.

"The elephant," he said at last, "is such a big animal it hardly ever gets lost."

●

TEACHER: "Millie, spell the word 'mouse'."

MILLIE: "M-o-u-s."

TEACHER: "But what's at the end of it?"

MILLIE: "A tail."

●

"Now boys," said the teacher, "tell me the signs of the zodiac. You first, Thomas."

"Taurus, the Bull."

"Right! Now you, Harold, another one."

"Cancer, the Crab."

"Right again. And now it's your turn, Albert."

The boy looked puzzled, hesitated a moment, and then blurted out, "Mickey, the Mouse."

Dopey Dames

MR. SIMPKINS: "You sure made a poor job of painting this door."

MRS. SIMPKINS: "Well, you declared only this morning that it needed painting badly."

FEMININE VOICE on phone: "Hello, City Bridge Department?"

MASCULINE VOICE: "Yes. What can we do for you?"

FEMININE VOICE: "How many points do you get for a little slam?"

●

COUNTRY HOSTESS to visitor: "Are you interested in art?"

CITY VISITOR: "Yes, whenever I visit a strange city, the first thing I do is look up an artery."

●

"I hear your grandson has a new automobile," said the neighbor. "What make is it?"

"I'm not sure," replied Grandma, "but I think he said it was a LALLAPALOOZA."

●

GRANDMA: "And how did Georgie do on his history examination?"

MOTHER: "Oh, not at all well. But it wasn't his fault. Why, they asked him about things that happened before he was born!"

●

"Are you the game warden?" asked a lady over the telephone.

"Yes, I am the game warden," was the reply.

"Oh, I am so glad," said the lady. "Will you please suggest some games for a little party I'm giving for my children?"

DORA: "Why didn't you ride in the Bridle Path?"

NORA: "I thought that was only for newly married couples."

•

MRS. BUTLER: "Did you meet your son at the station?"

MRS. WILKINS: "Oh, goodness no! I've known him for years."

•

NEIGHBOR: "I understand your son is on the football team. What does he play?"

MOTHER: "I think he's one of the drawbacks."

•

THEATER USHER: "How far down do you want to sit, madam?"

"Why, *all* the way, of course."

•

"Now, this plant," explained the horticulturist patiently to the vague sightseer, "belongs to the begonia family."

"Ah, yes," chirped the sweet old lady, "and you're looking after it for them while they're away on vacation?"

•

MISTRESS: "Selma, when you wait on the table tonight for my guests, please don't spill anything."

HIRED GIRL: "Don't you worry, ma'am, I never talk much."

77

FISH DEALER: "Lobsters, madam; nice lobsters? Look, they're all alive."
LADY SHOPPER: "Yes, but are they *fresh*?"

•

A tobacco farmer was showing a visiting lady around his plantation.

> "These are tobacco plants in full bloom," he explained.

> "Isn't that wonderful!" she gushed. "And when will the cigars be ripe?"

•

A not overly bright woman swept into a fashionable kennel shop. "I want a collar for Wilbur," she said. Timidly, the clerk inquired, "What size, please?"

> "You should know the size," she exclaimed. "Wilbur buys all his clothes here!"

Food
Fun

"Forty-eight hamburgers, please," the boy said to the clerk at the roadside stand.

"All for *you*?" gasped the clerk.

"Don't be silly," said the boy, "I have three friends waiting outside for me."

●

YOUNG HOUSEWIFE: "Is this milk fresh?"
GROCER: "Fresh? Why, three hours ago it was grass."

Why is it that you cannot starve in the Sahara Desert?

Because of all the sand which is there!

•

DINER: "Do you serve crabs here?"
WAITER: "We serve anyone; sit right down."

•

"This butter is so strong it could walk around the table and say hello to the coffee," said one diner to another in a restaurant.

"Well, if it does the coffee is too weak to talk back."

•

BRIDE: "The two best things I cook are meat loaf and apple dumplings."
GROOM: "Well, which is this?"

•

What has four wheels and flies?

A garbage wagon.

•

DINER in restaurant: "What's this leathery stuff?"
WAITER: "Why, that's filet of sole, sir."
DINER: "How about a nice tender piece from the upper part of the shoe?"

•

MRS. NAG: "I've got my husband to the point where he eats out of my hand."
MRS. GAG: "Saves a lot of dishwashing, doesn't it?"

BROKE: "Do you charge for bread?"
WAITER: "No."
BROKE: "Do you charge for gravy?"
WAITER: "No."
BROKE: "I'll take bread and gravy."

●

MOTHER: "Now Georgie, don't you know you are not supposed to eat with your knife?"
GEORGIE: "I know, Mother, but my fork leaks!"

●

What is the difference between a hungry man and a glutton?

One eats to live, the other lives to eat.

●

An out-of-town visitor went into a café and ordered breakfast. "Please bring me orange juice, two scrambled eggs, toast, and black coffee," he told the waitress. In a minute the waitress returned and said, "What do you mean by 'black coffee'?"

"Without cream or sugar."

"Oh," said the waitress, "we're out of cream—but we *can* serve it without condensed milk."

●

PAUL, in a restaurant: "Go see if the chef has pigs' feet."
SAUL: "I can't tell. He's got his shoes on."

What is the best butter in the world?
>*A goat.*

•

What has teeth and never eats?
>*A comb.*

•

JILL: "What kind of fish are they?"
BILL: "Jellyfish."
JILL: "What flavor?"

•

A peanut sat on a railroad track;
His heart was all a-flutter.
A train came speeding down the track.
Toot! Toot! Peanut butter.

•

PAUL: "With which hand do you stir your coffee?"
SAUL: "My right, of course."
PAUL: "*I* use a spoon!"

•

What aunt always provides a place for you to eat?
>*Restaurant.*

•

WAITER: "You ought to have some of our enthusiastic stew."
DINER: "Why do you call it that?"
WAITER: "Because the cook puts everything he has into it."

 82

Taken to the dentist for a checkup, young Jimmy was told he'd have to have a filling.

"Now, Jimmy," asked the dentist, "what kind of filling would you like for that tooth?"

"Chocolate, please," replied Jimmy promptly.

•

What most resembles half a cheese?

The other half.

•

What is it that stays hot even if you put it in a re-frigerator?

Pepper.

•

How can you change a pumpkin into another vegetable?

Throw it up into the air and it will come down squash.

•

If eight eggs cost twenty-six cents, how many eggs can you buy for a cent and a quarter?

Eight eggs.

•

What do ghosts eat for breakfast?

Ghost toasties and evaporated milk.

•

DINER: "Hey, Chef! This soup is spoiled."
CHEF: "Yeah, who told you?"
DINER: "A little swallow."

CUSTOMER: "That chicken I bought yesterday had no wish-bone."

BUTCHER, smoothly: "It was a happy and contented chicken, madam, and had nothing to wish for."

●

VISITOR: "Why is your dog watching me so intently while I eat?"

HOST: "Maybe it's because you're eating out of his plate."

Job Jests

SALESMAN: "Sonny, is your mother at home?"

LITTLE SAMMY: "Yes, sir."

SALESMAN (after knocking for some time and getting no answer): "I thought you said she was at home?"

LITTLE SAMMY: "Yes, sir, but I don't live here."

MINE FOREMAN: "How come you're carrying only one bag of coal at a time, while the other workers are carrying two?"

MINE WORKER: "Oh, that's because the others are too lazy to make two trips, like *I* do."

●

CASTING DIRECTOR: "That fellow wants a hundred dollars just to play the part of an Indian in the movie."

PRODUCER: "Why, that part is only worth fifty dollars. He's supposed to be a half-breed."

●

PAYMASTER: "How long have you been working here?"

OFFICE BOY: "Ever since the day the boss threatened to fire me."

●

Simpson suddenly became ill and was rushed to the hospital. His boss was among the first to visit him. "My dear George," said the boss soothingly, "don't worry about a thing. Everyone at the office is going to pitch in and do your work—as soon as we can find out what you have been doing."

●

COMEDIAN: "Look here, I do object to going on right after the monkey act."

MANAGER: "You're right. They may think it's an encore."

CHUCK: "Joe sure isn't afraid of work."
CHARLIE: "What makes you think so. I think he is real lazy."
CHUCK: "He can lie down beside work and fall fast asleep."

●

EMPLOYER: "Why were you late this morning?"
OFFICE BOY: "On account of my alarm clock. Everybody in the house got up except me."
EMPLOYER: "How was that?"
OFFICE BOY: "There are nine of us and the alarm clock was only set for eight."

●

The world is full of willing people: some willing to work, the rest willing to let them.

●

EMPLOYER: "I want a responsible boy for this job."
DOPEY: "Then I'm just the right person for you! In every place I ever worked, something went wrong and I was responsible!"

●

PERSONNEL MANAGER to a job hunter: "How old are you?"

"Eighteen," answered the young man.

"Well, what do you expect to be in, say, three years?"

"Twenty-one," the young man replied without hesitation.

A social worker met one of her charges on the street one very hot day.

SOCIAL WORKER: "What is your brother doing these days, Joe?"

JOE: "Selling snow shovels."

SOCIAL WORKER: "Snow shovels in summer? What's the idea?"

JOE: "Yeah. He figured there would be no competition."

●

PARKER: "Don't you ever take a vacation?"

BARKER: "I can't get away."

PARKER: "Why? Can't the firm do without you?"

BARKER: "And how! That's what I don't want them to find out."

●

HARRY: "Why aren't you working?"

LARRY: "The boss and I had a fight and he won't take back what he said."

HARRY: "What'd he say?"

LARRY: "He said, 'You're fired.' "

●

LENNY: "My father makes faces all day."

BENNY: "Why does he do that?"

LENNY: "Because he works in a clock factory."

●

Did you ever hear about the farmer who crossed his bees with lightning bugs so they could work at night?

MAN: "I read your ad for a man to retail canaries."
BIRD SHOP OWNER: "Yes, do you want the job?"
MAN: "No, I'm just curious as to how the birds lost their tails."

•

IRRITATED EMPLOYER: "*Where* have you been, this last hour?"
INNOCENT EMPLOYEE: "Out having my hair cut."
IRRITATED EMPLOYER: "Well! You can't have your hair cut on *my* time!"
INNOCENT EMPLOYEE: "And why not? It *grew* on your time!"

•

EMPLOYER, on pay day: "Here, Jones, is your pay—for loafing seven hours."
JONES, coolly: "Excuse me—*eight* hours."

•

A girl applied for a job as a stenographer and they gave her a test in spelling.

"How do you spell Mississippi?" she was asked.

"The river or the state?"

•

PATIENT: "What do you charge for extracting a tooth?"
DENTIST: "Five dollars."
PATIENT: "What! For only two seconds' work?"
DENTIST: "Well, if you wish, I can extract it very slowly."

BRIDE, to her neighbor: "You should meet my husband. He makes his living with his pen."

NEIGHBOR, impressed: "You don't say! You mean he's a writer?"

BRIDE: "No, he raises pigs."

•

WARDEN: "Boys, I've had charge of this prison for ten years and we ought to celebrate the occasion. What kind of a party would you suggest?"

PRISONERS, in a chorus: "Open house!"

•

CIRCUS OWNER: "Are you the famous lion tamer—the great Flambino?"

JOB APPLICANT: "No, I only comb the lions and clean their teeth."

Money Mumbles

Walking along a street a man was attracted by frightened screams from a house. Rushing in he found a mother frantic because her little son had swallowed a quarter. Seizing the child by the heels, he held him up, gave him a few shakes, and the coin dropped to the floor. The grateful mother was lost in admiration.

"You certainly knew how to get it out of him," she said. "Are you a doctor?"

"No, madam," the man replied, "I'm from the Internal Revenue Bureau."

SHOPPER: "How much are these tomatoes?"

GROCER: "Forty cents a pound."

SHOPPER: "Did you raise them yourself?"

GROCER: "Yes, ma'am, I certainly did. They were only thirty-five cents yesterday."

●

DOPE: "Would you sooner lose your life, or your money?"

DOPIER: "Why, my life, of course. I'll need my money for my old age."

●

A touring American businessman noticed an Indian chief lolling at the door of his wigwam on the reservation.

"Chief," suggested the tourist, "why don't you get a job in a factory?"

"Why?" grunted the chief.

"Well, you could earn a lot of money. Maybe thirty or forty dollars a week."

"Why?" insisted the chief.

"Oh, if you worked hard and saved your money, you'd soon have a bank account. Wouldn't you like that?"

"Why?" again asked the chief.

"I'll tell you," shouted the tourist. "With a bank account you could retire, and then you wouldn't have to work any more."

"Not working now," pointed out the chief.

 92

For many minutes there had been a violent ringing at the night bell of a drug store until finally the druggist, who lived above it, sleepily crawled into his clothes and went downstairs. A kilted Scotsman stood in front of the store.

"Five cents' worth o' bicarbonate of soda for indigestion, if ye please," the Scotsman requested.

"A nickel's worth of bicarbonate of soda at this time of night?" exploded the druggist. "Getting me up for that when a glass of warm water would have done just as well!"

"Weel, weel," returned the Scot, putting his money back in his pocket. "I thank ye for the advice, and I'll no' bother ye after all. Good night."

●

"Just tell me one good reason *why* you can't buy a new car now," said the persistent automobile salesman.

"Well, I'll tell you, sir," replied the farmer, "I'm still paying installments on the car I swapped for the car I traded in as part payment on the car I own now."

●

PAUL: "Could you loan me ten dollars?"
JOE: "I hate to do it, because when a fellow lends money it always breaks up a friendship."
PAUL: "Oh, come now! We haven't been *such* good friends."

93

A woman was trying to collect compensation for an accident. When the adjuster for the company called, she demanded loudly, "I want $20,000 for that lost thumb."

"But madam, that seems a lot of money for just a thumb."

"Well, it isn't," she insisted. "It's the one I kept my husband under."

●

"You know, I think everyone should divide his worldly goods with the other fellow," said one office worker to another.

"That's a good idea. If you had two thousand dollars, would you give me one half?"

"Sure."

"And if you had two automobiles, would you give me one?"

"Sure."

"And if you had two shirts, would you give me one?"

"No."

"Why?"

"Because I've *got* two shirts."

●

WOMAN SHOPPER at the counter: "I suspect that you're giving me awfully short weight for my money!"

BUTCHER: "Well, I'm positive you're giving me an awful long wait for mine."

😀 94

What did the adding machine say to the clerk?

You can count on me.

●

A business man from Texas who was a visitor in New York stood watching a building being constructed. After an hour or so, he noticed a rough-dressed man also standing by, also watching, and smoking one cigar after another. Finally he said,

"How many cigars do you smoke a day?"

"About ten," the man answered.

"What do they cost you?"

"Twenty-five cents apiece."

"My, that's two dollars and a half a day! How long have you been smoking?"

"Thirty years."

"Two-fifty a day for thirty years is a lot of money."

"Yes, it is."

"Do you see that office building on the corner?"

"Yes."

"If you had never smoked in your life you might *own* that fine building."

The man took the cigar out of his mouth, looked squarely at his questioner and said, "Do *you* smoke?"

"No, never did."

"Do you own that building?"

"No."

"Well, I *do*."

95

VISITING UNCLE: "If you're real good, Johnnie, I'll give you this bright new penny."

JOHNNIE: "Haven't you got a dirty old quarter?"

●

FRANK: "What do you find the most difficult thing on the piano?"

HANK: "To pay the installments."

●

JUDGE: "Now tell me, why did you steal that purse?"

PRISONER: "Your honor, I was not feeling well and I thought the change would do me good."

●

Two young men were discussing matrimony.

"You wouldn't marry a girl just for her money, would you?"

"No," said the other fellow, "but I wouldn't have the heart to let her die an old maid just because she had money, either."

Meet _these_ Menaces

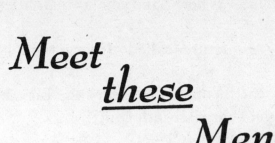

VISITOR: "And what will you do, dear, when you are as big as your mother?"

LITTLE GIRL: "Diet."

IMPATIENT FRIEND: "Where have you been all afternoon?"

DOPEY: "I saw a picture called 'Henry the Sixteenth'."

IMPATIENT FRIEND: "You mean 'Henry the Eighth'. Where did you get that sixteenth stuff?"

DOPEY: "I sat through it twice."

●

Little Polly counted her chestnuts carefully and then approached her grandma.

"Grammaw, can you eat nuts?" she asked.

"No, dear, I have no teeth," Grandma replied. Little Polly emptied her apron into grandma's lap, saying, "Then you can mind these till I come back from school."

●

SILLY: "I'm going to join a circus."

BILLY: "What are you going to do in a circus?"

SILLY: "I'm going to be a midget."

BILLY: "You're too big for a midget."

SILLY: "That's the idea. I'll be the biggest midget in the world."

●

JOE: "Say, Dad, that apple I just ate had a worm in it, and I ate that, too."

DAD: "What! Here, drink this water and wash it down."

JOE (shaking his head): "Naw, let 'im *walk* down!"

98

JOHN, JR.: "Hey, Pop—*that* man wasn't a painless dentist like he advertised."

POP: "Why? Did he hurt you?"

JOHN, JR.: "No, but he yelled when I bit his thumb, just like any other dentist."

•

BENJIE: "Mom, do you remember that vase you always worried I would break?"

MOM: "Yes, what about it?"

BENJIE: "Your worries are over."

•

HARRY: "A steam roller ran over my uncle."

LARRY: "What did you do?"

HARRY: "I just took him home and slipped him under the door."

PAUL: "See that house? That's where Uncle Tom lived."

SAUL: "Uncle Tom from 'Uncle Tom's Cabin'?"

PAUL: "Yes."

SAUL: "Never even heard of him."

●

LENNY: "What is that you're chewing?"

BENNY: "It's called 'Magic Gum'—the more you chew it, the smarter you get. I'm going to chew this piece second and have a lot of swell ideas."

LENNY: "Got any more?"

BENNY: "I've only got one stick left. I'll sell it to you for ten dollars."

LENNY: "Here's the ten dollars."

BENNY: "Here's the gum."

LENNY: "Boy, it's all right. It tastes good. Do you think I'll get smart from this? Funny. I don't feel any different. I think it's a joke."

BENNY: "Say, you're smart already!"

●

DOPEY: "My father can hold up an auto with one hand."

DOPIER: "He must be very strong."

DOPEY: "No, he's a cop."

●

TEACHER: "Give for one year the number of tons of coal shipped out of the United States."

TED: "In fourteen-hundred-ninety-two—none."

TOMMY: "I always do a good deed every day."

SUNDAY SCHOOL TEACHER: "That's fine—what good deed have you done today?"

TOMMY: "Why, there was only castor oil enough for one of us this morning, so I let my little brother have it."

●

A club of eccentric young college boys had for one of their rules that on Monday evenings any man in the clubroom who asked a question which he was unable to answer himself should pay a fine of one dollar. One evening Parker asked, "Why doesn't a ground squirrel leave any dirt around the top of his hole when he digs it?"

After some deliberation he was called upon to answer his own question.

"That's easy," he said. "The squirrel starts at the bottom and digs up."

"All very nice," suggested a member, "but how does it get to the bottom?"

"That's *your* question," answered Parker.

●

"Lady, could you give me a quarter so I can get to see my family?" asked the ragged little boy.

"Certainly, my boy," said the generous lady, as she handed the coin to him. "And where is your family?"

"At the movies," he answered, as he ran off.

RANDY: "Do you have any bloodhounds?"

ANDY: "Yes. Come here, Pooch."

RANDY: "But he doesn't look like a bloodhound to me."

ANDY: "Bleed for the lady, Pooch!"

●

Gerald was going to have a birthday party, and his mother insisted on his inviting, among others, a neighbor's boy with whom he had had a fight. He finally promised to do so, but on the day of the party the neighbor's boy failed to turn up.

Walter's mother became suspicious. "Did you invite George?" she asked, after the party.

"Of course I did, Mother. I not only invited him to come, I *dared* him to."

Lady at the Wheel

"I turned the way I signaled," said the lady indignantly, after the crash.

"I know it," retorted the man she'd hit. "That's what fooled me."

TRAFFIC OFFICER: "Now tell me, just what could the other driver have done to avoid this accident?"

WOMAN DRIVER, indignantly: "He could have gone down another street!"

●

The woman auto tourist posed for a snapshot in front of the fallen pillars of an ancient temple in Rome.

"Don't get the car in the picture," she pleaded, "or my husband will think I ran into the place!"

●

A woman driver was sailing along a country road when she noticed a couple of repair men climbing telephone poles.

"Dopes!" she exclaimed to her companion, "they must think I never drove a car before."

●

A woman driving in Chicago stopped her car for a red light. However, when the light turned green again, she just stayed right where she was. When the light had changed several times and she still hadn't moved, the traffic policeman finally went over and inquired politely, "Lady, ain't we got no colors you like?"

●

TRAFFIC COP: "Miss, you were doing seventy miles an hour!"

SWEET YOUNG THING: "Oh, isn't that splendid! And I only just learned to drive yesterday."

BOB: "Does your mother know much about cars?"

ROB: "Naw. She thinks you cool the motor by stripping the gears."

●

VISITING FRIEND: "Oh, Mabel, I do wish *I* could afford a car like this!"

MABEL: "So do *I*!"

●

GEORGE: "Is your wife having any better luck in learning to drive the car?"

JIM: "Well, the road is beginning to turn when she does."

●

The examiner was testing an applicant for a driver's license.

"What does it mean," he asked, "when a woman is holding out her hand?"

"It means," answered the applicant, "she's turning left, turning right, backing up, waving at somebody, or going to stop."

●

A woman drove a Ford into a service station to complain that her car was using too much gas. The attendant pointed to the choke which protruded from the dashboard: "Do you know what *this* is for?" he asked.

"Oh, *that* gadget," replied the woman airily. "I never use it, so I keep it pulled out to hang my handbag on."

105

POLICEMAN: "Don't you know that you should always give over half of the road to a woman driver?"
TIMID MALE DRIVER: "I always do—when I find out which half she wants."

●

COP: "What ya mean, goin' seventy miles an hour?"
PRETTY MOTORIST: "My brakes don't work and I was hustling to get home before I had an accident."

●

POLICEMAN: "How did you knock him down?"
LADY DRIVER: "I didn't! I stopped to let him go across, and he fainted!"

Oh, Doctor!

"Did you go to another doctor before you came to me?" asked the doctor.

"No," replied the patient, "I went to a drug-gist."

"And what foolish advice did *he* give you?"

"He told me to come to you," said the patient.

PHYSICIAN: "Shall I give your wife a local anesthetic?"

WEALTHY HUSBAND: "No. I'm rich—give her the best! Give her something imported."

●

Mrs. Peterson complained to her doctor that his bill was too high.

"Don't forget," the doctor reminded her, "that I made eleven visits to Johnny when he had the measles."

"And don't *you* forget," she replied, "that Johnny made you lots of money by giving the measles to the whole fourth grade!"

●

DOCTOR: "I don't like the looks of your husband."

WIFE: "I don't either, but he is good to the children."

●

LADY (standing in the middle of a busy street): "Officer, can you tell me how to get to the hospital?"

POLICEMAN: "Just stand where you are."

●

The famous surgeon and his wife were in their library.

"Robert," his wife exclaimed, "why did you tear the back part out of my new book?"

"Excuse me, dear," he answered, "the part you speak of was labeled 'appendix' and I took it out without thinking."

"Your pulse is as steady as a clock," announced the doctor to the worried patient.

"Well, but you've got your hand on my wrist watch," he replied.

•

DOCTOR: "What do you dream about at night?"
DOPEY: "Baseball."
DOCTOR: "Don't you dream about anything else?"
DOPEY: "No, just about baseball, night after night."
DOCTOR (puzzled): "Don't you ever dream about food?"
DOPEY: "What? And miss my turn at bat?"

•

DOCTOR: "How is your wife getting along with her reducing diet?"
MR. SMALL: "Fine. She disappeared last week."

•

PAUL: "What does he do for a living?"
SAUL: "He used to be a surgeon, but he had to quit."
PAUL: "Too hard on his nerves?"
SAUL: "No, too much inside work."

•

HOUSEWIFE: "Look here, my man, why do you always come to *my* house to beg?"
TRAMP: "Doctor's orders, madam."
HOUSEWIFE: "Doctor's orders?"
TRAMP: "He told me that when I found food that agreed with me I should stick to it."

"Doctor," said a patient, "it is mighty nice of you to come all this distance to see me."

"Oh, that's all right," said the doctor. "You see, I have another patient in this section so I thought I would just kill two birds with one stone."

•

DANNY: "Do you know what a vegetarian is?"

DOPEY: "Sure, a horse doctor."

DANNY: "No. That's a veterinarian."

DOPEY: "Oh, I thought a veterinarian was a soldier."

•

FUSSY LADY PATIENT: "Do you think raw oysters are healthy?"

WEARY DOCTOR: "I never knew one to complain."

Just Plain Dopey

Once there were two men riding in an airplane.
Unfortunately, one fell out.
Fortunately, there was a haystack below him.
Unfortunately, there was a pitchfork in the haystack.
Fortunately, he missed the pitchfork.
Unfortunately, he missed the haystack.

Three morons were arguing about which part of the human body was most important. One said it was the feet, "because yuh gotta go places."

"Naw," said the second. "It's your hands. How yuh gonna pick things up an' all?"

"No, sir," said the third, "the dimples in my knees—*that's* the most important part."

"Dimples in your knees, huh?" snickered the others, "an' whatcha say that for, huh?"

" 'Cause," insisted he, "I eat celery in bed, and that's where I keep my salt."

•

A city boy was looking, not too hard, for a job.

"I can get you a job digging potatoes," suggested a country friend.

"Why don't you get the man that planted them?" asked the city boy. "He knows where he hid them."

•

RONNIE: "Is your new hunting horse well-behaved?"
JOHNNIE: "He certainly is! He has such good manners that when we come to a fence, he stops and lets me go over first."

•

A handyman doing a hauling job was told that he couldn't get his pay until he made out a statement. After much thought, he handed in the following bill: "Ten comes and ten goes, at four bits a went, $10."

In the bank one day the little moron suddenly called out at the top of his voice, "Did anyone drop a roll of bills with a rubber band around it?"
Several people at different tellers' windows answered, "I did!"

"Well, I just now found the rubber band," said the little moron.

●

HARRY: "Here comes the parade now. Mary'll miss it if she doesn't come to the window. Where is she?"
CARRIE: "She's upstairs waving her hair."
HARRY: "For Pete's sake, hasn't she got a flag?"

●

FIRST MORON: "Are you crazy if you talk to yourself?"
SECOND MORON: "No, but you are if you listen."

●

CITY MORON: "Why does cream cost more than milk?"
COUNTRY MORON: "Because it's harder for the cows to sit on the small bottles."

A farmer was driving past an insane asylum with a load of fertilizer. An inmate of the asylum saw him and called, "What are you hauling?"

"Fertilizer," the farmer replied.

"What are you going to do with it?"

"Put it on strawberries."

"You ought to live in here; *we* get sugar and cream on them."

•

MECHANIC: "Have we any four-volt, two-watt bulbs?"

HELPER: "For what?"

MECHANIC: "No, two."

HELPER: "Two what?"

MECHANIC: "Yes."

•

SAM: "Joe, did you know that a cat has three tails?"

JOE: "Don't be silly."

SAM: "But I can prove it."

JOE: "Try it."

SAM: "Well, you'll have to agree that no cat has two tails."

JOE: "Right."

SAM: "And one cat has one more tail than no cat, hasn't it?"

JOE: "Of course."

SAM: "So, one cat has three tails."

CITY MORON: "Why does the cream rise to the top of the milk?"

COUNTRY MORON: "So the people can get it."

●

Two morons were gossiping. "Cal," said one, "tell me something. Is Mr. Oglethorpe worth any money?"

"I don't know what he's worth, but he saves fifty dollars a day."

"How does he save fifty dollars a day?"

"He goes in the post office every day and there's a big sign there—fifty-dollar fine for spitting—so he don't spit."

●

A country moron was on a trip to the big city. He went into a drug store to telephone a friend. There he saw a dial phone for the first time. He looked at it, studied it, looked at it again, then came out.

"I've got to get to another telephone," he said to his brother.

"Why, what's the matter with the telephone in there?"

"It's got holes in it."

●

TV FAN: "What's that you've got?"

MECHANIC: "An invention I'm making for a television set."

TV FAN: "What is it?"

MECHANIC: "A combination of nuts and wisecracks."

Did you hear the one about the moron who backed off the bus because he heard a lady say she was going to grab his seat as soon as he got up?

●

COXSWAIN: "How is your insomnia?"
SHIP'S COOK: "I'm getting worse. I can't even sleep when it's time to get up."

●

Why did the moron tiptoe past the medicine chest?
He didn't want to wake the sleeping pills.

●

A man got off a train at Albuquerque, New Mexico.
"I beg your pardon," he said to an Indian, "what's your name?"
"Me Running Deer."
"Is that your son there?"
"Yes."
"What's his name?"
"Ninety-eight Cents."
"Why do you call him Ninety-eight Cents?"
"Because he's no buck yet."

●

CUSTOMER: "I understand this is a second-hand store."
CLERK: "Yes, it is."
CUSTOMER: "Well, then, I want one for my watch."

The plane for Chicago was well on its way, when the pilot began to laugh hilariously.

PASSENGER: "What's the joke?"

PILOT: "I'm thinking of what they'll say at the asylum when they find out I have escaped."

•

Good old Dr. Make-you-well was trying to sell young Bobby the idea of including a few vegetables in his daily diet.

"Carrots," he said, "*that's* the ticket. They're good for your eyes."

"I don't believe that baloney," stated Bobby firmly.

"Well, did you ever see a rabbit with glasses?" asked the doctor.

•

A nurse noticed a mental patient with his ear close to the wall listening intently. Holding up a warning finger to be quiet, he beckoned the nurse closer and said, "Listen here." The nurse listened for some time and then said, "*I* can't hear anything."

"No," said the patient, "and it's been like that all day."

A be-bop bystander watching a goat who had fallen into a whirling cement mixer said, "Man, look at that crazy mixed-up kid!"

●

DOPEY: "Since you do not have any speedometer on your flivver, how do you tell how fast you are going?"

DOPIER: "That's simple; when I go ten miles an hour my tail light rattles; when I go twenty miles an hour my fenders rattle; when I go forty miles an hour my teeth rattle; when I go fifty miles an hour my bones rattle."

DOPEY: "What happens when you go sixty miles an hour?"

DOPIER: "I don't know, but I *think* I go to heaven."

Ouch!

"Yes," said the boastful young man, "my family can trace its ancestry back to the *Mayflower*."

"I suppose," remarked his friend, sarcastically, "next you'll be telling us that your ancestors were in the Ark with Noah?"

"Certainly not," said the other. "*My* people had a boat of their own."

SALLY: "I dreamed last night that I had invented a new type of breakfast food and was sampling it when—"

MOLLY: "Yes, yes, go on."

SALLY: "—then I woke up and found a corner of the mattress gone!"

●

VALET: "Sir, your car is at the door."

MASTER: "Yes. I can hear it knocking."

●

VISITING FRIEND: "Are the girls in this town pretty?"

HIS HOST: "Well, let me put it this way—we held a beauty contest and nobody won."

●

TEACHER: "Can anyone here tell me some of the uses of cowhide?"

PUPIL: "Well, it helps keep the cow together!"

●

BEN: "One of our little pigs was sick so I gave him some sugar."

DAN: "Sugar! What for?"

BEN: "Haven't you ever heard of sugar-cured ham?"

●

IRRITATED MAN, to the telephone operator: "Why *can't* you get me the zoo?"

OPERATOR, in a cool voice: "Because the lion is busy!"

A jeweler was taking a grandfather clock to his shop for repairs. On his way in a crowded street, he bumped into a lady and accidentally knocked several bundles from her arms.

"Why can't you be like other people," bellowed the infuriated lady, "and just wear a watch?"

•

DEAN: "Old Mr. Fussbudget flunked out of our school forty years ago and now he has died and left us a million dollars."

MRS. DEAN: "Ah, a very forgiving spirit."

DEAN: "I'm not so sure. The gift has a rather peculiar condition—it is to be used only for paying the transportation of students transferring to other institutions of learning."

•

FANNIE: "Are you going to take the car out in this rainstorm?"

DANNIE: "Certainly. It's a driving rain, isn't it?"

An immigrant, taking his test for naturalization papers, was asked, "Who is the president of the United States?"

"Eisenhower," he answered.

"Could *you* be president?" was the next question he was asked.

"No."

Nodding encouragingly, the questioner asked, "Why not?"

"I'm too busy right now," explained the immigrant gently.

●

Two eagles were lazily soaring over the desert when a jet-propelled plane sped by them, its exhaust spouting flame and smoke. As it went out of sight, one of the eagles remarked:

"That bird was really in a hurry."

"You'd be in a hurry too," said the other, "if *your* tail was on fire."

●

Why is a watermelon filled with water?

Because it's planted in the spring.

●

The little moron took a friend driving in the mountains. After a while his friend said, "Every time you race around one of those sharp curves, I get scared!"

"Then why don't you do what *I* do?" the little moron suggested. "Close your eyes."

MOTHER: "Have you filled the salt shakers?"

BETTY: "Not yet, Mother. It's hard pushing the salt through these little holes!"

•

A preacher dialed long distance to put a call through to a clergyman in a faraway town.

"Do you wish to place a station-to-station call?" asked the operator.

"No," he said. "Make it parson-to-parson."

•

TEACHER: "What was George Washington noted for?"

RUSTY: "His memory."

TEACHER: "What makes you think his memory was so great?"

RUSTY: "Because they erected a monument to Washington's memory."

BOSS: "Simpson, what are you doing with your feet on the desk?"

SIMPSON: "Economy, sir—my eraser wore out, so I'm using my rubber heels."

A huge elephant and a tiny mouse were in the same cage at the zoo. The elephant looked down at the mouse nastily and trumpeted in disgust, "You're the puniest, the weakest, the most insignificant thing I've ever seen!"

"Well," piped the mouse in a plaintive squeak, "don't forget, I've been sick."

An employer said to a man applying for a job: "You ask high wages for a man with no experience."
"Well," the prospect replied, "it's so much harder work when you don't know anything about it."

FIRST LADY: "My sister's baby swallowed a bottle of ink!"
SECOND LADY: "Incredible!"
FIRST LADY: "No. Indelible."

PAUL: "Your new overcoat is pretty loud, isn't it?"
SAUL: "Yeah, but I'm gonna buy a muffler to go with it."

FIRST WORKMAN (getting on bus): "It's going to be tough sleddin' today."

SECOND WORKMAN: "Why do you say that?"

FIRST WORKMAN: "Because there's no snow!"

•

PROUD MOTHER: "Yes, he's fourteen months old now and he's been walking since he was eight months old!"

BORED VISITOR: "Really? He must be awfully tired."

•

POLLY: "How did Santa Claus treat you?"

MOLLY: "He brought me this lovely woolen sweater."

POLLY: "That isn't wool. It's plainly marked 'cotton'."

MOLLY: "Yes, I know—that's to fool the moths."

•

Mrs. Newlywed was eager to prove to her husband what a good cook she was, and on the servant's day off, set about cooking a chicken for his dinner. She plucked the fowl carefully, arranged it neatly in a pot, and put it in the oven.

Two hours later she heard a loud banging on the oven door. She opened the door to find the chicken looking up at her piteously.

"Lady," it cried pleadingly, "either give me back my feathers or turn on the gas. I'm freezing to death in this oven!"

MRS. MORTIMER, to the new maid: "We'll have breakfast promptly at eight o'clock."
MAID: "All right, ma'am. If I'm not down on time, don't wait."

•

STRANGER: "I was born in South America."
NATIVE: "What part?"
STRANGER: "All of me, of course."

•

NEIGHBOR: "Where's your brother, Johnny?"
JOHNNY: "In the house playing a duet. I finished my part first."

•

"Wilt thou give me the pleasure of accompanying me in a game of croquet?" spake Sir Gawain.
"Nay, nay, I dast not,"
quoth the shy Lady Elinor.
" 'Tis a wicket game."

Ouch Again!

A man dropped in to pay a friend an unexpected visit, and was amazed to find him playing chess with his dog. The man watched in silence for a few minutes, then burst out with: "That's the smartest dog I ever saw in my life!"

"Oh, he isn't so smart," was the answer. "I've beaten him three games out of four!"

When the clock strikes 13, what time is it?
Time to get it fixed.

●

DOOPEY: "I hope the rain keeps up."
LOOPEY: "Why?"
DOOPEY: "So it won't come down."

●

"Mother," said the baby moth, "I just found a tiny moth crying."
Mother answered, "Who ever heard of a moth crying?"

"Oh, Mommy," said the baby moth, "haven't you ever seen a moth ball?"

●

A lady went into a store and asked, "May I try on that dress in the window?"

"Well—" said the new clerk doubtfully. "Don't you think it would be better to use the dressing room?"

●

Why are fishermen so stingy?
Because their business makes them sell fish (selfish).

●

BILL: "I wish you boys wouldn't call me Big Bill."
PHIL: "Why not?"
BILL: "Those college names stick—and I'm going to be a doctor."

DOPEY: "If *I* had a thousand men, and *you* had a thousand men, and we had a war, who would win?"
DOPIER: "I give up."
DOPEY: "*I* win! You just gave up!"

•

PAUL: "What is the best way to make a coat last?"
SAUL: "Make the vest and trousers first!"

•

GOLF STUDENT: "Well, how do you like my game?"
PRO: "I suppose it's all right, but I still prefer golf."

•

Why is a pair of skates like an apple?

> *They both have to do with the fall of man.*

•

The telephone bell on a prominent economist's desk rang insistently. When he answered, a voice informed him,

> "You're all wet about the cost of living reaching a new high! My wife and I live sumptuously—eating everything we like—on sixty-eight cents a week."

> "Sixty-eight cents a week!" echoed the economist. "I can't believe it! Won't you tell me how? And to make sure I get the story straight, please speak louder."

> "I *can't* speak louder," came the answer. "I'm a goldfish."

129

FIRST PELICAN: "That's fine fish you have there."
SECOND PELICAN: "Well, it fills the bill."

•

PAUL: "I saw a fellow strike a girl today."
SAUL: "You didn't let him get away with it, did you?"
PAUL: "I went up to him and said, 'Only a coward would hit a woman—why don't you hit a man?'"
SAUL: "Then what happened?"
PAUL: "That's all I remember."

Ouch! Ouch! Ouch!

"Herbert," said a mother to her six-year-old son, "are you teaching the parrot to use slang after I asked you not to?"

"No, Mama," replied Herbert. "I was just telling him what not to say."

Two voices were heard in the park one beautiful evening.

"I love you," said one.

"Ouch!" yelled the other.

"I love you."

"Ouch!"

It was two porcupines necking.

•

When is it easy to read in the woods?

When autumn turns the leaves.

•

Could you light a candle if you had a box of candles and no matches?

Just take a candle out of the box and you will make the box a candle lighter.

•

How many balls of string would it take to reach the moon?

Only one—if it were long enough.

•

PAUL: "Why Saul, where did you get that nice Easter tie?"

SAUL: "What makes you think it's an Easter tie?"

PAUL: "It's got egg on it."

•

How do sailors get their clothes clean?

They throw them overboard and they are washed ashore.

BRAGGY: "Where I come from they do things in a hurry. Why, they put up buildings quicker than in any other city. They start a twenty-story building one day and in a week it's finished."

BRAGGIER: "That's nothing—you should come down to our town. I was going to work one morning and they were laying the cornerstone of a building. When I came home from work that night, the landlord was putting tenants out for not paying their rent."

●

WILLIS: "Why do you comb your hair before going to bed?"

PHYLLIS: "To make a good impression on the pillow."

●

Why is a locomotive like a stick of gum?

> *One goes choo choo, the other goes chew chew.*

●

DAN: "In a couple of years you will all have to look up to me."

NAN: "How's that?"

DAN: "I'm going to be a window cleaner."

●

PHIL: "Didn't I tell you about Mrs. Spitz? She had triplets and two weeks later she had twins."

BILL: "That's impossible. How did it happen?"

PHIL: "Well, one of the triplets got lost."

MOPEY: "My hair is getting thin."
DOPEY: "Well, who wants fat hair?"

•

DONNIE: "Isn't nature wonderful?"
CONNIE: "Why do you say that?"
DONNIE: "Well, thousands of years ago she didn't know man was going to invent glasses, yet look how conveniently she placed his ears!"

•

You tell 'em, mountain . . . I'm only a bluff!

•

MR. MEEK, to the barber: "My hair is coming out—what can I get to keep it in?"
BARBER: "A paper bag."

•

PAUL: "I saw something last night I'll never get over."
MOLL: "What was that?"
PAUL: "The moon."

Lilliputian Logic

Dorothy, aged six, was watching her mother put cold cream on her face.

"What's that for, Mummy," she asked.

"It's face cream, dear, to make me beautiful."
A little while later, after the cold cream had been wiped off, Dorothy looked at her mother for a minute, shook her head, and remarked sadly, "Didn't work, did it, Mummy?"

Five-year-old Bettina was getting ready for bed. Suddenly she turned to her mother and asked, "Mother, are we going to move tomorrow?"

"Yes, dear, this is the last night you will sleep here."

"Then," said Bettina, kneeling beside her bed, "I'd better say good-by to God now if we're moving to Cleveland in the morning."

●

Little Victoria, watching the farm hands spreading out a stack of hay to dry, could contain her curiosity no longer, so she politely asked, "Is it a needle you're looking for?"

●

HOSTESS (at a children's birthday party): "Jackie, does your mother allow you to have two pieces of cake when you are at home?"

JACKIE (who has just asked for a second piece): "No, ma'am."

HOSTESS: "Well, do you think she'd like you to have two pieces here?"

JACKIE, confidentially: "Oh, *she* wouldn't care. This isn't *her* cake!"

●

A little boy who had been used to receiving his older brother's old toys and clothes recently remarked,

"Mom, will I have to marry his widow when he dies?"

136

Three-year-old Patty's mother sent her for a switch to be punished with. Patty was gone quite a while, and when she finally came in her mother asked her for the switch.

Patty sobbed a little and said, "The tree was too big for me to reach, but here's a wock you can fwow at me."

●

Lenny's mother was trying to explain to him that the neighbor's dog was a good dog and wouldn't bite.

"Well, if he did eat me up would I go to heaven like a good boy?" the child asked.

His mother said that of course he would.

"Well, then," the boy said after a moment's thought, "wouldn't that dog have to go too?"

●

"Look, Mother!" cried little Danny, "there's a big bear in the back yard."

"You know perfectly well that's Johnny Jackson's dog. Now go to your room and ask God to forgive you for telling a lie."

In a few minutes Danny was back downstairs.

"Did you ask God to forgive you?" his mother asked.

"Yes, I did," said Danny. "And he said it was all right. God said the first time He saw Johnny Jackson's dog He thought it was a bear Himself!"

"Can any of you children tell me who lived in the Garden of Eden?" asked the Sunday-school teacher.

"Yes, teacher," said a little girl, "I think it was the Adamses."

●

Teacher: "Randy, if you put your hand in one pants pocket and you find seventy-five cents and you put your hand in the other pants pocket and you find twenty-five cents, what would you have?"
Randy, promptly: "I'd have somebody else's pants on!"

Dumb Question, Dumb Answer

JACK: "Today I saw a baby that gained ten pounds in two weeks by drinking elephant's milk."

MARY: "You don't say! Whose baby was it?"

JACK: "The elephant's."

"My father died at sea. My grandfather died at sea. And my great-grandfather died at sea," related the sailor.

"My, my," remarked the visiting sentimental old lady, "if all your ancestors died at sea, how did you *dare* enlist in the navy?"

"Ma'am," responded the sailor, "where did *your* father die?"

"In bed."

"Your grandfather?"

"In bed, too."

"Your great-grandfather?"

"He also died in bed."

"Then," said the seaman, "how do you *dare* go to bed, since all your ancestors died there?"

●

BRIDE: "Harry! Harry! Wake up! I just heard a mouse squeak!"

GROOM, drowsily: "What do you want me to do—get up and oil it?"

●

A court official, after explaining the history of the American flag to a group of aliens seeking citizenship papers, asked one of them, "Tell me—what flies over the City Hall?"

The foreigner thought a moment, then, "Peejins!" he shouted triumphantly.

Mr. and Mrs.

WIFE: "I think you might talk to me while I sew."
HUSBAND: "Why don't you sew to me while I read?"

●

SHE: "Then you'll take me for a drive on Thursday?"
HE: "Yes, but suppose it rains?"
SHE: "Come the day before, then."

She had just received a beautiful skunk coat as a gift from her husband.

SHE: "I can't see how such a nice coat comes from such a foul-smelling beast."

HE: "I don't ask for thanks, dear. But I do think I deserve respect."

●

She came to the police station with a picture in her hand. "My husband has disappeared," she sobbed. "Here is his picture, I want you to find him."

The inspector looked up from the photograph. "Why?" he asked.

●

BOOK-STORE CLERK: "Here's a new book called *How to Help Your Husband Get Ahead*."

BRIDE: "Oh, no thank you. My husband already has one."

●

HUBBY: "What's the matter with this suit I just bought? What don't you like about it? The store said it was a perfect fit."

WIFE: "It looks more like a convulsion."

●

YOUNG WIFE: "I really managed to save something this month. I put a hundred dollars in the bank."

YOUNG HUSBAND: "Wonderful! It wasn't so hard, was it?"

YOUNG WIFE: "It was easy. I just tore up the bills."

What is the difference between a kiss, color television, and a monkey?

> *The kiss is so dear, color television is too dear, and the monkey is you, dear.*

●

SMITH: "Who is your wife going to vote for?"
JONES: "For whoever I vote for."
SMITH: "Who are you going to vote for?"
JONES: "She hasn't decided yet."

●

BRIDEGROOM: "My wife and I have a joint checking account."
BEST FRIEND: "Isn't that hard to keep straight?"
BRIDEGROOM: "No. I put in the money and she takes it out."

●

DOCTOR: "I'm sorry to tell you that your wife's mind is completely gone."
MR. PECK: "I'm not surprised. She's been giving me a piece of it every day for twenty years."

●

WIFE: "Wait a minute—did you shave?"
HUSBAND: "Of course I shaved."
WIFE: "Next time, stand a little closer to the razor."

●

HUSBAND TO WIFE: "Well, in a way, it's a two-week vacation . . . I take a week and then the boss takes a week."

WIFE: "Goodness, Henry, this isn't *our* baby."

HENRY: "Shut up! It's a better buggy!"

●

A multimillionaire, being interviewed about his self-made fortune, said: "I never hesitate to give full credit to my wife for her assistance."

"In what way did she help?" the reporter asked.

"Well, if you want the whole truth," replied the man, "I was curious to find out if there was any income she couldn't live beyond."

●

What sentence of three words which reads the same backward and forward did Adam use when he introduced himself to Eve?

"Madam, I'm Adam."

Bloopers and Blunders

In a midwestern cemetery, this sign appears:
"It is forbidden for any persons to pick flowers from any but their own graves."

The unfortunate woman was killed while cooking her husband's breakfast in a horrible manner.

News note in a COUNTRY PAPER

•

"Father," said the adoring mother, "Jonathan's teacher says he ought to have an encyclopedia."

"Encyclopedia, my eye," grumbled his father. "Let him *walk* to school, like I did."

•

Columbia, Tennessee, which calls itself the largest outdoor mule market in the world, recently held a mule parade headed by the governor.

NEW YORK MAGAZINE

•

A four-year-old girl was taken to church for the first time, and was very much impressed by it all. And when everyone knelt down, she whispered, "Mummy, what are they doing now?"

"Shhh!" cautioned her mother, "they're getting ready to say their prayers."

"*What?*" yelled the child in amazement, "with all their *clothes on?*"

•

SANDY: "We've got a new baby at our house."
MANDY: "Where did you get it?"
SANDY: "We got it from Doctor Brown."
MANDY: "We take from him, too."

146

What did the big firecracker say to the little fire-cracker?

"My pop is bigger than your pop."

●

BILLY: "I got a new little baby brother."

MILLY: "*Another* one? Gee, you've got about nineteen already, haven't you?"

BILLY: "Yeah."

MILLY: "What's his name?"

BILLY: "We called him Joe for two days."

MILLY: "For two days? Then what happened?"

BILLY: "After two days my father and mother found out we've already *got* a Joe in the family."

●

Little five-year-old Betty was taken to church for the first time. As she walked out of the church with her parents, the preacher stopped her, leaned over, and asked her how she liked church.

"I liked the music okay," said Betty, "but the commercial was too long."

●

A lady decided to have the little neighbor boy stay for lunch one day. As the meal got under way, she watched his struggles to manipulate his knife and fork and, hoping to be helpful, finally asked him,

"Are you sure you can cut your steak?"

"Oh yes," he replied. "We often have it this tough at home."

The visiting governor of Maine was addressing a group of the inmates of a penitentiary.

"Fellow citizens," he began, then stopped short, because they were not citizens.

"Fellow convicts," he began again, then realized he was again off the beam.

"Well, boys," he finally said, "I don't know what to call you, but I'm mighty glad to see so many here."

●

Dr. Carson Carter, noted health authority, who was to speak at the Century Club on "How to Keep Well," could not appear because of illness.

THE CALIFORNIA (PA.) SENTINEL

●

A patient was convalescing from an appendectomy. A friend came to see him. "How you doing?"

"I'm doing all right, but the day after the operation they opened me up again to take a sponge out of me they left in there. Yesterday they opened me up again and took out a scalpel that they forgot."

Just then the doctor walked in. "Has anyone seen my hat around here?" he asked.

●

Mrs. Millie Mock broke her arm recently. She is recovering nicely under the car of Dr. Leatherman.

THE CALIFORNIA (PA.) SENTINEL

An extremely nervous man carried his twins up to the baptismal font for the christening.

"What are the names of the little boy and girl?" asked the minister.

"Steak and Kidney," stuttered the embarrassed father.

"What?"

"Their names," corrected the wife icily, "are Kate and Sidney."

•

"Now that you've seen my new son," said the proud new father, "which side of the house do you think he resembles?"

"Well," said his embarrassed bachelor friend, "I came in the front door and really didn't notice either side of the house."

•

HOSTESS (at a dinner party): "What, going already, Professor Bennett? And must you take your dear wife with you?"

PROFESSOR: "Indeed, I'm sorry to say I must!"

•

As a steamer was leaving Athens, a woman went up to the captain and, pointing to the distant hills, inquired:

"What is that white stuff on those hills?"

"That is snow, madam," replied the captain.

"Well," said the lady, "I thought so myself. But a gentleman just told me it was Greece."

At a formal dinner the hostess, who was seated at the far end of the table from a very famous actress, wrote a note to the actress and had the butler deliver it.

The actress couldn't read without her glasses, so she asked the man at her left to read it to her. "It says," he began, 'Dear, do me a favor and please don't neglect the man at your left. I know he's a bore, but talk to him.' "

•

STARTLING STATEMENTS FOUND ON EXAMINATION PAPERS:

"Daniel Boone was born in a log cabin he built himself."

"An Indian baby is called a caboose."

"The mother of Abraham Lincoln died in infancy."

They Say It
Happened to —

James Whitcomb Riley and Bill Nye used to go
about the country together lecturing. Once when
they were traveling by train, Bill Nye, who was very
fond of playing jokes on his friend, happened to spy
Mr. Riley's ticket protruding from his coat pocket.
He reached over and removed it without Riley's
knowledge.

When the conductor entered the car for fares, Bill Nye remarked innocently, "Here comes the conductor. Get out your ticket."

Mr. Riley searched first in one pocket and then another, but with no success. At length he turned to his friend and explained that he had lost his ticket, and asked him for a loan since he had spent all his money buying the ticket. But Bill Nye professed to be bankrupt also.

The conductor was fast nearing their seat and the situation was becoming acute, when Bill Nye innocently suggested a way out. "I tell you what, Riley," he said, "just crawl down under the seat and I'll put my coat over you and he'll never know you're there."

Riley was a small man and the situation was desperate: the conductor was almost upon them. Hurriedly he followed Nye's suggestion. When the conductor reached their seat Bill Nye held out both their tickets.

"*Two* fares?" asked the conductor in doubt.

"Yes," solemnly answered the wicked Bill Nye.

"Two?" repeated the train official. "Who's the other one for?"

With a mischievous twinkle in his eye, Bill Nye bent over, lifted the coat from his friend and said,

"It's for my friend here, but he's a little queer. He prefers to ride under the seat."

Daniel Webster, the great American statesman, was once sued by his butcher for a very much overdue bill. Before the suit was settled he met the butcher on the street, and to the butcher's embarrassment said, "Why have you not sent around for my order?"

"Why, Mr. Webster," said the man. "I did not think you wanted to deal with me when I brought this suit."

"Tut, tut," said Webster, "sue all you wish, but for heaven's sake don't try to starve me to death!"

•

Gutzon Borglum, the sculptor who created the tremendous Mount Rushmore Memorial in South Dakota, was once asked if he considered his work perfect in every detail.

"Not today," he replied. "The nose of Washington is an inch too long. It's better that way, though. It will erode to be exactly right in ten thousand years."

•

When Calvin Coolidge was a boy, an acquaintance tried to borrow a couple of dollars from him—and was turned down. When Coolidge was President the same person visited the White House and renewed his request for a couple of dollars. Again Coolidge refused. The chum drawled, in reluctant admiration,

"I got to hand it to you, Cal; success ain't changed you a bit!"

Gary Cooper was asked during an interview if he uses any word other than his famous "Yup."

"Yup," replied Gary.

"What is it?" asked the newsman.

"Giddy-up!" said Cooper.

•

Walking with a friend one day, Fritz Kreisler passed a large fish shop where a fine catch of cod-fish, with mouths open and eyes staring, were arranged in a row. Kreisler suddenly stopped, looked at them, and clutching his friend by the arm, exclaimed:

"Heavens! That reminds me—I should be playing at a concert!"

•

RED GRANGE: "I once carried a hundred-pound load on my back for a mile."

FAN: "It got heavier with every step, I bet."

RED GRANGE: "No—it was ice."

A very amusing story, still going the rounds, is told about Calvin Coolidge when he was Vice-President. The Coolidges lived in the Willard Hotel in Washington. A fire alarm in the middle of the night brought every guest into the lobby, in a variety of negligees and fancy pajamas. Mr. Coolidge speedily surmised that there was no danger and started to trudge back to his room. "Nothing doing!" said the fire marshal, "get back in that lobby!"

"You are speaking to the Vice-President," said Coolidge with some dignity.

"Okay, then," said the marshal. "Go ahead." A moment later he called suspiciously, "What are you Vice-President of?"

"The United States," said Coolidge.

"Come right back here!" ordered the marshal. "I thought you were Vice-President of the hotel."

●

THOMAS JEFFERSON: "What did Franklin say when he discovered electricity in lightning?"

GEORGE WASHINGTON: "Nothing, he was too shocked."

In the course of one of his lecture trips Mark Twain arrived at a small town. Before dinner, he went to a barber shop to be shaved.

"You're a stranger?" asked the barber.

"Yes," Mark Twain replied, "this is the first time I've been here."

"You chose a good time to come," the barber continued. "Mark Twain is going to lecture tonight. You'll go, I suppose?"

"Oh, I guess so."

"Have you bought your ticket?"

"Not yet."

"But everything is sold out. You'll have to stand."

"How very annoying!" Mark Twain said, with a sigh. "I never heard of such luck! I *always* have to stand when that fellow lectures."

 156

Gobs of Humor

A pink-cheeked young Ensign reported for duty on a battleship. The gruff old Captain stared at him in disapproval.

"Well!" he said at last. "I guess they decided to send the fool of the family to sea."

"No, sir, not at all," said the Ensign. "That custom has been stopped since your time, sir."

FIRST MATE: "Have you cleaned the deck and polished the brasses?"

GOB: "Yes, sir, and I've swept the horizon with my telescope."

●

The proprietor of a restaurant was reprimanding a careless waiter. "During dinner," he said, "you spilled soup on the Admiral's coat."

"But the Admiral didn't mind, sir, it was Navy Bean soup," answered the waiter.

●

SAILOR: "This coffee tastes like mud."

COOK: "It should. It was ground this morning."

●

A sailor went wearily into the barber shop early one morning and slumped down in a chair. "Give me a shave," he said.

The barber told him that he was too far down in the chair for a shave.

"All right," said the sailor with a sigh, "give me a haircut."

●

The captain of H.M.S. DIAMOND by some navigation error hit the cruiser SWIFTSURE bows on. As the SWIFTSURE went astern, the admiral signaled:

"What do you intend to do now?"

"Buy a farm!" was the reply from the DIAMOND'S captain.

A dim-witted girl was visiting a sailor in the hospital.

"Where were you wounded?" she asked.

"In the Solomons, miss," he answered.

"How terrible!" she exclaimed. "Are they any better?"

The sailor came on board carrying a cardboard box punched full of holes.

"What's in the box?" asked his shipmate.

"A cat," said the sailor.

"What do you want of a cat aboard ship?"

"I dream of mice every night, and I'm scared of mice. I've brought along a cat to catch them."

"But you only imagine the mice!"

"Ah, yes," said the sailor. "But the cat in this box is imaginary, too!"

FIRST GOB (in his first battle at sea): "The enemy ships are thick as peas. What shall we do?"

SECOND GOB: "Shell them, of course."

●

MESS COOK: "Did you say you wanted these eggs turned over?"

DISGUSTED GOB: "Yes! Turn them over to a museum!"

●

A sailor was bragging to his girl. "A shell fragment went right through my chest," he boasted.

"Goodness!" she said. "How did it miss your heart?"

"My heart was in my throat at the time," said the sailor modestly.

Old lady (stopping a wounded sailor on the street):
"How were you wounded, poor man?"
Sailor: "By an enemy shell, madam."
Old lady: "Did it explode?"
Sailor: "No. It followed me up the gangplank and bit me."

●

A naval officer, who had been very strict with his men, fell overboard. He was rescued by a deck hand.

"What can I do to reward you, my good fellow?" asked the officer.

"The best way, sir," said the deck hand, "is to say nothing about it. If the other fellows knew I'd pulled you out, they'd chuck me in."

BRIEFING OFFICER: "Why is it important not to lose your head in an attack?"

GREEN GOB: "Because then I wouldn't have any place to put my cap."

●

The teacher called on little Charlie. "Tell me what you know about George Washington. Was he a soldier or sailor?"

"I think he was a soldier," replied Charlie.

"Why do you think he was a soldier?"

"I seen a picture of him when he crossed the Delaware and any sailor knows enough not to stand up in a rowboat."

●

The chaplain aboard a troop ship said that on the next Sunday he would preach a special sermon. Before then he wanted all the sailors to read the seventeenth chapter of St. Mark. The next Sunday he asked how many sailors had done as he asked. Nearly all of them raised their hands.

"Splendid!" said the chaplain. "My sermon will be on honesty. There are only sixteen chapters in the book of St. Mark."

●

FIRST SAILOR (at mess): "I'm hungry enough to eat a horse."

SECOND SAILOR: "That's what we're getting in a few minutes."

An officer on board a battleship was drilling his men.

"I want every man to lie on his back, put his legs in the air and move them as though he were riding a bicycle," he explained. "Now begin!" After a few minutes one of the men stopped.

"Why did you stop, Smith?" demanded the officer.

"If you please," said Smith, "I'm freewheeling for a while."

"We're a tough outfit," boasted the Marine. "We eat our steak raw and our beans with the shells on. We boil our coffee until it's so thick you can't stir it with a spoon."

"That so?" drawled the Gob. "Well, in the Navy, when we make coffee, we drop the anchor in, and if it sinks, we put in more coffee."

Once upon a time there were two naval recruits. Now there are gobs of them.

•

CAPTAIN: "If the boat foundered, whom would you save first, the children or me?"

READY-WITTED GOB: "Me."

•

BARBER: "Haven't I shaved you before, sir?"

SAILOR: "No, I got that scar at Guadalcanal."

Musical
Monkeyshines

An old man at a party bowed his head and wept quietly but profusely while a young lady sang the plaintive ballad, "My Old Kentucky Home," in a high soprano voice.

The hostess tiptoed up to him and inquired sympathetically, "Pardon me, are you a Kentuckian?"

"No, madam," the tearful one replied, "I'm a musician."

PAUL: "My brother can play the piano by ear."
SAUL: "That's nothing. My grampaw fiddles with his whiskers."

●

Moisha Rabinovoff began his musical education almost before he could talk. For over twenty years he studied in practically every conservatory in the world. After that he played in concerts in every big European capital—London, Vienna, Rome, Paris. Finally he came to New York to play under Leopold Stokowski. On the first day when he was playing with Stokowski, the great conductor noticed he had a grouchy look on his face.

"Hah!" he thought. "This guy is a sourpuss."

"Why have you got that sour look on your face?" Stokowski demanded. "Don't you like me?" he continued.

"It's not that," answered Rabinovoff.

"Maybe you don't like the other musicians?"

"No, it isn't that."

"Well, maybe you don't like the piece we're playing?"

"No, it's not that."

"Maybe you don't like Carnegie Hall?"

"That isn't it."

"Well, there must be *something* wrong. What is it?"

"*I just don't like music!*" exploded Rabinovoff.

 166

DAN: "Did you hear that Jones is making a hundred dollars a night playing the violin?"
NAN: "Imagine! Twenty-five dollars a string!"
DAN: "Yeah, if I were him I'd get a harp."

●

FRED: "You say your son plays the piano like Paderewski?"
TED: "Yes. He uses both hands."

●

DOPEY: "What is your occupation?"
DOPIER: "I used to be an organist."
DOPEY: "And why did you give it up?"
DOPIER: "The monkey died."

●

Walter Damrosch, composer of the opera CYRANO DE BERGERAC, arrived one day at the Met to see his opera. Due to the sudden illness of the tenor, LA BOHÈME was substituted for CYRANO without notifying Damrosch. The latter sat quietly through the first act, then turned to the manager and asked, "Who changed the scenery?"

●

HOSTESS: "They tell me you love music."
GUEST: "Yes, I do. But never mind—keep right on playing."

●

VISITOR: "Does your son play on the piano?"
MOTHER: "No. Not yet. He can't climb that high."

167 ☺

GUEST at a musicale: "That's a very, very difficult number that contralto is struggling with!"

OTHER GUEST: "*Difficult?* I wish it were downright *impossible!*"

●

PRETTY YOUNG STUDENT: "Professor Boschovich, do you think I will ever be able to do anything with my voice?"

WEARY TEACHER: "Well it might come in handy in case of fire or shipwreck."

●

POLITE VISITOR: "Your Georgie is making really good progress with his violin since I heard him last. He is beginning to play quite nice tunes."

GEORGIE'S MOTHER: "Oh, do you really think so? His father and I were afraid that we'd merely got used to it."

Legal Giggles

LAWYER: "Among other things, your uncle left you over five hundred clocks."

HEIR: "Oh, dear! It will take a long time to wind up his estate, won't it?"

The lawyer came over to the railroad station when his client sent a messenger, and found a doctor setting the client's leg in splints.

"How did you break your leg, Tom?" asked the lawyer.

"Do you see those six steps over there?" asked Tom.

"Yes," said the lawyer.

"Well, I didn't!" said Tom.

A man was suing his wife for assault.

"She hit me with an oak leaf," he said.

"Surely *that* wouldn't have hurt you!" said the Judge.

"It sure did!" said the man. "It was an oak leaf from the dining-room table!"

BURGLAR (just released from jail): "Thanks, Judge. I'll drop in on you some time."

JUDGE: "All right, but make it in the daytime, please."

●

MIKE: "Why does a judge have so little time left for himself?"

IKE: "Because he's so busy, I guess."

MIKE: "Wrong! It's because he hands out so much time to other people."

●

JUDGE: "You say you robbed the delicatessen because you were hungry. With all that food around, why didn't you make yourself a sandwich instead of robbing the cash register?"

PRISONER: "I'm a proud man, Judge. I like to pay for what I eat."

In a back-woods domestic-relations court the judge listened carefully to both sides in a case against an elderly man who was charged by his wife with non-support.

After all the evidence was in, the judge told the defendant:

"You haven't taken proper care of this good woman, and I'm going to grant her forty dollars a month."

The defendant beamed with pleasure. "That's mighty nice of Your Honor," he said, "and I'll give her a dollar or two from time to time myself."

●

Have you heard the story of the rancher who had occasion to telephone the legal firm of Rasmussen, Rasmussen, Rasmussen and Rasmussen? The conversation went as follows:

"Hello. I'd like to talk to Mr. Rasmussen."

"Mr. Rasmussen is in court arguing a case."

"Oh. Then I'll talk to Mr. Rasmussen."

"Mr. Rasmussen can't come to the phone. He's in conference with an important client."

"Oh. Then I'll talk to Mr. Rasmussen."

"Mr. Rasmussen isn't in today. He's playing golf at South Hills."

"Oh. In that case, can I talk to Mr. Rasmussen?"

"Speaking."

"I'll have to give you ten days in jail or twenty dollars," said the judge.

"I'll take the twenty dollars, Judge," said the prisoner.

•

JUDGE: "How could you swindle people who trusted you?"

PRISONER: "But Judge, people who don't trust you can't be swindled!"

•

LAWYER: "Why did you run away from the scene of the accident?"

CLIENT: "I was running to stop a fight."

LAWYER: "But nobody was fighting!"

CLIENT: "Me and the other driver were!"

•

CLIENT: "My wife's been throwing things at me ever since we were married."

LAWYER: "But why didn't you complain before?"

CLIENT: "This is the first time she's ever hit me."

JUDGE: "Have you ever appeared as a witness before?"

JOE: "Yes, your honor."

JUDGE: "In what suit?"

JOE: "My tan gabardine."

●

Sammy Topper was a bit of a smart-aleck and practical joker, and frequently found himself before the local judge in his small town.

This time the judge told him indignantly, "Look now! You've been warned lots of times. But I'm sorry for your poor long-suffering family, so I'll just fine you now . . . but if this happens again tomorrow, I'll toss you in jail."

"I get it," said Sam. "Fine today . . . cooler tomorrow."

HELLO, JUDGE

Hillbilly Hoaxes

HILLBILLY (to four-year-old son): "Ira, quit pointin' that thar gun at yore little brother. Hit might go off and kill one of them hawgs he's playin' with."

•

SOCIAL WORKER: "Goodness! doesn't your little boy swear terribly?"

HILLBILLY MAMA: "Yes'm, he sure does. He don't put no expression in it at all."

UNCLE BOSKIE: "I've got a cow I want to sell you, Oscar."

UNCLE OSCAR: "Yeah? Would she fit into my herd?"

UNCLE BOSKIE: "No; I dunno as she would."

UNCLE OSCAR: "Does she give lots of milk?"

UNCLE BOSKIE: "No; I can't say as she gives lots of milk, but I can tell you this: she's a kind, gentle, good-natured old cow, and if she's *got* any milk she'll *give* it to you."

•

MA SNOOKER, a backwoods woman, the soles of whose feet had been toughened by a lifetime of shoelessness, was standing in front of her cabin fireplace one day when her husband addressed her.

PA SNOOKER: "You'd better move your foot a mite, Maw; you're standing on a live coal."

MA SNOOKER: "Which foot, Paw?"

•

A hillbilly on a construction job stood reading a letter to another hillbilly. His ears were stopped up with cotton, stuck on with adhesive tape.

The boss came over and said, "What kind of horseplay are *you* two fellows up to?"

"My buddy here," said the hillbilly, "got this here letter his gal writ him, boss, but he kain't read, so he gets me to read it for him, but he stops up my ears so's I kain't hear what his girl writ him."

A hillbilly walked into a hotel and registered for a room. The bellhop took his bags and led him across the lobby to the elevator. As they were going up, the new guest took a quick look around and complained, "It sure is an awful small room for five dollars!"

●

HOTEL CLERK in big city: "Why don't you wipe the mud off your shoes when you come in here?"
HILLBILLY: "*What* shoes?"

●

TOURIST: "I see you raise hogs almost exclusively about here. Do you find that they pay better than corn and potatoes?"
HILLBILLY (slowly): "Wal, no, ma'am; but yer see, ma'am, hawgs don't need no hoeing."

●

FIRST HILLBILLY: "My Uncle Boskie wants me to he'p him with his income tax."
SECOND HILLBILLY: "*You* help him? Why, how can *you* help him—you can't even read or write."
FIRST HILLBILLY: "Oh, he don't want me to read ner write. He wants me to pay it fer him."

●

UNCLE OSCAR: "What became of the hired man you got from the city?"
UNCLE BOSKIE: "He crawled under a mule to see why it didn't go."

A hillbilly was complaining about the housing shortage. "I wouldn't mind having all my kinfolk living with me," he moaned. "If it wasn't for their doggone *pets*! Cousin Boskie has six dogs, Aunt Omalia has nine cats. And when they all get to fightin', it disturbs Uncle Jasper's eight hogs so bad, they wake up cousin Chick's dozen goats. It's terrible, especially since the windows are always down."

"Why don't you raise your windows?" asked a friend.

"*What!*" objected the hillbilly, "and let my thirteen buzzards escape!"

●

POLICEMAN (to hillbilly who has been whipping his horse): "Don't whip him, man—*talk* to him!"
HILLBILLY (to horse, by way of opening the conversation): "*I* come from up in the Cumberland mountains. Where *you* from?"

Egging on the Elders

FOND GRANDMA: "Dear, I have a real treat for you. I'm going to take you to the fair and let you ride on the merry-go-round!"

MODERN CHILD: "All right, Grandma, I don't mind, if it will amuse you."

VISITOR: "Are you a good boy, Benjie?"
BENJIE: "No, ma'am. I'm the kind of boy Mom doesn't want me to play with."

•

"Why don't you finish your alphabet soup, Daniel?" asked his mother. "There's a few letters left in your plate."

"I know, but they spell spinach," answered Danny firmly.

•

TOMMY: "Pop, can you help me with this arithmetic?"
POP: "I could, but it wouldn't be right, would it?"
TOMMY: "No, I don't suppose so—but you could try, anyhow!"

•

The scoutmaster was very bossy, but he did insist that the boys should have good food at camp. One day he saw two Scouts carrying a large soup kettle.

"Get me a spoon. I want to taste that," he ordered. The boys started to object, but the scoutmaster broke in, "Now, don't give me any arguments. Do as I say!"

They brought a spoon, and he took a large mouthful. Sputtering angrily, he yelled, "You don't call this *soup*, do you!"

"No, sir," one of the Scouts answered. "We *tried* to explain. It's dishwater."

"I'll be good for a nickel, Mother," coaxed little George hopefully.

"Oh, Georgie," replied his mother, "why can't you be like your big brother? He isn't good for a penny. He's good for nothing."

●

A very prim old lady had a few words of advice for her granddaughter. "My dear," she said, "I wish you would do something for me. There are two words I wish you would promise me never to use. One is 'swell' and the other is 'lousy.' Would you promise me that?"

"Why sure, Granny," said her granddaughter. "What are the words?"

●

JOHNNY: "Mom, what was the name of the last station our train stopped at?"

MOTHER: "Don't bother me, I don't know. Don't you see I'm reading?"

JOHNNY: "Well, it's too bad you don't know, because Little Brother got off there."

●

"Didn't you promise me to be a good boy?"

"Yes, Father."

"And didn't I promise you no spending money if you weren't?"

"Yes, Father. But since I've broken my promise, you sure don't have to keep yours."

MOTHER: "What do you want to take your cod-liver oil with this morning, Elmer?"

ELMER: "A fork."

●

Young Billy had been to a birthday party, and, knowing his weakness, his mother looked him straight in the eye and said, "I hope you didn't ask Mrs. Parker for a second piece of cake?"

"No," replied Billy. "I told Mrs. Parker I wanted the recipe so you could make some like it, and she gave me two more pieces without my asking at all!"

Boy meets Girl

MOLL: "I dreamed about the funniest thing last night. Wasn't it a funny dream?"

PAUL: "How do *I* know what your dream was about?"

MOLL: "You *ought* to know. You were in it!"

CLEO: "What makes you like Pauline so much?"

LEO: "Nutty haircut, goofy manners, no brains, and too much make-up."

CLEO: "Why, I'm astonished! That certainly describes most of the girls, but surely not *Pauline*!"

LEO: "I know it—that's why I like her so much."

●

DAN: "Do you know the difference between taxis and a bus?"

NAN: "No."

DAN: "Good—then we'll take a trolley."

●

SAUL: "Say, I hear that Jack kissed you last night!"

MOLL: "He did not! And besides, he promised not to tell."

●

"I'd like a box of pencils," said the high-school boy to the clerk in the stationery shop.

"Hard or soft?"

"Soft. They're for writing love letters."

●

Willis called on Phyllis on date night, carrying a package under his arm.

"What have you got there?" said Phyllis.

"Do you like candy?" said Willis.

"I love it," said Phyllis.

"Well, I brought a pan," said Willis, "let's make fudge."

184

They were strolling through a country lane when Claude got romantic. "Ah Maude, look at the cow and the calf rubbing noses in the pasture. That sight makes me want to do the same," he said softly.

"Well, go ahead," his girl answered, "it's *your* cow."

●

Eskimo: "What would you say, darling, if I told you I pushed my dog team for a thousand miles through ice and snow just to tell you that I love you?"

Eskimoette: "I'd say that was a lot of mush."

●

A fellow was having his first date with a new girl. Things were going along pretty well, as they rode along in his car, when she turned to him and coyly asked: "Do you want to see where I was operated on?"

"Why—uh—yeah. Sure!" he gulped.

"Well, all right," said the girl. "We're just two blocks from the hospital now."

●

Fresh young man in an elegant roadster: "How about a little ride, cutie?"

Bright young thing: "Are you going north?"

Fresh young man: "Yes, I am."

Bright young thing: "Good! Give my regards to the Eskimos."

DORA: "My sweetie took me down to the picture show last night and we had to ride on a crowded streetcar. Gee! Was he mad!"

NORA: "Because you had to ride on the crowded streetcar?"

DORA: "Well, that's part of the reason, but the thing that made him the sorest was that there was only one seat when we got on, so I had to stand up all the way downtown."

●

There was a young man so benighted,
He never knew when he was slighted;
    He would go to a party,
    And eat just as hearty,
As if he'd been really invited!

●

Why should pretty girls set a good example?
    Because boys are so apt to follow them.

●

GIRL, on the phone: "Is Hugh there?"

KID SISTER, answering: "Hugh *who*?"

GIRL: "Yoo-hoo yourself!"

●

BOB came to class with a black eye.

JIM: "Who gave you that shiner?"

BOB: "My girl friend."

JIM: "I thought she was out of town."

BOB: "I thought that too"

CLAUDE: "Going to have dinner anywhere tonight?"

MAUDE, eagerly: "Why, no, not that I know of."

CLAUDE: "Gee, you'll be awfully hungry by morning!"

•

NEW DATE: "I said, you *have* been out with worse-looking fellows than I am, haven't you?"

POPULAR GIRL: "I heard you the first time. I was trying to think."

•

SWEET YOUNG THING to suitor: "If people ask what I see in you, Herbert, what shall I tell them?"

•

JOHNNY: "Lawrence is just bashful. Why don't you give him a little encouragement."

BONNIE: "Encouragement? *He* needs a cheering section!"

•

PRETTY GIRL at concert: "What's that book the conductor keeps looking at?"

INTELLECTUAL DATE: "That's the score of the overture, of course!"

PRETTY GIRL, excitedly: "Oh, really? Who's winning?"

•

JACK: "Betty doesn't seem to be very intelligent."

JOHN: "No, she didn't pay any attention to me, either."

NEW BOYFRIEND: "I'll only marry a girl that can cook well, keep our home attractive, and help me save my money."

ANNOYED GIRLFRIEND: "Fine. You must meet our maid—she's got all those requirements."

●

YOUNG MAN: "Mr. Jones, your daughter has promised to be my wife."

MR. JONES: "That's your own fault—what else did you expect if you kept hanging round here every night?"

Regional Roundup

TOURIST (to Indian in heart of reservation): "White man glad to see red man. White man hope big chief feel tip-top this morning."

INDIAN (calling to a friend): "Hey, Joe, come here and listen to this square. He's really hep!"

Uncle Ike Hubbard was once eating supper at the roundup wagon and at the same time complaining about the grub. Finally the cook got so sore that he became quite sarcastic.

"Do you think you kin manage to eat the biscuits, Uncle Ike?" he said with strained sweetness.

"They ain't so bad," answered Uncle Ike. "If you put a lot o' this butter on 'em you can't taste 'em quite so much. 'Course, you can taste the butter, but I'm purty strong myself, as the feller says, and anyhow, your coffee's weak enough to bring up the general average."

●

A tourist traveling through western Kansas saw a man sitting by the ruins of a house that had been blown away.

"Was this your house, my friend?" he asked sympathetically.

"Yep."

"Any of your family blown away with the house?"

"Yep, wife and four kids."

"Great Scott, man, why aren't you hunting for them?"

"Well, stranger, I've been in this country quite a spell. The wind's due to change this afternoon. So I figure I might as well wait here till it brings 'em back."

A tourist driving through Maine wasn't sure he was on the right road. He stopped his car and asked a farmer plowing a field, "Which way is it to Bar Harbor, please?"

"Don't know," the farmer answered.

"Well, then, which way is it to Boothbay Harbor?" the tourist asked.

"Don't know."

In irritation the tourist snapped, "Don't you know *anything*?"

"Well," said the farmer, "*I* ain't lost."

●

"Is this a healthy town?" asked a tourist from New York of a native of Enterprise, Oregon.

"It sure is," replied the native. "When I came here, I hadn't the strength to say a word; I had hardly a hair on my head; I couldn't walk across the room, even with help; I even had to be lifted in and out of bed."

"That's wonderful!" exclaimed the tourist. "How long have you been here?"

"I was born here."

●

TALKATIVE LADY TOURIST: "Shame on you! A big man like you catching poor little helpless fish!"

VERMONT FISHERMAN: "Well, if this fish had kept his mouth shut, he wouldn't be on the end of this hook."

191

A group of tourists in New Mexico came upon an Indian brave riding a pony. A heavily burdened squaw walked beside him.

"Why doesn't the squaw ride?" asked a tourist of the brave.

"She got no pony."

●

An old Vermont storekeeper was dying, and his sorrowful family was assembled at his bedside.

"Is Ma here?" he asked wearily.

"Yes, Zeke," she replied.

"And my oldest son, Aaron?"

"Yes."

"And the other four boys?"

"Yes."

"And all the girls?"

"Yes, Zeke."

The dying man shot up to a sitting position. "What's the big idea?" he shouted. "Who's tending the store?"

●

Some friends were trying to cheer an old Oklahoma cowman who had lost everything he had, including his home.

"You don't need to sympathize with me," he said. "*I'm* all right. I'll come back. I came here fifty years ago with only sixty-five cents and asthma, and I still got the asthma."

A tourist stopped at a combination service station and general store in the back country. While his car was being serviced, he noticed an oldtimer basking in the sun holding a short piece of rope in his hand.

The tourist walked over to him and asked, "What have you there?"

"This is a weather gauge, sonny."

"How can you possibly tell the weather with a piece of rope?" the tourist wanted to know.

"It's simple, sonny. When it swings back and forth it's windy. When it gets wet, it's raining."

•

A mob in Montana once hanged a man because he was supposed to have stolen a horse. After quite a few hours, one of the men broke the news to the dead man's widow in this manner:

"We hanged Sam for stealing a horse, but it turns out he didn't do it after all, so I guess the joke's on us."

•

Two Indians were riding at eighty miles an hour.

FIRST INDIAN: "I think we should slow down."

SECOND INDIAN: "Why?"

FIRST INDIAN: "Because I think we must be getting near the reservation."

SECOND INDIAN: "Why?"

FIRST INDIAN: "Because we're hitting too many Indians."

A visitor from New York was visiting a Californian. They were standing out in the open.

"Looks like rain," said the New Yorker.

"Won't rain here," replied the Californian.

"Well, look at those clouds up there."

"Those clouds don't mean anything. They're empty. They're coming back from Florida."

●

What was the greatest feat of strength ever performed in the United States?

Wheeling West Virginia.

●

Two close-mouthed Vermont farmers met each other every morning for twenty years in the village store without ever speaking to each other.

One day, Farmer Perkins turned down the street when he went out, instead of up the street as usual.

"Where ya goin'?" asked his startled neighbor.

"None o' yer durn business," snapped Perkins. "And I wouldn't tell yer *that* much if yer warn't an old friend."

Quick Quips

"What do you believe is the reason for your long life, Uncle Ebenezer?" asked the reporter on Uncle Ebenezer's 102nd birthday.

Uncle Ebenezer thought for a moment or two, then, "Well, I guess it's because I was born a long time back, I guess," he said reflectively.

A woman came up to a policeman and said:

"Oh, officer! There's a man following me and I think he must be crazy."

The officer took a good look at her. "Yes," he answered, "he must be!"

●

What always has an eye open but can't see anything?
A needle.

●

A night watchman heard noises in the dark warehouse. Drawing his revolver, he went to the door and called,

"Come out with your hands up, so I can see who you *are*. If you don't, I'll come in and see who you *were*."

●

What word is always pronounced wrong?
Wrong.

●

Why does a chicken cross the road?
For fowl purposes.

●

What is the best material for kites?
Flypaper.

●

"I wish *I* had a pretty, intelligent and helpful wife," said the bachelor.

"So do I," said the husband.

196

ELEVATOR BOY: "Here's your floor, son."

INDIGNANT PASSENGER: "*Son!* How dare you call me that!"

ELEVATOR BOY: "Well, I brought you up, didn't I?"

•

"This tonic will grow hair on a billiard ball."

"Who *wants* hair on a billiard ball?"

•

DOPEY: "Why did the cow get a divorce?"

DOPIER: "She got a bum steer."

•

What is worse than finding a worm in an apple?
Finding only half a worm.

•

The bald-headed man would like very much to part with his comb and brush.

•

Didja hear about the comic who told the same jokes three nights running—he wouldn't dare tell them standing still.

•

Two boll weevils came from the country to the city. One became rich and famous. The other remained the lesser of the two weevils.

•

Have you heard of the woman who was such a good cook she graduated from cooking school with flying crullers?

A visitor at a state prison asked one of the prisoners, "What's your name?"

"9742," the prisoner sneered.

"Is that your *real* name?"

"Naw," he said, "just me pen name."

●

How many peas in a pint?

One.

●

Why would a barber rather shave ten men from New York than one from San Francisco?

Because he would get ten times as much money.

Dizzy-
Daffy-
Nitions

TEACHER: "Frankie, can you define nonsense?"
FRANKIE: "Yes, teacher—an elephant hanging over a cliff with his tail tied to a buttercup."

●

What is a professor?

A textbook wired for sound.

What's the difference between a mother and a barber?

> *The barber has razors to shave. The mother has shavers to raise.*

●

What is the difference between a beached ship and an airplane?

> *One grounds on the land, and the other lands on the ground.*

●

BENNY: "What part of an automobile kills the most people?"

KENNY: "The nut behind the wheel!"

●

What makes more noise than a pig caught under a fence?

> *Two pigs.*

●

What is the difference between fog and a falling star?

> *One is mist on earth, the other is missed in heaven.*

●

An egoist is someone always me-deep in conversation

●

TEACHER: "George, what is a synonym?"

GEORGIE: "A synonym is a word you use when you can't spell the other one."

TEACHER (to bring out the idea of size): "Mention a difference between an elephant and a flea."

TOMMY: "Well, an elephant can have fleas, but a flea can't have elephants."

●

What is the difference between the earth and the sea?

One is dirt-y, the other is tide-y.

●

Paul and Saul were trying to define the word "collision."

"Collision," said Paul, "is when two things come together unexpectedly."

"I know," brightly replied Saul. "Twins."

Child's definition: An adult is one who has stopped growing except in the middle.

●

Tomorrow: One of the greatest labor-saving inventions of today.

●

A hard-boiled egg is hard to beat.

●

A dentist is a man with a lot of pull.

Laughs

Across the Oceans

ENGLISHMAN, to visiting AMERICAN: "Odd names your towns have. Such as Hoboken, Skaneateles, Walla Walla, Oshkosh, Albuquerque."

AMERICAN: "I suppose they do sound queer to English ears. Do you live in London all of the time?"

ENGLISHMAN: "No, indeed. I spend part of my time at Chipping Norton, and divide the rest between Bigglewade, Bournemouth, and Leighton Buzzard."

VISITING AMERICAN: "How come you Scotsmen are so thrifty?"
SCOTTISH HOST: "It is a gift."

●

SANDY: "I want a cheap coat hanger."
SALESPERSON: "Here's one for three pence."
SANDY: "Three pence! I want something much cheaper."
SALESPERSON: "The nail department is down two aisles to the left."

●

"Ah, it was different in the old days," whispered the old professor in a café in Warsaw, glancing cautiously around the room. "Then we could lie as we pleased. Now we have to lie as we are told."

●

VISITING AMERICAN TOURIST: "James, I am afraid that, by mistake, I tipped His Lordship instead of you."
ENGLISH BUTLER: "I'll never see the tip now."

●

"Russia," cried the Soviet agriculture expert at a Paris meeting, "is an agricultural paradise, with *four wheat crops* a year."
Incredulous listeners demanded how this could be.

"It's easy," he explained. "We have one from Poland, one from Hungary, one from Czechoslovakia, and one from Russia."

Andrew Carnegie was born in Scotland, and came to America as a boy. When he returned for a visit after he had become one of the richest men in the world, two of his townsmen were discussing the famous visitor.

SANDY: "I hear that Andrew Carnegie is worth $400,000,000!"

MAC: "Weel! He sure must have had a saving woman!"

•

An American in Hong Kong on business, was placed next to a Chinese at a banquet. At the end of the first course, the American turned to his neighbor and said, "Likee soupee?"

The Chinese grunted, "Yes."

At the end of the meat course the American said, "Likee meatee?"

The Chinese again grunted, "Yes."

Then the Chinese man was introduced and spoke eloquently for half an hour in perfect English.

When he sat down he turned to his American neighbor and said, "Likee speechee?"

•

The story is that the Grand Canyon was caused by a Scotsman dropping a dime.

•

MAC: "How much candy can you eat?"

JOCK: "Any given amount."

TIM: "How does your new short-wave radio work?"
CHARLIE: "Perfectly—I got China when I turned it on at three o'clock this morning."
TIM: "China and what else?"
CHARLIE: "Flowerpots, milk bottles, and old shoes."

•

A newspaper correspondent assigned to cover the Paris peace meetings bumped into an old acquaintance whom he knew to be a secret agent.

"Hello," he said. "What are you doing here?"

"Oh, just looking for scraps of information," answered the agent. "And what are you doing here?"

"Oh, I'm just looking for information of scraps," replied the correspondent.

•

GUIDE, on a safari in Africa: "Quick, m'lord! Shoot that leopard on the spot!"
LORD KILBRACKEN: "Be specific, my man: *which* spot?"

•

Food is more plentiful in Paris with the summer season, but not so with meat, which accounts for a restaurant patron's complaint to the waiter that his pork chop was too little and too hot.

"Why don't you blow on it?" the waiter none too politely inquired.

"I am afraid to," said the diner. "It might blow away."

GESUNDHEIT

An immigration officer asked a small Chinese man
his name.

"Sneeze," replied the man proudly.

"Is that Chinese?" asked the officer.

"No," said the man, "it's my American name."

"Then," asked the officer, "what is your native
name?"

"Ah Choo!" replied the Chinese man.

FIRST ACTOR, in a London Club: "I'd rather play to
an English audience than an American audience."

SECOND ACTOR: "What's the difference between an
Englishman and an American?"

FIRST ACTOR: "Well, an Englishman first laughs out
of courtesy; second, when the rest of the audience gets
the joke; and third, when he gets it himself."

SECOND ACTOR: "What about an American?"

FIRST ACTOR: "Oh, he never laughs at all—he's heard
it before."

A fellow, carrying a hundred-pound bomb, got on a London bus and sat down.

"What's that you've got in your lap?" asked the conductor.

"It's a delayed-action bomb I'm taking to the police station," came the answer.

"Coo!" exclaimed the conductor. "You don't want to carry a thing like that on your lap! Put it under the seat!"

●

ENGLISH PROFESSOR, at dinner: "It was Sir Walter Raleigh who first introduced your American turkey into Britain."
AMERICAN GUEST, trying to cut his portion: "And this one must be the very one he introduced."

●

A Frenchman asked a German guest how they told the difference in Germany between an optimist and a pessimist.

"Very simple," the German explained. "The optimist is learning English, the pessimist is learning Russian."

●

A railroad agent in Africa had been bawled out for doing things without orders from headquarters. One day his boss received the following startling telegram: "Tiger on platform eating conductor. Wire instructions."

The cockney innkeeper of the HAND AND ANCHOR objected to the way a painter had painted his sign:

"There ought to be more space between 'and and and and 'and and Anchor!"

●

An Arab stood on a weighing machine in the light
   of the lingering day
A counterfeit penny he dropped in the slot and
   silently stole a weigh.

●

AMERICAN TOURIST in France: "Waiter, bring me some of this—see, here on the menu."
WAITER: "Madam, the orchestra is playing it now."

●

FRENCHMAN greeting friend at boat: "Did you have any difficulty with your English in America?"
RETURNING FRIEND: "No—but the Americans did."

●

GUIDE, in England: "This tower goes back to William the Conqueror."
TOURIST: "Why, what's the matter with it? Isn't it satisfactory?"

●

FIRST ENGLISHMAN: "Charley, did you hear that joke about the Egyptian guide who showed some tourists two skulls of Cleopatra—one as a girl and one as a woman?"
SECOND DITTO: "No, let's hear it."

209 😀

George's father was one of those rich self-made men who have no use for learning unless it helps business. But George wanted to go to Paris to learn the language and study art. At last he got permission to leave. Six months later, his father went to Europe on business and visited George in Paris. The boy took him to an expensive restaurant and they had a fine dinner. After coffee he spoke a few words in French to the waiter.

"Is that all the French you've learned?" asked the old man.

"It's enough," George replied. "I told him to give you the check."

•

An Englishman was traveling with an American through the corn belt. "My dear man," he said, "what are you doing with all this corn?"

"Well," said the American, "we eat what we can and what we can't, we can."

The Englishman found this hilarious. As soon as he was back in London he told his friends in the club about the abundance of corn and his question about it. "And you know what the Yankee said?" he asked. " 'We eat as much as we can and what we cannot eat we put into tins.' "

Trip Talk

An excited young man ran madly down the ferry landing, leaped across six feet of water, and landed with a crash on the deck of the ferry.

"Well," he gasped, as he picked himself up, "I made it!"

"What's your hurry?" asked a deck hand. "This boat's comin' *in*."

PASSENGER: "Is this bus on time?"

BUS DRIVER: "No, but we're on the right road."

•

TRAVELER: "How much will you charge to take my baggage to Canal Street?"

TAXI DRIVER: "Half dollar for you, sir. Your luggage goes free."

TRAVELER: "Okay, then. You just take the luggage, and I'll walk."

•

FRANK: "You must have had a terrible accident last night. The front of your car is all smashed in. What did you hit?"

HANK: "Last night I was driving and hit a cow——"

FRANK: "A Jersey cow?"

HANK: "I don't know—I didn't see her license plate."

•

The Browns were just back from a vacation trip to New Jersey.

"How did you find the mosquitoes?" asked a friend.

"I didn't," said Mr. Brown. "*They* found *me*."

•

"Do you have hot and cold water in this hotel?" inquired a visitor.

"Yes, hot in the summer and cold in the winter," the clerk informed her.

A city youngster, who was more accustomed to man-made wonders than to the marvels of nature, was taken on a vacation to Niagara Falls. There he saw his first rainbow. As the boy stood and gazed upon the gorgeous sight, he was full of wonder and surprise.

"Mother," he finally exclaimed, "it's certainly beautiful but what does it advertise?"

●

The bore was giving the story of his travels in the Swiss Alps and droned on, and on, and on. At one point he remarked: "There I stood, with the abyss yawning before me."

"Excuse me," interjected a bored listener, "but was that abyss yawning before you got there?"

●

A fat lady with her arms full of bundles wedged herself in the bus and fumbled for her purse in her coat pocket to pay the fare. She struggled and struggled. A man standing next to her suddenly handed her a dime. "Take this, lady," he said unhappily, "and pay your fare. I'm getting tired of you buttoning and unbuttoning my suspender buttons."

●

HOTEL GUEST: "Is there an Encyclopaedia Britannica in the hotel?"
DESK CLERK, politely: "I'm so sorry, sir. We haven't one—but what is it you wish to know?"

One night at a party at the Elwells, Mrs. Barker was telling of their novel vacation plan. "You see," said Mrs. Barker, "last year a few of us cooked up such a satisfactory vacation plan that we're going to do it again this year."

"What was it?" asked Mrs. Elwell.

"Well," said Mrs. Barker, "six couples of us pooled our vacation money and rented a big house at the seashore for the season. Each couple spent two weeks there, taking care of the kids. All told, there were seventeen of them."

"Well!" exclaimed Mrs. Elwell. "I wouldn't call taking care of seventeen children a *vacation*— but I suppose the kids loved it."

"Oh," said Mrs. Barker quickly, "those two weeks were a *nightmare*! What *was* a vacation was the ten weeks at home without our kids."

•

RIDER, on way to station: "Why did they build this station so far out of town?"

DRIVER: "They wanted it to be near the railroad."

•

HOTEL CLERK (to guest parading through lobby in pajamas): "Here, what are you doing?"

GUEST (awakened): "Oh, I'm *so* sorry! But I'm a somnambulist."

HOTEL CLERK: "Well, you can't walk around here like that, no matter *what* your religion is."

A man rushed off a train and ran up to a little boy standing on the platform.

"We've only got a short stop here," he said. "Here's a quarter. Go in that lunchroom and get me a sandwich, will you? And here's another quarter. Get a sandwich for yourself, too."
The boy was gone so long the man began to get nervous. Just as the conductor hollered "All Aboard!" the kid dashed out of the lunchroom and ran over to the man.

"Here's your quarter," he said. "They only had one sandwich."

•

Have you heard about the man who took a vacation to forget everything? The first night at the hotel he opened his suitcase and discovered he *had* forgotten everything.

•

STUFFY AUNT: "Well, Horace, you haven't honored us with your presence for a long time. Just what brought you to town *this* time?"
HORACE: "Well I just came to see the sights, and thought I'd call on you first."

•

SUMMER BOARDER: "What became of that other windmill that was here last year?"
FARMER: "There was only enough wind for one, so we took it down."

A Spaniard, an American, and a Scotsman were discussing what they would do if they awoke one morning to discover that they were millionaires.

The Spaniard said he would build a bull ring.

The American said he would go to Paris to have a time.

The Scotsman said he would go to sleep again to see if he could make another million.

●

RUSTY: "So you missed your train?"

BUSTER: "Yes!"

RUSTY: "By how much did you miss it?"

BUSTER: "I missed it by just a minute."

RUSTY: "Well, don't get so excited. The way you're carrying on, it's as if you missed it by an hour."

Travel Teasers

Severely jostled in the thundering herd of New York's subway rush hour, a girl was finally crammed among the standees. Her sense of humor was not impaired, however. She poked her face close to the ear of the man standing next to her.

"Look," she demanded tartly, "my rib—is it crushing your elbow?"

LADY: "Can you give me a room and bath?"
HOTEL CLERK: "I can give you a room, madam, but you'll have to take your own bath."

●

A train ran off a big bridge recently and no one was killed or injured. How can this be?

> *It ran off the bridge at one end as usual and went on its way along the tracks.*

●

What is it that is found in the very center of America and Australia?

> *The letter* R.

●

Why should a man always wear a watch when he travels in a desert?

> *Every watch has a spring.*

●

Why are weary people like automobile wheels?

> *Because they are tired.*

●

PAUL: "What's your hurry, Saul?"
SAUL: "I'm going to the airport to catch the 5:30 plane."
PAUL: "Well, what's your hurry? It's only 2:30 now."
SAUL: "I *know* that. But I always have to figure on a few dopes stopping me to ask me why I'm hurrying."

What is the richest country in the world?

> *Ireland, because its capital is always Dublin.*

●

What is the difference between the North Pole and the South Pole?

> *All the difference in the world.*

●

What state is round at both ends, and high in the middle?

> *Ohio.*

●

When does an automobile go exactly as fast as a train?

> *When it is on the train.*

●

You can always tell the English;
You can always tell the Dutch;
You can always tell the Yankees—
But you cannot tell them much!

●

A midget belonging to a circus got on the sleeper at Chicago to go to New York. He had an upper berth. He went into the diner and drank a large cup of coffee. About two hours later the man in the lower berth rang loudly for the porter.

> "Porter!" he shouted. "I can't sleep. Someone is pacing overhead."

A motorist speeding along a highway at eighty miles an hour was stopped by a policeman. "Was I driving too fast?" asked the motorist apologetically.

"Oh no," replied the policeman. "You were flying too low."

●

"What's the matter with you, are you blind?" said the pedestrian.

"Blind?" snapped the driver. "I *hit* you, didn't I?"

Girls, Girls, Girls

PRETTY YOUNG GIRL, to friend: "Not only has Jack broken my heart and wrecked my whole life, but he has spoiled my entire evening!"

●

A young lady after a broken engagement returned all her friend's letters marked, "Fourth Class Male."

TESS: "I was horseback riding yesterday and from the after-effects I think I'll learn to ride side-saddle."
BESS: "Why do that?"
TESS: "It saves you a little place where you can sit down the next day."

•

ETTA: "Do you believe in free speech?"
GRETTA: "I certainly do."
ETTA: "Then may I make a long distance call on your telephone?"

•

Three girls are under an umbrella, but none of them gets wet. How can this be?
It isn't raining.

•

Ring! Ring!
"Hello, Betty, this is Nettie—are you wearing your pedal pushers tonight?"
"Why, yes, I'm afraid I am."
"Good. Then you won't mind lending me your formal."

•

DORA: "Where is your brother?"
CORA: "He's in the hospital—his girl threw him over."
DORA: "That shouldn't have made him go to a hospital."
CORA: "Yes, but *this* girl threw him over a cliff."

BELLA: "Did anyone ever tell you how wonderful you are?"
STELLA: "Don't believe they ever did."
BELLA: "Then where'd you get the idea?"

•

MOLLY, at a picnic: "We've got thousands of things to eat."
POLLY: "Gee—what?"
MOLLY: "Beans."

•

JOAN: "Did Evelyn inherit her beauty?"
JANE: "Yes, her father left her a drug store."

•

TILLY: "He's worth in the neighborhood of Fifty Thousand Dollars, I've heard."
BILLIE: "Good! That's my favorite neighborhood."

•

"Have you seen Sally's new dress?"
"No, what does it look like?"
"Well, in many places it's a lot like Sally."

•

HELEN: "I don't see how football players ever get clean!"
RUTH: "Silly, what do you suppose the scrub teams are for?"

MABEL: "How is your new boy friend?"

MARY: "He is very fast with a buck—then he slows down."

•

MARY: "She sure gave you a dirty look."

LOUISE: "Who?"

MARY: "Mother Nature."

•

JOAN: "Hasn't Jack ever married?"

JEAN: "No, I don't think he intends to, because he's studying for a bachelor's degree."

•

BETTY: "Who is that guy with the long hair?"

MARY: "He's the sophomore from Yale."

BETTY: "Oh, I've often heard of those Yale locks."

Goofy Guys

"I went hunting the other day," said Simpson, "and the dogs got in the way of a skunk. Finally they gave up the chase."

"Did they lose the scent?" asked his friend.

"They gave up the skunk, but I don't think they will ever lose the scent," Simpson answered with feeling.

LENNY: "Do you believe it is seven years' bad luck if you break a mirror?"

BENNY: "No, indeed not. My cousin broke one and he didn't have seven years' bad luck."

LENNY: "He didn't?"

BENNY: "No, he was killed in an explosion the same day."

•

"Why is this train late?" an irritated lady asked the conductor.

"Well, lady," explained the conductor, "the trouble is that the train in front is behind and this train was behind before besides."

•

As he paid his hotel bill the departing guest turned and yelled to the bellboy, "Quick, boy, run up to room 999 and see if I left my brief case and overcoat. *Hurry up*, because I've got just six minutes to catch my train."

Four minutes later the bellboy was back, all out of breath. "Yes, sir," he reported, "they're up there."

•

BILLY: "How's your father coming with his new dairy farm?"

SILLY: "Grand. He makes all the cows sleep on their backs."

BILLY: "What's the idea?"

SILLY: "So the cream will be on top in the morning."

Shingles were coming loose on Mr. Lazyman's house, and he complained of the leaks.

"Why don't you mend the roof?" asked the neighbor next door.

"I can't today—it's pouring rain."

"Well, why don't you mend it in dry weather?"

"It don't leak then," said Mr. Lazyman.

●

FARMER: "What are you doing up in that tree, young fellow?"

BOY: "One of your apples fell down, and I'm trying to put it back!"

●

CIRCUS MANAGER: "Well, *now* what's wrong?"

INDIA-RUBBER MAN, pitifully: "Every time the strong man writes a letter he uses me to rub out the mistakes."

●

BELLBOY: "Telegram for Mr. Portocopondolous! Mr. Portocopondolous!"

MR. PORTOCOPONDOLOUS: "Boy! What initial, please?"

●

LOUIE: "How did you like the play last night?"

HUGHIE: "I saw the first act, but not the second."

LOUIE: "Why not?"

HUGHIE: "I couldn't wait that long. It said on the program—second act, two years later."

SCOUTMASTER: "George, are all the rest of the boys out of the woods yet?"

GEORGE: "Yes."

SCOUTMASTER: "All seven of them?"

GEORGE: "Yes, all seven of them."

SCOUTMASTER: "And they're all safe?"

GEORGE: "Yep, they're all safe."

SCOUTMASTER: "Then, by golly, I've shot a deer!"

●

DOPE: "I can climb *anything*."

DUPE (throwing a flashlight beam upward): "Well, then climb that!"

DOPE: "Well—I could. But it would be just like you to turn it off when I was twenty-five feet up. Then where would *I* be!"

●

MAN calling on telephone. "Hello, this is Andy."

DEAF MAN answering: "Eh?"

FIRST MAN: "This is Andy! *A* for Adam, *N* for Ned, *D* for Dan and *Y* for ——"

DEAF MAN, interrupting him: "Yes, yes! I know all you guys, but *which* one is talking *now*?"

●

EDDIE: "My brother stands in front of a mirror with his eyes closed."

TEDDIE: "What for?"

EDDIE: "Oh, he just wants to see what he looks like when he is asleep."

228

A boy was down on his hands and knees looking for something on the sidewalk when a policeman approached.

"What are you doing?" said the cop.

"I lost a silver dollar on Third Avenue," was the answer.

"But this is Fourth Avenue," the cop pointed out. "If you lost the dollar on Third Avenue, why are you looking for it on Fourth?"

"Because there's more light here," said the boy.

●

A hillbilly was taken to the hospital after an accident. He had his temperature taken and was then left alone in the ward until the house doctor made his rounds.

"Well," said the doctor, "how do you feel?"

"Okay, boss."

"Had any nourishment?"

"What did you say?"

"I said, have you taken anything in the way of food?"

"Well, a while ago a lady give me a piece of glass to suck."

●

ACTOR: "Why did you quit the stage?"

COMEDIAN: "Ill health."

ACTOR: "What do you mean, ill health?"

COMEDIAN: "I made people sick."

Dope and Dupe stepped out of the plane as it landed in Pittsburgh. Suddenly Dope let out a cry.

> "Dupe," he groaned, "I think I've lost my wallet!"
>
> "Did you look in your pockets?" asked Dupe.
>
> "All but one," replied Dope, unhappily.
>
> "Well, for goodness' sake, why don't you look there?"
>
> "Because," Dope moaned, "if it's not there, I'll die!"

●

An applicant for citizenship wasn't too clear about the judge's question, "Do you solemnly swear to support the Constitution?"

Finally he answered, "Judge, I'd like to, but I already have a wife and six children in Europe."

Troubles, Troubles, Troubles

A pigeon came home very late for dinner one evening, with his feathers bedraggled, and his eyes bloodshot. "I was out minding my own business," he explained, "when—bingo! I get caught in a badminton game!"

A man once decided that he wanted to commit suicide, so he made very elaborate preparations, to be *sure* nothing would defeat his purpose. He went out on a very high bridge, and took along a can of gasoline, a match, a rope, and a revolver.

He tied the rope around his neck, then tied it to the bridge. Next he poured gasoline over his clothes. Then he lit a match to himself. Finally, just as he jumped off the bridge, he shot off his revolver.

The revolver shot cut the rope; his fall into water put out the fire; and if he hadn't known how to swim, he would have drowned!

●

"Oh, did I find a dreamy apartment!" said Mrs. Gush to her friend. "It has a wonderful living room, a wonderful balcony, a wonderful dining room, a wonderful bedroom, and the kitchen—the kitchen is out of this world!"

FRIEND: "Isn't that a little bit inconvenient?"

●

GRACIE ALLEN: "They put my brother in jail for stealing, but it wasn't his fault."

GEORGE BURNS: "Oh, it wasn't his fault?"

GRACIE ALLEN: "No, how did he know the woman didn't mean what she said?"

GEORGE BURNS: "What did the woman say?"

GRACIE ALLEN: "Well, he was helping her house clean and she gave him a rug and told him to beat it."

REPORTER: "What made you risk your life to save your friend?"
BOY HERO: "I *had* to do it. He was wearing my skates."

•

FIRST COMMUNIST: "Nice weather we're having."
SECOND COMMUNIST: "Yeah, but the rich are having it, too!"

A banquet speaker went on and on with his speech. The Mayor nodded, and, after a while, rested his head on the tablecloth. The chairman reached over and bumped him lightly on the head with his gavel.
MAYOR: "Hit me harder—I can still hear him."

Two little boys were playing noisily in a train. The conductor finally told their father that the children must behave or he would make trouble for him. The boy's father said, wearily:

"Trouble—you don't know what trouble *is*! My wife's in the hospital. I have the itch. I am on my way to see my sick mother-in-law; my daughter has just had triplets; one of the boys has just smashed his finger and the other has chewed up our tickets. And that's not all—I just discovered we are on the wrong train."

Whoppers, Whoppers, Whoppers

The New Yorker said, "I once had an old mare that licked the fastest express train on a forty-mile run."

"That's nothing!" said the Texan. "I was out about thirty miles from my house on my farm one day, when a frightful storm came up. I turned the pony's head for home and, do you know, he raced the storm so close for the last ten miles that I didn't feel a drop—while my dog, only ten yards behind, had to swim the whole distance!"

235

A cowboy was raving about his horse. "I got the smartest horse you ever saw!" he declared. "One day while riding I fell off and broke my leg."

"Wait a minute," interrupted another cowboy. "You're not going to tell me he picked you up and put you back in the saddle."

"No, but he dragged me to my bunk, then galloped five miles to get me a doctor. There was only one catch: he came back with a *horse* doctor!"

●

South Dakota is noted for very sudden changes of temperature. One summer day it got so hot that a field of popcorn started popping—it really caused a flurry! The cows in the next field thought it was snowing, and froze to death watching!

●

DOPEY: "My grampa made a scarecrow so terrible that it frightened every single crow off the place."
DOPIER: "You think *that's* something? *I* made one that scared 'em so much they brought back the corn they stole last year!"

●

One year at the Liar's Club meeting where everyone told their biggest whopper the prize was won by a member who merely said: "I never told a lie."

A hunter was out in the forest. It was late in the day and getting colder. A bear appeared. The hunter grabbed his gun—there was no ammunition left! He wiped the sweat off his brow and put it in the gun— it shot out as an icicle and pierced the head of the bear and the bear died of water on the brain!

EXECUTIONER to prisoner: "Have you any last words?"
PRISONER: "Yes! This will be a lesson to me."

•

There once was a lawyer who joined a nudist colony and never had a suit afterwards.

•

POLICEMAN (to boy sitting on top of oak tree): "Hey! What are you doing up there?"
BOY: "I don't know. I must have sat on an acorn."

"It was so cold where we were," boasted the Arctic explorer, "that the candle froze and we couldn't blow it out."

"That's nothing," said his rival. "Where we were the words came out of our mouths in pieces of ice, and we had to fry them to see what we were talking about."

●

An Easterner and a Westerner were walking one day near the foot of one of the Catskill mountains. The Easterner, wishing to impress the visitor, produced a famous echo to be heard in that place. When the echo returned clearly after nearly three minutes, the proud Easterner, turning to the Westerner, exclaimed:

"There, you haven't anything like *that* out your way!"

"Oh, I don't know," said the Westerner, "I guess we can better that. Why, in my camp in the Rockies, when I go to bed I just lean out the window and call out, *'Time to get up; wake up!'* and eight hours afterward the echo comes back and wakes me."

Stretching
the Baloney

(We had to fill up these
last few pages *somehow!*)

The two tramps were stretched out on the green grass. Above them was the warm sun, beside them was a babbling brook. It was a quiet, restful, peaceful scene.

"Boy," mused the first tramp contentedly, "right now I wouldn't change places with a guy who owns a million bucks!"

"How about five million?" asked his companion.

"Not even for five million," drowsed the first tramp.

"Well," persisted his pal, "how about ten million bucks?"

The first tramp sat up.

"That's different," he admitted. "Now you're talking real dough!"

●

A floorwalker, tired of his job, gave it up and joined the police force. Several months later a friend asked him how he liked his new job. "Well," he replied, "the pay and the hours are good, but what I like best is that the customer is always wrong."

●

"How can I ever show my appreciation?" gushed a woman to a famous lawyer, after he had solved her legal troubles.

"Madam," he replied, "ever since the Phoenicians invented money there's been only one answer to that question."

Then there's the story of the angry wife of a movie star who had gone off fishing and left her alone. Asked where her husband might be, she replied, "Just go down to the bridge and look around until you find a pole with a worm on each end!"

•

Hetty, the little daughter of a tire salesman, had seen triplets for the first time in the daily paper.

"Oh, Mummy!" she called out, "What do you think it says here?"

"I can't imagine, dear. What?"

"It tells about a lady that had twins—*and a spare!*"

•

At a dinner for a child star who was a big box-office attraction a movie producer got up, patted the little girl on the head, and said, "We wish to pay homage to our little star." Then, placing his hand on the shoulder of the star's mother, he continued, "But we don't want to forget the goose that laid the golden egg."

•

A little girl at her first church wedding suddenly whispered loudly to her mother: "Mummy, has the lady changed her mind?"

"Why, dear, whatever do you mean?" her mother asked.

"Well, Mummy, she went up the aisle with one man and came back with another!"

"Don't throw banana peels on the edge of the Grand Canyon," cautioned a ranger to a careless tourist. "You don't want somebody to slip and fall three miles, do you?"

•

There was a young lady of Niger
Who smiled as she rode on a tiger.
> They came back from the ride
> With the lady inside
And a smile on the face of the tiger.

•

When the train stopped at the little Southern station, the tourist from the North got out and strolled around a bit. He gazed curiously at a lean animal with scraggy bristles which was rubbing itself against a scrub-oak.

"What do you call *that*?" he asked curiously of a farmer on a hay wagon.

"A razorback hawg, suh," the farmer replied.

"What is he doing, rubbing himself against that tree?"

"He's stropping hisself, suh; jes' stropping hisself."

 242

PUNS, PUNS, PUNS

Edited by **HELEN HOKE**
With **BORIS RANDOLPH**

Illustrated by **SEYMOUR NYDORF**

Range Places

WALL: "Why do all bank cashiers run to Canada?"
STREET: "I give up."
WALL: "Because that's the only place they have To-ronto."

MAUDE: "I don't Bolivia."

CLAUDE: "Denmark my words, you'll regret it."

●

SAGE SAM especially likes the Swiss slogan: every little bit Alps.

●

A proud Tennessean calls his home CHATEAU NOOGA. He probably did not care for sweets or he would have made it CHATEAU NOUGAT.

●

Meet some of the Sister States: MARY LAND, IDA HO, LOUISA ANNA and MINNE SOTA.

●

HILDA: "I don't mean to Russia, but Venice she leaving?"

TILDA: "Well, she said she wasn't going to Rumania here another day."

●

SUE: "Are you going to see him Samoa?"

PRUE: "Don't be Sicily, he's Spain in the neck."

●

CURIOUS CARL wants to know, are the Mich*iganders* any relation to the Portu*guese*, and if so, how much, and what?

●

GUIDE: (pointing) "That's where they Hong Kong."

TOURIST: "Oh! Did Shanghai?"

ED: "Jamaica any money on the deal?"
NED: "No! Egypt me!"

●

MAY, setting a candle aslant: "This reminds me of the leaning tower of Pisa."
JAY, in all seriousness: "But that is a tower in Italy, while this is a tower in grease."

●

SAGE SAM declares, "Annapolis what keeps the doctor away."

●

STUPE: "What do you say when you greet a person geographically?"
DUPE: "Hawaii."
STUPE: "And when you're taking leave of him?"
DUPE: "Abyssinia."

FROSH: "What did you do last summer?"
SOPH: "I worked in Des Moines."
FROSH: "Coal or iron?"

●

The late, famous Joseph Henry Jackson, of San Francisco, invented a new game: the idea is to think up fictitious place names that go with abbreviations of state names. For instance: Shapeless, Mass.; Apples, Ida.; Oola, La.; and Goodness, Me. Pennsylvania offers a rich variety, ranging from Poison, Penn. to Grandpa, Pa. These days someone was bound to think of Income, Tex. Of those about Illinois, Mr. Jackson awarded first place to Deathly, Ill. He's fond of Hittor, Miss. and Praise, Ala. Others are Proan, Conn.; Coco, Colo.; Either, Ore.; and Farmerina, Del. For the culture-minded, there are Paderoffs, Ky. and Turge, Nev.

●

FIRST HAM: "Wonderful thing, radio; why, with my little one-valve set I got London and Paris the other night."
SECOND HAM: "With your window open or shut?"
FIRST HAM: "Open; but why do you ask?"
SECOND HAM: "Oh, I only asked because with my window open I get Chile every night."

●

DROOP: "Swell town you got. Lotta big men born here?"
STOOP: "No. Only babies."

A vaudeville routine used by Harry Vokes and Hap Ward way back in 1902, went like this:

"Where did you get those pants?"

"Pantsylvania."

"The coat?"

"North Dacoata."

"The vest?"

"Vest Virginia."

"The collar?"

"Collarado."

"The hat?"

"Manhattan."

ANGRY AGNES to the grocery clerk: "Please call the Bosphorus. A Canada stuff we bought here yesterday was no good."

•

WAITRESS: "Are you very Hungary?"
DINER: "Yes, Siam."
WAITRESS: "Well, we'll be glad to Fiji. What can I Serbia?"
DINER: "I'll have some Chile and Aix and coffee. And be sure to Sweden the coffee with a Cuba sugar."

•

Groucho Marx on a broadcast: "In Africa, the tusks are too firmly rooted, but in Alabama, of course, Tuscaloosa."

•

COCKNEY: "What a boat ride! First we stops in Cuba, and then we puts in at Haiti."
New Yorker: (politely) "And what comes after Haiti?"
COCKNEY: "H'eighty-one."

•

The young man met her at Friendship, Missouri, followed her to Love, Virginia, and asked her to name the day at Ring, Arkansas. They were married at Church, Iowa, and settled down at Home, Oregon, but the twins were born at Boise, Idaho.

Love Is Pun

DOPEY DAN'S so dumb he thinks a *courtship* is a *royal boat*.

When a boy and girl are about to elope, the young man asks, "Does your mother know your route?"

•

NAÏVE: "I just received a letter from my sweetheart and she put a couple of X's at the bottom of it. What does *that* mean?"

CYNIC: "It means she's double-crossing you."

•

BUD: "I understand he takes her to mystery plays instead of dances."

JUD: "Yep. They tell me they love each shudder."

PETER PENNILESS: "Will you marry me, my love?"
PATTY PAYCHECK: "No, I'm afraid not, Peter."
PETER PENNILESS: "Oh, come on, be a good support."

●

DORIS: "Do you really love me, dear?"
BORIS: "You know I do, sweetheart."
DORIS: "Would you die for me?"
BORIS: "No, my pet. Mine is an undying love."

●

MR. SIXTY: "Women are a delusion."
MISS TWENTY: "Yes, but men are always hugging some delusion or other."

●

ROMANTIC RENA always says, "love is a wonderful sting."

●

JOE: "If you don't marry me, I'm going to hang myself from that lamp post in front of your house."
ZOE: "Oh, please don't do that. You know father doesn't want you hanging around here."

●

CAUTIOUS CATHIE advises that it's now generally acknowledged that the best way for a girl to keep her youth is not to introduce him around to other girls.

●

CAUTIOUS CATHIE also warns that the girl who marries a title very frequently turns her fortune to a count.

JACK: "Are you a suitor for Miss Juliet's hand?"
MACK: "Yes but I didn't."
JACK: "Didn't what?"
MACK: "Suit her."

●

KEN: "Darling, when I think that tomorrow is your birthday, and when I think that I didn't know you a year ago—"
JEN: "Sweetheart, don't let's talk about our past. Let's talk about my present."

●

JEEPERS: "She sat on my lap for at least two hours."
PEEPERS: "Quite a lapse of time, eh?"

●

ANDY: "What ever happened to that correspondence romance you were having with the girl you'd never seen?"
RANDY: "It ended when we exchanged pictures."
ANDY: "Oh, I see. A sort of photo finish."

●

When a friend called at the home of a deb who was planning to be married, there was no one there except the maid.

"No, ma'am," said the maid, "she's not here. She's down at the Y.W.C.A. taking the course."

"What do you mean, 'the course'?"

"For pity's sake," came the reply, "I thought you'd know *that*. It's the course in domestic silence."

TOMDICK: "I'd like to find some girl who's a good housekeeper who'd be willing to marry me."
ANDHARRY: "Ah! You want one ready maid."

•

DAN: "I'll stick to you like glue, my darling."
NAN: "The feeling is mucilage, my love."

•

TOM: "Are you still in love with that girl?"
HARRY: "No, it was just a passion fancy."

•

CLAUDE: "Will you marry me in spite of my trouble?"
MAUDE: "Why, darling, what *is* your trouble?"
CLAUDE: "Alas, falling hair."
MAUDE: "Why you darling boy! To how much?"

•

GENTLEMAN, entering a very full bus: "Can we squeeze in here, dear?"
LADY FRIEND (faintly): "No—let's wait."

•

ROMANTIC RENA went to a real swell wedding. They threw puffed rice.

•

GEORGIE: "May I see you pretty soon?"
GEORGETTE: "Don't you think I'm pretty *now?*"

•

DON: "What is more tempting than a beautiful girl to behold?"
JUAN: "A girl to be held, of course."

13

WISE WILFRED knows that when an old-fashioned girl
sees any night life—she sprays insect powder on it.

●

LESLIE: "Where can I get hold of your sister?"
FREDDIE: "I don't know. She's ticklish."

●

JACK: "Please give me a kiss, darling!"
JILL: "No!"
JACK: "Don't you believe in the hereafter, darling? I
want a kiss!"
JILL: "What's the hereafter got to do with a kiss?"
JACK: "That's what I'm hereafter!"

JENNY: "I think you'd better put the jello in the refrigerator before you kiss me, dear."

JOHNNY: "Why, honey?"

JENNY: "It's so jellous."

●

OUTRAGED RIGHTEOUS (to persistent Casanova): "If you don't leave now, I'll call the whole fire department to put you out."

●

SHE, on tiptoes: "There! I am about your size."

DISCONSOLATE LOVER: "On the contrary, my sighs are about you."

●

SUITOR: "May I marry your daughter?"

STERN FATHER: "What is your vocation?"

SUITOR: "I'm an actor."

STERN FATHER: (angrily) "Then get out before the foot lights."

●

ROMANTIC RENA is a May bride . . . she may or may not be married.

●

BILLY: "Darling, if I should ask you in French if I might kiss you, what would you answer?"

MURIEL (thinking quickly): "Billet doux."

●

JAY: "Wilt thou?"

GAY: "Only in hot weather."

JANE (reaching for her half of the wishbone): "Oh, but I don't really know what to wish for."

JOHN: "Well, then, may *I* wish for you?"

JANE: "Oh, John, this is so sudden, but I would not disappoint you for worlds."

●

FIRST CHAP: "Didn't you used to have Miss Flyfly's photo in that frame there?"

SECOND CHAP: "Yes, but I got rid of it when I proposed and she gave me the negative."

●

HE (dejectedly): "You've played the deuce with my heart."

SHE (archly): "Well, didn't you play the knave?"

●

MOTHER: "Kate, I'm wondering about that young man that comes to see you every evening. What are his intentions?"

KATE: "I don't know, Mother. He keeps me in the dark."

●

PAT: "What do you suppose becomes of all those love triangles you hear about?"

PETE: "Most of them turn into wrecktangles, I guess."

●

JIM: "I want to know how long girls should be courted."

TIM: "The same as short ones."

GERT: "I didn't see John at the dance last night but I hear he acted the part of a thoroughbred."
TRUDE: "What part?"

•

JOHN: "Don't you think I'm rather good looking?"
JANE: "In a way."
JOHN: "What kind of a way?"
JANE: "Away off."

•

MOANIN' JOE: "My girl is a draftsman. Every time I make plans she draws the line."

•

HENRY: "So you liked me because I ignored you?"
HENRIETTA: "Yes, it was love at first slight."

17

FIRST MAN: "How did you get on with Miss Smart after the dance last night?"

SECOND MAN: "Well, I asked her twice if I could see her home, and she said that as I was so keen on seeing her home she would send me a photograph of it."

●

ANGRY AGNES declares: "He had the manners of a gentleman. I *knew* they didn't belong to him."

●

FLORRIE: "But surely you didn't tell him straight out that you loved him?"

LAURIE: "Goodness, no! He had to squeeze it out of me."

Medicine Jest

A man called at a doctor's office and the door was opened by the maid.

"Is the doctor in?" the man asked.

"No, sir," the maid answered.

"Will he be in soon?" the man continued.

"Prob'ly no," said the maid. "He went out on an eternity case."

Feeling rundown one winter, Joe went to his doctor for a check-up.

"There's nothing radically wrong with you," said the medico after a thorough examination. "All you need is a little sun and air."

"Yes, I guess so," said Joe, "but we can't afford him yet."

●

PATIENT: "I want to see a doctor. Is this the place?"
DOCTOR: "This is where I practice."
PATIENT: "Don't want no person to *practice* on me; I want a doctor to *cure* me.

●

THANKFUL HUSBAND: "She took a bad turn in the middle of the night. If I didn't take the turn with her . . . I'd have fallen out of the bed."

●

A doctor's son and a lawyer's son were arguing about their fathers.

"A little bird told me what kind of lawyer *your* old man is," said the doctor's son. "It said, 'Cheep! Cheep!'"

"Yeah," said the lawyer's kid. "Well, a duck told me what kind of doctor *your* old man is. It said, 'Quack! Quack!'"

●

SAGE SAM says: "A psychopath is where a psycho walks up and down."

DOCTOR: "Now, what is your best trick?"

MAGICIAN: "I saw a woman in half."

DOCTOR: "Is it difficult?"

MAGICIAN: "It's child's play. I learned it as a child."

DOCTOR: "Are there any more children at your home?"

MAGICIAN: "I have several half-sisters."

21

JERRY: "I once laughed all through an operation."

TERRY: "Is that so?"

JERRY: "Yeah, the doctor had me in stitches."

●

"How did you happen to become a chiropodist?" he was asked.

"Oh," he replied, "I always was at the foot of my class at school, so just naturally drifted into this profession."

●

PATIENT: "I feel like a new man."

PSYCHIATRIST: "Yeah? Anyone I know?"

●

MUTT: "Why is a physician who doesn't drink like a shipyard?"

JEFF: "Because he is a dry doc."

●

The young man in white passed a pretty girl in a Los Angeles hospital corridor. He cauterize and winked. She interne winked back.

●

DOPEY DAN thinks the phrase "false doctrine" means giving people the wrong medicine.

●

DOCTOR (to cockney patient): "Now, my man, what about this ear?"

PATIENT: "This 'ere *wot?*"

🙳 🙲

MISSIONARY: "Why do you look at me so intensely?"
WITCH DOCTOR: "I'm the tribe's food inspector."

•

"I see you gave that little debutante a private room," observed the first surgeon.
SECOND DOC: "Yes, she was too cute for wards."

PSYCHIATRIST: "How do you make your living?"
SELF-DELUSIONED: "I built three million fabricated homes."
PSYCHIATRIST: "That's a lie!"
SELF-DELUSIONED: "I *told* you it was fabricated."

•

ITCHY: "Doctor, did you say eating radishes would make my skin break out?"
DOCTOR: "No. I never make rash promises."

Animal
Punorama

JOEL: "Here's a telegram from the boss in Africa. He says he is sending us some lions' tails."

NOEL: *"Lion's tails?* What are you talking about?"

JOEL: "Well, read it yourself. 'Just captured two lions. Sending details by mail.'"

BILL: "You don't mean to tell me that fishes are musical?"

PHIL: "Certainly. Did you never hear of the piano tuna?"

●

A sea gull soared and landed on a channel marker. Buoy meets gull.

●

IZZY: "I saw a man-eating shark at the aquarium."

DIZZY: "That's nothing; I saw a man eating herring in the park."

●

MOE: "I'll put my rabbit in the other room."

JOE: "You don't mean to say you have a *rabbit* in the house?"

MOE: "I can't let him out."

JOE: "Why."

MOE: "This is an ingrown hair."

●

WISE WILFRED states: "The crow is not so bad a bird after all. It never shows the white feather and never complains without caws."

●

FIRST PELICAN: "Pretty good fish you have there."

SECOND PELICAN: "Well, it fills the bill."

●

JOHNNY'S TEACHER: "What's a myth?"

JOHNNY: "A myth is a young female moth."

DOPEY DAN laughs: "Sister Diana went horseback riding yesterday, and now she has to eat fundamental."

●

Mama Skunk was worried because she could never keep track of her two children. They were named In and Out, and whenever In was in, Out was out, and if Out was in, In was out. One day she called Out to her and told him to go and bring In in. So Out went out and in no time at all he brought In in.

"Wonderful!" said Mama Skunk. "How, in all this great forest, could you find In in so short a time?"
"It was easy," said Out. "In stinct."

NICE NEIGHBOR: "Willie, do you know what a panther is?"

LITTLE WILL: "O, yeth, ma'am. It'th a man who maketh panth."

●

ALEX: "Use these words in one sentence: bear, boys, bees."

ALICE: "Boys bees bare in the old swimming hole."

●

"If you want your parrot to talk, you should begin by teaching it short words."

"That's strange. I supposed it would take quicker to polly-syllables."

STUDENT-EDITOR of high school paper: "That big brown bear at the zoo just had a little baby bear, and they want us to write a story about it."
ASSISTANT STUDENT EDITOR: "Tell them we'll send over the cub reporter."

•

BIRD LOVER: "Did you hear the story about the peacock?"
A FRIEND: "No."
BIRD LOVER: "It's a beautiful tale."

•

EDUCATED EDDIE knows that until the baby birds are old enough to fly, asparagus and gets food for them.

•

OPPORTUNIST: "There's a cattle boat sailing for South America and I can get you on. I'm a personal friend of the head cow."
EQUALLY SO: "I think you're giving me the wrong steer."
OPPORTUNIST: "I just thought I'd horn in."
EQUALLY SO: "Well, we certainly milked that one."

•

Even *Dopey Dan* knows that mosquitoes are things you pat on the back.

•

"Have you much fish in your basket?" asked a neighbor one evening of a returning fisherman.

"Yes, a good eel," was the rather slippery reply.

HAPPY HARRY: "The roosters do the strutting while the hens do the laying. But that old hen wasn't doing anything so I'm gladiator."

•

A group of students in the biology class decided to play a joke on the professor. They used the body of a Japanese beetle as a chassis, substituted for its legs those of three grasshoppers, and glued on the feelers of a moth. They presented this Rube Goldberg-ish concoction to the professor and told him they were unable to identify it. He peered at it for a few seconds and then declared:

"Gentlemen, this is indeed a rare find. It is an insect rarely encountered in the insect world. Some people call it a humbug."

PROUD BUSINESSMAN TO HIS COUSIN AT ELLIS ISLAND: I'm rich! I got assets. Do you know what assets mean?"

NEW ARRIVAL: "Sure. Assets is little donkeys."

●

REX: "Have you a monkey wrench here?"

TEX: "Naw. My brother's got a cattle rench over there; my cousin got a sheep rench down there; but it's too cold for a monkey rench here."

●

DOPEY DAN complained: "My sister wanted to give me some Red Cross seals at Christmas time, but I told her I didn't want them—why I wouldn't even know how to feed them!"

Sheer Foodishness

WAITER: "How did you find your steak, sir?"

SOURBALL: "I looked under a slice of onion and there it was."

FIRST WIT: "What does a punster use for bread?"
SECOND WIT: "Punpernickel."

●

DINER: "Here, waitress, take this chicken away; it's as tough as a paving-stone."
WAITRESS: "Maybe it's a Plymouth Rock, sir."

●

"Boo-hoo," boo-hooed the bride. "To think my cake would turn out this way when I put my heart into it!"

"Never mind, honey," comforted the groom, "next time try baking one when you're light-hearted."

●

GROCERYMAN: "Pat, do you like apples?"
PAT: "Sure, sor, Oi wudn't ate an apple for the world."
GROCERYMAN: "Why how is that?"
PAT: "Ough! didn't me poor ould mother die av apple plexy?"

●

It was in a hotel dining room. The guest called out sharply, "Waiter!"

"Yes, sir."

"What's this?"

"It's your soup, sir."

"Yes, but what kind of soup?"

"It's bean soup," said the waiter with dignity.

"I'm not asking what it's *been*. I'm asking what it is *now!*"

WAITER: "Waffle you have, sir?"

CUSTOMER: "Waffle a waffle."

WAITER: "I wouldn't have a waffle if I were you, sir. They taste waffle."

CUSTOMER: "Waffle I have then, if I don't have one of your waffle waffles?"

WAITER: "Waffle I care waffle you have! Waffle you think I am, a mind reader?"

CUSTOMER: "Waffle goodness sake! Waffle you getting so mad about, anyhow?"

●

HUSBAND: "I thought that lamb was a little tough."

TIRED HOUSEWIFE: "Oh, let's not talk chop."

●

He was a waiter who had known years of stomach trouble. When he recognized that the customer was ordering a bland diet, he jotted down the order and then in a moment of abstraction, asked, "Will that be ulcer?"

●

NOODLE: "Will you join me in a bowl of soup?"

NOGAN: "Do you think there'd be room for both of us?"

●

PIGGY: "May I have fruit for breakfast in addition to examine bacon?"

WIGGY: "Oh well, eat all you want. There's an extradition the pantry."

DOPEY DAN is so dumb he thinks rhubarb is a French street.

•

MISS SMARTY is a vegetarian. She only goes out with men who have plenty of lettuce.

•

SIMPLE-TOM: "Yes, I know fish is brain food, but I don't care so much for fish. Ain't you got some other brain food?"
ALERT WAITER: "Well, there's noodle soup."

WAITER, as the boiled tongue slipped off the plate: "Please pardon the slip of the tongue."

•

MR. HEADHIGH: "I read today that in Alaska they have no food so they have to cut up their shoes and make soup out of them."

MRS. HEADHIGH: "Hush! The cook may hear you and we'll have goulash soup and filet of sole hash for dinner."

•

FIRST TRAMP: "Looks like rain today, doesn't it?"

SECOND TRAMP: "Yes, but it smells like coffee."

•

HOSTESS: "Do you feel like a cup of tea?"

GUEST: "Of course not. Do I look like one?"

•

DOPEY DIANA bought three loaves of bread to economize because she saw a sign in the baker's window that read: *Raisin bread tomorrow.*

•

WANTS-TO-KNOW: "Why do you eat dessert first?"

O.K., WILL-TELL: "My stomach's upset."

•

SAGE SAM advises—"It makes no difference which side bread is buttered on . . . eat both sides."

•

IN A HURRY: "Where are my spareribs?"

PLAIN TRUTH: "Lady I'm a butcher, not a doctor."

Eric von Stroheim, when in New York, used to eat at Lindy's, where most of the waiters are German. His waiter invariably greeted him with "Wie geht's, Herr Stroheim?", always omitting the *'von'*.

At last Stroheim got angry and said: "My name is *von* Stroheim, as you ought to know. Have you put down my order?"

"Jawohl, Herr Stroheim," said the waiter.

"*Von* herring,
Von schnitzel,
Von applecake, and
Von beer."

EARL: "Name me three kinds of nuts."
SHIRL: "That's easy! Peanuts, walnuts and forget-me-nuts."

●

REPORT: "How do the foreign dishes compare with American ones?"
HER: "Oh, they break just as easily."

●

BORE: "What are you having?"
POOR: "Calves' brains and ox-tail soup."
BORE: "That's one way of making ends meet."

●

Two bopsters went into a hash joint. One ordered a piece of pie.

"Sorry," says the waitress. "The pie is gone."

"Oh, that crazy pie!" cried the bopster. "I'll take two pieces!"

●

JOEY: "You look sweet enough to eat."
CHLOE: "I do eat. Where'll we go?"

●

MOLLY: "Our butcher certainly is an awkward fellow."
POLLY: "Yes, I notice his hands are always in his weigh."

●

WISE ALFRED states "We can't have archaic and eat it too."

AMAZED: "Why have you got your hand in the alphabet soup."

CRAZED: "I'm groping for words."

●

DOPEY DAN thinks synonym is what they put on a certain kind of breakfast roll.

●

LANDLADY: "I think you had better board elsewhere."
BOARDER: "Yes, I often have."
LANDLADY: "Often had *what?*"
BOARDER: "Had better board elsewhere."

●

WAITRESS: "What's making you cough, sir?"
DINER: "Why the coffee, of course."

Ladies and Pungents

Max Beerbohm once declined to be lured into a hike to the summit of a Swiss Alp. "Put me down," he said firmly, "as an anti-climb Max."

William Shakespeare, a master wit as well as a master playwright, used many puns in his plays. Mercutio, the swashbuckling, devil-may-care fellow who would steal the play in "Romeo and Juliet" if he were not killed, dies with a pun on his lips: "Ask for me tomorrow and you shall find me a grave man."

●

Thomas R. Marshall, Vice-President under Wilson, was a great admirer of the President. One of the books Marshall wrote was dedicated: "To President Woodrow Wilson from his only Vice."

●

Will Rogers once said: "The nation is prosperous on the whole, but how much prosperity is there in a hole?"

●

John Kendrick Bangs: "She would rather fool with a bee than be with a fool."

●

An editor met the late Sir James Barrie, the famous author of *Peter Pan*, at a dinner.

"Sir James," he said, "I suppose some of your plays do better than others. They are not all successes, I imagine."

Barrie said confidentially, his eyes twinkling, "No, some Peter out and some Pan out."

●

Robert Frost: "A successful lawsuit is the one worn by a policeman."

Samuel Goldwyn had heard of Dorothy Parker's quick wit and he determined to have her come to Hollywood and write for him.

"But," objected one of his assistants, "don't you think she's rather caustic for this job?"

"What do *I* care how much she costs," shouted Goldwyn. "*Get* her!"

●

Alec Templeton, the blind piano virtuoso, is credited with having the last word in the following story. A woman waylaying him after the radio broadcast, gushed:

"Oh, Mr. Templeton, that last selection you played was divine. May I ask who was the composer?"

"Bach, madam," Templeton replied.

"Wonderful," the lady burbled, "and is he composing at present?"

"No," the pianist answered, "he is decomposing."

●

Cornelia Otis Skinner, during a lecture: "One learns in life to keep silent and draw one's own confusions."

●

WISE WILFRED always remembers that the great Mark Twain said sagely: "Some money is twice tainted: 'taint yours and 'taint mine."

●

John Galsworthy: "He's not worth my wiles."

Theodore Roosevelt prided himself on his memory of names and faces. At a White House reception he stood shaking hands with a long line of visitors. At length there stood before him a little man from New York, a haberdasher who specialized in making shirts to order.

"Do you remember me, Mr. President? asked the visitor. "I made your shirts."

"Major Schurtz? Why, of course, I remember, Major," boomed the great man heartily. "And how are all the boys of the old regiment?"

●

Arthur "Bugs" Baer once said: "He was so quiet, you could hear a pun drop."

Abraham Lincoln could turn a neat pun on occasion. The governor of a Middle Western state was describing a small stream named Weeping Water. For Mr. Lincoln the name had humorous possibilities.

"No doubt," he suggested, "the Indians out there call it Minneboohoo."

"Why?" the governor asked.

"Well," said Lincoln, "isn't it logical when they call Laughing Water, Minnehaha?"

●

Clare Booth Luce: "The politicians were talking themselves red, white, and blue in the face."

●

Benjamin Franklin: " 'Tis against some men's principle to pay interest, and seems against others' interest to pay the principal."

Phineas Taylor Barnum: "Every crowd has a silver lining."

•

Big Jim Farley, ace politician of the early Roosevelt regime at a big dinner once referred to Henry Kaiser, the outstanding shipbuilder of World War II, as "SIR LAUNCHALOT."

Kleptomaniacts

Bop: "What makes you think that having been a drummer in a swing band will make you a good policeman?"

Ster: "I'm used to pounding a beat."

OLE: "I went out with a copple of robbers last night."

KNUT: "You did?"

OLE: "Yah, it was raining."

●

POLICE: "How do you earn your living? Do you pick pockets?"

MAN: "No, sir. I take 'em as they come."

●

Clifton Fadiman says that William Cole waits in calm and certain expectation of the day when he will be taken to police headquarters, shown two sets of fingerprints, and be moved to comment, "Why they're whorls apart!"

●

"You were thrown out," remarked the ash barrel. "That's what you get for being so crooked."

"The crookedness is not my fault," said the nail. "I was driven to it by a woman."

●

BEN: "I saw your brother riding down the street and he had a pinched look."

LEN: "Yeah? I wonder why?"

BEN: "He was riding in the patrol wagon."

●

MRS. BROWN (with newspaper): "John, it refers here to some gunmen taking a man for a ride. What kind of a ride?"

BROWN: "A slay ride, my dear."

Half Moon, the Indian detective, stooped low as he ran along the railroad ties. His assistant, Quarter Moon, caught up with him.

"What you lookin' for, Chief?" he inquired.

"Lookin' for Big Chief who own railroad," he grunted.

"Think you'll find him?" asked his assistant.

"Sure. Me on his track," asserted Half Moon.

●

Ex-convict instructing his boy: "No, son, a safe-cracker is not something you buy on the Fourth of July, nor is forgery the work of a blacksmith."

●

#688,712: "How is Joe spending his spare time while he's in jail?"
#1,101,262: "Oh, he's writing his alibiography."

●

ADDLE: "That forger is a very moral person."
PATE: "What do you mean?"
ADDLE: "He is always ready to write a wrong."

●

"I am at your service, ma'am," the burglar said when the lady of the house caught him stealing her silver.

●

"What a lovely sirenade," exclaimed the hold-up man to his driver as six more police cars took up the chase.

🄳🄴

Con: "My brother is connected with the police department."

Dick: "Police Department? How?"

Con: "By a pair of handcuffs."

●

Prisoner: "I had the picture in my hand and one of the officers busted the picture over my head.

Cell-Mate: "And you still think you were double-crossed?"

Prisoner: "Sure—I was framed."

●

"I caught her in the kleptomaniact," shouted the storekeeper to the crowd, as he held onto the girl.

FIRST HOBO: "Have you spent many nights in police stations?"

SECOND HOBO: "No. Sleeping in them is only all right in a pinch."

•

SHERLOCK: "If a man smashed a clock, could he be accused of killing time?"

HOLMES: "Not if he could prove that the clock struck first."

•

FIRST ENGLISHMAN: "Why is a gasoline carrier like a police car?"

SECOND ENGLISHMAN: "That's easy. It's a petrol wagon."

•

SCOTLAND: So you're a detective in your home town?"

YARD: "Yes, I am. Here's a picture of me at work."

SCOTLAND: "This is a picture of you in bed."

YARD: "Yeah, I'm an undercover man."

Slicktionary
Daffynitions

ALIMONY: Merely a contraction of "all his money."

AMAZON: An expletive to go at the first part of a sentence (Example: AMAZON of a gun!).

ASPERSION: A burro in Persia.

AUTOMATON: A person who eats in the auto-
               mat.

BABY: Newly-wet.

BELL: One who lives a date-to-date ex-
               istence.

FAD: In one era and out the other.

FIREPLACE: An office used for discharging
               people.

GOLD DIGGER: A gal who likes to go buy-buy.

GOSSIP: A prattlesnake.

GUBERNATORIAL: A peanut in swimming.

INCONGRUOUS: Where the laws are made.

KLEENEX: Your daily nose-paper.

LEMON JUICE: An introduction: Lemon juice you to Miss Lyon.

NIGHTCLUB: Where they take the rest out of restaurant, and put the din in dinner.

OPERETTA:	A girl who works for the telephone company.
PRESS AGENT:	One who has hitched his braggin' to a star.
PSEUDO:	Counterfeit money.
STUCCO:	What a lot of house hunters are getting these days.
UNDER-RATE:	Seven.
WOLF:	A big dame hunter.
WEASEL:	It blows at noon.

Disrepunable Verse

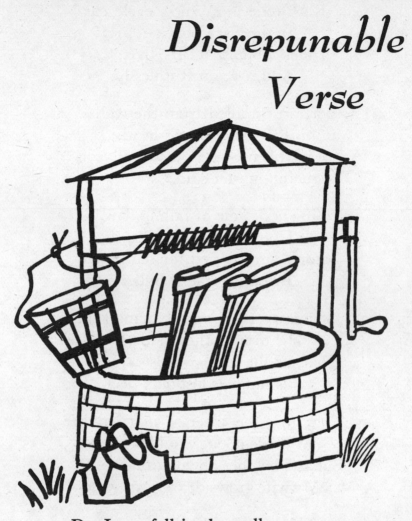

Dr. Jones fell in the well
    And died without a moan.
He should have tended to the sick,
    And let the well alone.

Ruth rode in my new cycle car
In the seat in back of me;
I took a bump at fifty-five,
And rode on Ruthlessly.

●

The portrait tumbled from the wall
And hit the young man's head.
"A striking likeness!" That was all
The rueful punster said.

●

Sing not to me of falling dew
Upon the purple hills,
For I am worried far too much
By falling due of bills.

●

The lawyer fell on a banana skin,
His torn clothes made him feel
That, as the legal words explain—
His suit was lost on a peel.

●

They told me when I married her
My ardent love would fade away,
But as I buy her gowns I find
My wife grows dearer every day.

●

The bachelor is a cagey guy,
And has a lot of fun;
He sizes all the cuties up
And never Mrs. one.

When Jonah interviewed the whale
  and haunted his internals,
As erst it is recorded in
  The truthfulest of journals,
What monarch did he symbolize?
  (A far-fetched joke you'll style it.)
It seems to us he might have been
  A sort of paunch's pilot.

●

"I'd rather not," Augustus said,
  The truffles quick rejecting:
"How now, my dear," said she, "what fresh
  Conceit are you affecting?
I do not wish t'ruffle you.
  Nor yet to make a pun, Gus;
But then I surely thought that you
  Were fond of any fun-Gus."

●

A famous judge came late to court
  One day in busy season;
Whereat his clerk, in great surprise,
  Inquired of him the reason,
"A child was born," his Honor said,
  "And I'm the happy sire."
"An infant judge?" "Oh, no," said he,
  "As yet he's but a crier."

There was a little lawyer man
    Who gently smiled as he began
The widow's husband's will to scan;
    And thinking of his coming fee,
He said to her quite tenderly,
    "You have a nice fat legacy."
Next morning as he lay in bed
    With bandages on his broken head,
He wondered what-in-heck he'd said.

As he walked with baby
He had to confess
That marriage with him
Was a howling success.

●

Brown has a lovely baby girl,
The stork left her with a flutter;
Brown named her "Oleomargarine,"
For he hadn't any but her.

●

He who courts and goes away,
May court again another day;
But he who weds and courts girls still
May go to court against his will.

●

Flo was fond of Ebenezer—
"Eb," for short, she called her beau.
Talk of "tide of love" — great Caesar!
You should see 'em, Eb and Flo.

●

Ladies, to this advice give heed:
In controlling men,
If at first you don't succeed,
Just cry, cry again.

Deep-Art-ment

EGBERT: "He said you were a sculptor but you should wash more often."

CUTHBERT: "Are you sure that's what he said?"

EGBERT: "Well, he said you were a dirty chiseler."

CRITIC: "The picture of the horse is good, but where is the wagon?"
ARTIST: "Oh, the horse will draw that."

•

PABLO: "Do you think Lautrec painted Toulousely?"
PICASSO: "If he did I'm sure Van can Gogh him one better."

•

MORRIS: "Do you call *that* a portrait?"
NORRIS: "Yes, sir. All the poor traits are showing."

•

TITIAN: "This drawing looks amateurish."
MICHELANGELO: "Well, it's a matter of sketch as sketch can.

•

WISE WILFRED says that it's all right to pick an artist's pocket because he has pictures.

•

STUDENT: "Is it hard to learn to paint?"
TEACHER: "No, I think you'll find it's easely-y done."

Musical
Punes

MUSIC STUDENT: "That
piece you just played is by
Mozart, isn't it?"
HURDY-GURDY MAN:
"No, by Handel."

MARIE: "Can you sing opera?"

MARIO: "Of course!"

MARIE: "Do you sing FAUST?"

MARIO: "I sing faust or slow—any kind you want."

●

Louis Untermeyer: "I was thinking about the American composers who keep borrowing from modern French music. I like to call them American Debussy-bodies."

●

JANE (discussing operas with a friend in a street car): "I simply love Carmen."

CONDUCTOR: "Try the motorman, Miss. I'm a married man."

●

JASCHA: "This expensive violin is worth one hundred dollars, but I'll take $10.00."

MISCHA: "There must be a string attached to it."

●

"Fred," said Ned, after listening to an especially tall story, "do you know why you are like a harp struck by lightning?"

"No," said Fred, "I give up."

"Because a harp struck by lightning is a blasted lyre," said Ned.

●

ELVIS: "That girl across the hall has a singular voice."

PELVIS: "Thank heaven it isn't plural!"

WISE WILFRED says that a bandleader is a man who can face the music.

OSSIP: "I have an uncle that's conceited. He's seven feet tall and plays the flute."

GOSSIP: "What makes you think he's conceited just because he's seven feet tall and plays the flute?"

OSSIP: "Well *that's* high-flutin', isn't it?"

AUDITIONEE: "What do you think of my execution?"
AUDITIONER: "I'm in favor of it."

●

BELLYRINA: "I'm a finished dancer."
STAGE MANAGER: "I'll say."

●

"She must be very musical."
"How can you tell?"
"By the chords in her neck."

●

EDUCATED EDDIE tells us: "The grasshopper is something of a singer, but the potato bug is the most indefatigable musician. He plays on the tuber."

Welded Bliss

SOLOMON'S 999TH WIFE: "Solomon, are you really and truly in love with me?"
SOLOMON: "My dear, you are one in a thousand."

GUS: "You say his wife's a brunette? Didn't he marry a blonde?"
FERGUS: "He did, but she dyed."

●

OLIN: "I hear you've signed up as skipper on the good ship matrimony."
COLIN: "No, my wife is the skipper. I married a widow. I'm her second mate."

●

A man, whose daughter had married a man by the name of Price, was congratulated by one of his friends, who remarked: "I am glad to see you have got a good price for your daughter."

●

WIFE (trying on hats): "Do you like this turned down, dear?"
HUSBAND: "How much is it?"
WIFE: "Sixty dollars."
HUSBAND: "Yes, turn it down."

●

SALLY: "Were you excited when you first asked your husband for money?"
POLLY: "Oh, no, I was calm—and collected."

●

MASTERFUL WIFE: "This mountain air disagrees with me."
MEEK HUSBAND: "Why, darling," he protested mildly, "I don't see how it would dare."

A man's idea about marriage:
BEFORE: Spooning around with a cute dish.
AFTER: Forking over.

•

MRS. BRAGGERT: "My husband wrecks houses."
MRS. NOSEY: "Make much?"
MRS. BRAGGERT: "He pulls down a few thousand a year."

•

IKE: "What would you consider a long marriage?"
MIKE: "One that has lasted at least twenty-awed years."

•

OFFICE BUDDY: "How could you endure talking to that homely woman without laughing in her face?"
HIS PAL: "That's easy. She's my wife."
OFFICE BUDDY: "Oh, my mistake."
HIS PAL: "No, mine."

•

They were writing thank-you letters for their wedding presents.
HONEY: "What's the matter, dear?"
MOONER: "I had it on the tip of my tongue, and now it's gone."
HONEY: "Just think hard and it's bound to come back to you."
MOONER: "Fat lot of good that will do. It was a four-cent stamp."

MILLY: "Did you hear about the awful fright George got on his wedding day?"

TILLY: "Oh, yes; I was there. I *saw* her."

●

BLENDA: "What's your husband's average income?"

GLENDA: "Oh, around midnight."

It was plain to be seen that the groom was nervous; the ceremony had flustered him even more. At the end there was an awkward pause, during which all three looked at each other self-consciously. Bending forward the groom whispered—far too loud—to the minister, "Ain't it kisstomary to cuss the bride?"

"Alas! Sometimes it is," responded the minister sadly, "but that doesn't usually come till later."

•

WIFE (back-seat driving): "What happened, George?"
GEORGE: "Puncture."
WIFE: "You should have watched out for it! The guidebook warned us there was a fork in the road about this point."

•

JOE: "How did you meet your wife?"
SCHMOE: "Oh, we got caught in a revolving door and started going around together."

•

DIRK: "What was Mrs. Jones's maiden name?"
KIRK: "Why, her maiden aim was to get married, of course."

•

PECK: "I've been married five years, and I've got a bushel of children."
SNIFF: "How's that?"
PECK: "My name is Peck. I've got four children. Don't four pecks make a bushel?"

WISE WILFRED says a bachelor life is just one undarned thing after another.

•

"Her father married her mother for the bread she made, now her suitor wants to marry her for the dough she's got."

•

LITTLE WOMAN: "I think this a lovely hat you bought me, George, but really it's a sin to pay $50.00 for it."
DOTING HUSBAND: "Well, the sin is on *your* head, not mine."

You Auto Go for These

TRAFFIC COP: "What do you think you're doing crawling along at ten miles an hour with that load of hogs?"
TRUCK DRIVER: "I'm looking for a porking place."

ADDLE: "If you had a horse you wouldn't have to drive a car."

PATED: "Aw go on . . . horses can't drive cars."

●

SAGE SAM defines a pedestrian as a man who falls by the wayside.

●

WISE WILFRED contends that a pedestrian is a person who should be seen and not hurt.

●

WISE WILFRED also advises that, while a little jack can lift up an automobile, it takes a lot of jack to keep it up.

●

RIGGS (in history class): "Think of those Spaniards going 3,000 miles on a galleon!"

JIGGS: "Aw, forget it. Yuh can't believe all yuh hear about them foreign cars."

●

EDUCATED EDDIE says that even in Bible times a blowout was a great annoyance, for do we not read in Isaiah XXIII, 5: "They shall be sorely pained at the report of Tyre?"

●

PAT: "Odd how a single policeman can dam the flow of traffic, isn't it?"

NAT: "Yeah, but you should hear some of the motorists that are held up."

CYNICAL CYRUS defines fluid drive: "When there's a drip at the wheel."

●

POLICE: "Here's a ticket for parking."
MAN: "Thanks. Where's it playing?"

●

FRANTIC: "My engine's smoking."
MECHANIC: "Well, it's old enough."

●

FRANKIE: "Use the word 'Cadillac' in a sentence."
JOHNNY: "Well, a cadillac mean if you pull its tail."

●

DON: "What kind of oil do you use in your car?"
JUAN: "I usually begin by telling them I'm lonely."

●

OFFICER (to couple in parked auto): "Don't you see that sign, 'Fine for parking'?"
DRIVER: "Yes, Officer, I see it and I heartily agree with it."

●

HAPPY HARRY says, "A taxi driver is a man who drives away customers."

Outstanding Exam-bulls

Vesuvius is a volcano, and if you climb up to the top you can see the creator smoking.

The equator is a menagerie lion running around the earth.

●

A buttress is a female butler.

●

A pullet surprise is given in America every year for the best writings.

●

A pulmotor is an engine that pulls an automobile.

●

Asperity is the drug from which aspirin is made.

●

An autobiography is a history of motor cars.

●

To germinate is becoming a naturalized German.

●

History calls people Romans because they never stayed long in one place.

●

Louis xvi was gelatined during the French Revolution.

●

Equinox is derived from two Latin words. Equus means a horse, and nox means night. Therefore it is a nightmare.

●

The *World Almanac* is a book of sadistics.

●

As she is going to be married next month, she is very busy getting her torso ready.

Sense of Humus

ALFRED: "Hey, boy, where's your brother?"
JED: "In the barn, shoein' horses."
ALFRED: "Where's your mother?"
JED: "In the backyard, shooin' chickens."
ALFRED: "Where's your father?"
JED: "In the hammock, shooin' flies."

FIRST HEN: "That big rooster has been making love to me."

SECOND HEN: "Did you give him any hencouragement?"

FIRST HEN: "Well, I *did* egg him on a bit."

●

A farmer was trying to sell his horse after exercising it. He exclaimed to his prospective buyer: "Don't you admire his coat?"

"Coat's all right," said the prospect, "but I don't care for the pants!"

●

ROB: "How many heifers have you got?"

RUBE: "Heifer dozen."

A teacher in a country schoolhouse was instructing her class in the use of antonyms. "Now, children," she said, "what is the opposite of sorrow?"

"Joy!" shrieked the class in unison.

"What is the opposite of pleasure?"

"Pain."

"And what is the opposite of woe?"

"Giddap."

A city boy, visiting his country cousin, was walking through the pasture when he heard a peculiar buzzing sound. He looked around to find out what it was.

"Come away from there!" the cousin shouted. "It's a rattlesnake! If you go near it, it will strike."

"Gosh," said the city boy, "do *they* have unions, too?"

HAY: "Anything new in your neighborhood?"
STRAW: "Yes, the whole neighborhood is stirred up."
HAY: "What's the cause?"
STRAW: "Ploughing."

●

A husband puttered around in the backyard with some boards and nails while his wife lay in bed with a very bad cold.

"How's the wife?" asked a neighbor.
"Not so good."
"Sorry. Is that her coughin'?"
"Oh, no. This here's a chicken coop."

●

CUSTOMER: "Is the milk from this dairy pasteurized?"
WAITRESS: "It sure is. Every morning they turn their cows out to pasture."

●

FLO: "What are you doing these days?"
EB: "Working on a ranch where they raise hornless goats."
FLO: "But—"
EB: "There are no butts."

●

DOLEFUL DONALD sighs: "A Gentleman Farmer is a city guy who can only raise his hat."

●

ARITHMETIC TEACHER: "What comes before six?"
EARLY RISER: "The milkman."

When visitors came, Susie, age five, took them to see the pigs in their electric fence enclosure, explaining,

"When the piggies back into the 'lectric fence there'll be a short circus."

●

Roy: "Say, how come your team isn't bridled?"
Rogers: "Oh, they take their harness as a big yoke and laugh it off."

JEB: "Why were all your chickens out in your front yard yesterday?"

ZEKE: "They heard that men were coming here to lay a sidewalk, and they wanted to see how it was done."

●

COUNTRYFOLK: "I like to go to bed and get up with the chickens, don't you?"

CITYFOLK: "No, I like to sleep in my own bed."

●

COW: "What kind of saddle do you want—one with a horn or one without?"

BOY: "Without, I guess. There doesn't seem to be much traffic around here."

●

DUDE: "Did you take my toothpaste?"

HILLBILLY: "No, I did not take your toothpaste. I don't need it. My teeth ain't loose."

●

OLD TIMER: "Why is this clover older than you?"

YOUNG FELLOW: "It isn't."

OLD TIMER: "It is, though, because it is pasturage."

●

The farmer's boy who used to growl at the cows, as he drove them up, now stands wide-eyed at the corner appraising the calves.

●

A mother named her sons' cattle ranch "Lens" because it was "where the sons raise meat."

🜚 🜚

TIMMY had just refused to spend his holidays on a farm in the country.

PLEADING MOTHER: "But why, dear?"

TIMMY: "It's pretty awful here, where they cane by hand, but there they've got thrashing machines, and I ain't going to chance it."

●

Some years ago a woman clerk in the Department of Agriculture in Washington noticed a farmer lad wandering aimlessly about the lobby. "Perhaps," she suggested helpfully, "you'd like to see the forty-foot mural on the floor above. It's really quite interesting."

Half an hour later came an irate call from the Bureau of Animal Husbandry: "Who the heck," a voice inquired, "sent a guy up here looking for a forty-foot mule?"

●

A farmer was explaining to an elegant city lady guest what a menace insects are to farm products—how potato bugs ruin potato crops and corn borers destroy corn.

The lady listened attentively, then exclaimed: "And the poor dairy people. How the butterflies must bother them."

Daze and Nights

Weather report from Mexico:
Chili today and hot tamale.

BIRTHSTONES:

>For the laundress, the soapstone.
>For the surgeon, the bloodstone.
>For the politician, the blarneystone.
>For the borrower, the touchstone.
>For the locksmith, the keystone.

●

"The evening wore on," droned the man who was telling the story.

"Excuse me," interrupted a bored listener, "but can you tell us *what* the evening wore on that occasion?"

"I don't know that it is important," replied the story-teller. "But if you must know, it was the close of a summer day."

●

The bigger the summer vacation, the harder the fall.

●

TOAST: Here's to winter—may we always be coaled.

●

SUN: The oldest settler in the West.

●

MOON: It affects the tide and the untied.

●

JACK: "I don't like this cold weather."
FROST: "Oh, it's nothing."
JACK: "What are you talking about?— It's zero."
FROST: "Well, *that's* nothing."

DOPEY DIANA thinks the four seasons are pepper, salt, vinegar and oil.

•

As spring approaches, boys begin to feel gallant, and gals buoyant.

A poet on the Old Farmer's Almanac staff has a low opinion of Maine weather. He begins an unpleasant review of the whole year with:

> Dirty days has September,
> April, June, and November.

●

MATT: "Boy, that was really some horrorscope that sour-looking astrologer set up for me!"
NAT: "Well, then, why don't you look for a happy medium?"

●

Round the week:

> "When did you get your husband?"
> "On Manday."
> "And when did he select you for his bride?"
> "On Chooseday."
> "And you got married?"
> "On Wedsday."
> "And when the children came, when were they
>   happiest?"
> "On Toysday."
> "But you finally had to consult a psychologist?"
> "On Freuday."
> "Because you found yourself feeling low?"
> "On Sadderday."
> "And were avoiding everybody?"
> "On Shunday."

TRAMP (pathetically): "You see, lady, it's impossible to get a day's work at my old job."
KIND LADY: "What was your occupation?"
TRAMP: "I was a night watchman."

●

WONDERING DREAMER: "Why do poets always speak of the moon as silver?"
PRACTICAL REALIST: "It's because of the quarters and halves, I suppose."

Politricks

Some political speeches are a good deal like the horns on a healthy Texas steer—a point here and a point there, with a lot of bull in between.

●

Many a campaign argument is sound—just sound.

Commissioner Cox dictated a memo for the budget director, setting forth the duties of a new male assistant and thereby justifying his presence on the payroll. When the mimeograph of his memo was returned to him the commissioner nearly swooned!

It read, "The principal activities of this senior clerk is to take care of some of the cuties of the commissioner."

●

A teacher asked one of her pupils to give an example of the opposite uses of pro and con, and the boy replied promptly, "Progress and Congress."

●

"If all the women were taken out of circulation," said the feminine candidate, "what kind of a nation would this be?"

"Stag-nation," came the reply from a gallant young man in the back row.

●

When the public speaker asked the chairman how long he should speak he was told to watch the audience's reaction.

"If you haven't struck oil in five minutes," the chairman said, "quit boring."

●

WARD: "What is a political pie?"

HEDER: "It's a lot of crust, with applesauce and plums."

DUMB: "But why are you going to the North Pole?"
CLUCK: "They told me if I wanted to vote I'd *have* to go to the poles."

●

An irate tax payer in Boston addressed his check to:

City Haul
BOSTON, MASS.

●

When it comes to taxes we all have to be paytriotic.

●

MAYOR MOPPUS says, "I went to a good school where some of our foremost politicians learned their three R's—*this* is Ours, *that* is Ours, *everything* is Ours."

●

POLITICIAN (speechifying): "I want reform . . . I want land reform . . . I want housing reform . . . I want educational reform . . . I want . . ."
From the audience: "Chloroform."

●

The Chairman of the Management Board replied in a few appropriated words.

●

PAT: "Here, have some candy. It's political taffy."
MATT: "Political taffy? Why do you call it that?"
PAT: "Because it has a lot of pull."

●

CURIOUS CARL wants to know if a politician makes up his own bunk.

Watson a Name

ABE: "Have you ever met my sister, Louisa?"
SEE: "Yes. She's rather plump, isn't she?"
ABE: "I have another at home—Lena."

LOLITA: "You must be mighty proud of your husband Juan. He is so big and strong."
PEPITA: "Pah! You should have seen the Juan who got away!"

•

JOHN: "Darling, in the moonlight your teeth are like pearls."
DAWN: "Oh, indeed! And when were you in the moonlight with Pearl?"

•

CURT: "Who's your cook now?"
BERT: "Della."
CURT: "Della who?"
BERT: "Della Katessen."

•

WISE: "Have you heard about my friend Kersch?"
CRACK: "Kersch who?"
WISE: "Gesundheit!"

•

CLERK: "What can I do for you?"
CUSTOMER: "I want a hat."
CLERK: "Fedora?"
CUSTOMER: "No—for me."

•

Any parent of a three-year-old, we feel sure, will be quick to sympathize with the German mother who always felt better prepared to receive company after she had washed her Hans.

One of the most frustrating conversations in history is recorded by *Theatre Arts* magazine.

A subscriber dialed "Information" for the magazine's number.

"Sorree," drawled the lady, "but there is nobody listed by the name of Theodore Arts."

"It's *not* a person; it's a publication," insisted the subscriber. "I want *Theatre Arts*."

The operator's voice rose a few decibels. "I *told* you," she repeated, "we have no listing for Theodore Arts."

"Confound it!" hollered the subscriber, "the word is 'Theatre' : T-H-E-A-T-R-E."

"*That*," said the operator with crushing finality, "is *not* the way to spell Theodore!"

JED: "Do you know Art?"
FRED: "Art who?"
JED: "Artesian."
FRED: "Sure. I know Artesian well."

● If Ireland would sink, what would float?—Cork.

A teacher took over a new class.

"What's your name?" she asked one little boy.

"Jule," he replied.

"Not Jule," she said. "You shouldn't use contractions or nicknames. Your name is Julius."
She turned to the next boy.

"What's your name?"

"Billious," he replied.

"Knock! Knock!"
"Who's there?"
"Oscar."
"Oscar who?"
"Oscar if she loves me."

"Knock! Knock!"
"Who's there?"
"Celeste."
"Celeste who?"
"Celeste time I'm going to ask you."

"Knock! Knock!"
"Who's there?"
"Chester."
"Chester who?"
"Chester minute and I'll see."

•

"Knock! Knock!"
"Who's there?"
"Valencia."
"Valencia who?"
"Valencia a buck would you pay it back?"

•

"Knock! Knock!"
"Who's there?"
"Tarzan."
"Tarzan who?"
"Tarzan stripes forever."

•

"Knock! Knock!"
"Who's there?"
"Minerva."
"Minerva who?"
"Minerva's wreck from all these knock-knocks."

-and Last Names Too!

"What did Cleopatra say when Mark Antony asked if she was true to him?"

"Omar Khayyam."

●

A merchant in Dallas, Texas, asked the police to help him decipher the almost unreadable signature on a worthless check. The police did. It was, "U. R. Stuck."

Over the British telephone:

"Are you there?"

"Who are you, please?"

"Watt."

"What's your name?"

"Watt's my name."

"Yes, what's your name?"

"My name is John Watt."

"John what?"

"Yes."

"I'll be around to see you this afternoon."

"All right. Are you Jones?"

"No. I'm Knott."

"Will you tell me your name then?"

"Will Knott."

"Why not?"

"My name is Knott."

"Not *what?*"

●

"Do you know Nat Cohen?"

"One of the cloak-and-suit Cohens?"

"No, he's one of the ice-cream Cohens."

●

"Dr. Jekyll, tell me more about your alter ego."

"Scram, son, you're getting under my Hyde."

●

A Texas newspaper on the morning of the 1944 national election predicted the weather: "Not Dewey."

An American tourist met Bernard Shaw one morning
on Piccadilly and stopped him with a "Say, are you
Shaw?"

"Positive," replied G.B.S.—and walked on.

Strange, Moore, and Wright, three notorious punsters, were on a certain occasion dining together, when Moore observed, "There is but one knave among us, and that's Strange."

"Oh, no!" said Wright, "there is one Moore."

"Ah, yes!" said Strange, "that's Wright."

•

British epitaph on Meredith, an organist at St. Mary Winton College, Oxford:

Here lies one blown out of breath,
Who lived a merry life, and died a Merideth.

•

MAMIE: "Did you know that Xantippe, wife of one of the greatest of ancient philosophers, was a great scold?"

JAMIE: "Certainly. But just think what a great tease her husband was."

MAMIE: "A great tease?"

JAMIE: "Yes, Socrates."

•

The proceedings were delayed in a certain court by the failure of a witness named Sarah Mony to arrive. So the court was adjourned without Sarah-Mony.

•

A man by the name of Dunlop once defied a famous punster to perpetrate a pun on his name.

"Easy enough!" cried the wit. "Just lop off the last syllable and it's Dun!"

Domestic Depuntment

MRS. HIFALUTIN (to the new maid): "Sometimes, my dear, you'll have to help the butler upstairs. Understand?"

FIFI: "Yes, Madam. I've worked with drunken butlers before."

WIFEY: "Don't we always exchange presents?"
HUBBY: "I always exchange yours."

●

FED-UP HUSBAND (to free-and-easy club friend who has dropped in to supper uninvited): "Will you please understand, sir, that I won't have you use bad language before my wife!"
FREE-AND-EASY FRIEND (unabashed): "Well, how should I know she wanted to swear first?"

●

MR. FOOLISH: "How *could* you have a son that age?"
MRS. LOGICAL: "I didn't. When I had him he was just a baby."

●

DAVID: "Old Scrooge is dead at last, and I understand that his son will get a quarter of a million. If he doesn't paint the town red, now, then I miss my guess."
DORA: "I should think that anybody with a quart of vermillion might paint a town very red indeed."

●

A GENTLEMAN: "If the devil should lose his tail, where would he go to get it repaired?"
HIS WIFE: ? ? ?
THE GENTLEMAN: "In the place where they re-tail bad spirits."

●

LITTLE GIRL: "Ma, where is the state of matrimony?"
MOTHER: "It is one of the united states."

ENGLISHMAN (reading THE TIMES): "As far as I can see, the Empire is going to the dogs. It is really!"

EMPTY-HEADED SON: "That's quite right. I've noticed it myself for a long time. They give a much better show at the PALLADIUM or the COLISEUM nowadays."

•

HAIR-IN-CURLERS: "You should enter the cat show."

SLEEPY BREAKFASTER: "Why?"

HAIR-IN-CURLERS: "You've got such a long puss this morning."

•

MR. STUFFLY: "It's one of the first things a man should learn—his station in life."

MRS. STUFFLY: "Indeed! There's nothing more exasperating than being carried on to the one beyond."

•

OBLIGING PAPA: "I always help with the diapers. It's a good way to make a little change."

History-cal Hoists

A king's jester made puns until the ruler could stand him no longer and sentenced him to be hanged. As the jester stood on the gallows with the rope around his neck, the king relented to the extent of saying that if he'd promise never to make another pun, his life would be spared. But the jester just couldn't resist it.

"No noose is good news!" he exclaimed, so they went ahead and hanged him.

A nobleman at court claimed that he could make a pun on any subject.

"Make one about the king," someone quickly challenged him.

"The king is not a subject," was the immediate reply.

●

From the 1739 Joe Miller:
A gentleman was saying one day at the Tilt Yard Coffee-house, when it rained exceedingly hard, that it put him in mind of the general deluge. "Zoons, sir," said an old campaigner, who stood by, "who's that? I have heard of all the generals in Europe but him!"

●

Charles Lamb was one day accosted by a friend who said, "Mr. Lamb, make me a pun."

"Upon what, Sir?" was Lamb's reply.

●

To fool the giant Polyphemus, the wily Odysseus gave his name as Outis (Greek for Nobody). When Odysseus later attacked Polyphemus in the cave, the latter called to his fellow Cyclops for help, crying, "Nobody is killing me!"

●

The oldest pun is said to have originated in the Garden of Eden when Eve asked Adam, Now, tell me: "what's wrong about eating this apple?" and Adam answered, "I'll bite."

Charlemagne was in need of amusement.

"Why," they asked him, "do you have such a large number of court jesters in constant attendance on your royal person?"

"Because," he replied, with a right regal chuckle, "I could not earn the surname of 'The Great' were I not careful to keep my wits about me."

●

The Saxon flunkey entered.

"Sire," he said to his master, "Lady Godiva rides without."

Milord glanced out of the window, and re-marked:

"Very tactfully put, my man."

Capital Grins

BENNY: "What makes your sister so fat lately—she used to be very thin?"

DENNY: "She's working down in a photographer's."

BENNY: "Why, how does that make any difference?"

DENNY: "Well, you see, she's in the developing room most of the time."

At one time *Dopey Diana's* uncle operated an escort service—he was a bouncer.

•

A dentist in New York had once been defrauded in cashing a check. So he doesn't cash them any more.

"Sorry," he always explains laughingly, "but I am like the farmer in Czechoslovakia during the hated Hitler regime. One night a midget pounded on the farmer's door and asked to be hidden from the pursuing Gestapo. 'I can't,' said the farmer, 'I'd get in trouble if I were to cache even a small Czech.' "

•

JESTER: "My uncle is a southern planter."
LESTER: "You mean he owns a plantation?"
JESTER: "No. He's an undertaker in South Carolina."

•

Business Reports:

"My business is looking up," said the astronomer.
"Mine is going up in smoke," complained the cigar maker.
"Mine is all write," chuckled the author.
"Mine is just sew, sew," remarked the tailor.
"Mine is growing," the farmer boasted.
"Mine is pretty light," snapped the electric light man.
"Mine is picking up," smiled the cheerful ragpicker.
"Mine is looking better," opined the optician.

Greeting card for a businessman: Money happy returns of the day.

•

JOHN: "Was his bankruptcy due to a lack of brains?"
DON: "Yes, a lack and a lass."

•

EDUCATED EDDIE told us that Adam and Eve were the first bookkeepers: they invented the loose-leaf system.

•

After pointing out the many advantages of the house he was trying to sell to an Englishman, the salesman gestured proudly and enthused, "Now, sir, that is a house without a flaw."
The prospective customer looked amazed. "Remarkable," he said, "but what in heaven's name does one walk on?"

•

FRANK: "My uncle owns ten gasoline stations and not one of them has a roof."
HANK: "What's the idea?"
FRANK: "No overhead."

•

Mr. Bootstrap was dictating to his stenographer and he was in doubt on the phraseology needed. He looked at her and asked,
        "Do you 'retire' a loan?"
Her eyes flashed. "I'll have you know I sleep with Mama!"

BARRY: "How would you classify a telephone girl? Is hers a business or a profession?"

LARRY: "Neither. It's a calling!"

•

STENO: "Boss, will you advance me my next week's salary?"

BOSS: "Certainly not. I never make advances to my stenographers."

COMMERCIAL TRAVELER: "I have come about the attachment for your typewriter."
CLERK: "Well, I'm sorry she is out, and, what's more, she and I are engaged."

●

CASH: "He's cleaned up a fortune in crooked dough."
CREDIT: "What was he, anyhow? A counterfeiter?"
CASH: "No, a pretzel manufacturer."

●

BUSINESSMAN (on the phone): "I'm very sick. I have laryngitis."
SALESMAN: "Then why ain't you whispering?"
BUSINESSMAN: "Why should I? It ain't no secret."

●

CLERK: "Sir, I'd like my salary raised."
BOSS: "Well, don't worry. I've raised it somehow every week so far, haven't I?"

●

CYNICAL CYRUS says contemptuously:
    "Ha! dollars: The jack of all trades."

●

DIGBY: "My ancestors all followed the medical profession."
ODELL: "Doctors?"
DIGBY: "No. Undertakers."

●

SAGE SAM knows that a woman's face is her fortune only when it draws a lot of interest.

JOE: "What business did you say your uncle was in?"

MOE: "He runs a clinic."

JOE: "He's a doctor at a clinic?"

MOE: "Not *that* kind of clinic—a clinic and pressing joint."

From Words to Words

AVENUE: I avenue baby sister.

ARREARS: My brother and I both hate to wash in back of arrears.

DENIAL: Cleopatra lived and loved on denial.

DIABETES: That baseball team has sworn they'll either diabetes.

EVANESCENT: Well, evanescent my old pal Oscar!

FALSIFY: When I put a book on my head it falsify move.

HOODOO: Hoodoo you think *you* are?

INSULATE: How come you got insulate?

JEOPARDY: My uncle is a jeopardy sheriff.

LILAC: He's a nice kid but he can lilac anything.

LOQUACIOUS: She bumped into me and I told her to loquacious going.

MONSOON: I've been single for a long time, but I hope to get a monsoon.

SECONDARY: I couldn't get any milk at the first milk shop so I went to a secondary.

TERRORIZE: If Katie doesn't stop pulling my hair I'll terrorize out of her head.

Inci-dentally

JENNY: "I can never remember my friend's address—230 River Drive."

DICK: "Just think of the Chinese Dentist."

JENNY: "How's that?"

DICK: "Tooth Hurty."

A boy and his mother stood looking at a dentist's show-case.

"If I had to have false teeth, mother, I'd take that pair," said the small boy, pointing.

"Hush, James," interposed the mother quickly, shaking his arm, "Haven't I told you it's bad manners to pick your teeth in public?"

●

COMEDIAN NUMBER ONE: "I'm dining with the upper set tonight. Some class, eh?"
COMEDIAN NUMBER TWO: "The steak may be tough. Better take your lowers, too."

●

CYNICAL CYNTHIA says, "the only painless dentist is the one with a broken window."

●

MRS. CURIOUS: "How is it that the little hole in my tooth feels so big to my tongue?"
RESIGNED DENTIST: "Well, you know how a woman's tongue exaggerates."

●

DICK: "Your face is terribly swollen. What's wrong with it?"
CEDRIC: "One of my teeth is driving me to extraction."

●

DENTIST: "That's a fowl-looking tooth you have there, sir."
PATIENT: "Well, go ahead and pullet, then."

WENDELL: "Why do dentists get fat?"
RENDELL: "Nearly everything they touch is filling."

●

DOC: "Will you take a local anesthetic?"
JOCK: "No. I want this over quickly. I better take the express."
But he took the local anyway, because the doctor was expressionless.

●

"A bad case of molaria, as anyone can see," said the dentist, looking into the patient's mouth.

●

MOLAR: "How was your trip to the dentist—exciting?"
DOLAR: "Oh, I had a *drilling* time."

PRODDER: "Have you been to the dentist yet?"
SORELOSER: "Yes, it was quite a battle."
PRODDER: "Who won?"
SORELOSER: "It was officially declared a draw."

Bright Slayings

TEACHER: "Give me a sentence with the word diploma in it."

SALVATORE: "When the sink is stopped up, Mama always says go get diploma."

•

ALF: "In what language did Balaam's ass speak?"

RALPH: "He-bray-ic."

Dorothy brought a mite box from the missionary meeting.

"Why is it called a mite box?" asked mother.

"Because you might put money into it and you might not," she said.

•

"Son, how often must I tell you it is bad manners to dip your bread in the gravy?"

"Yes, father, but it is such good taste!"

•

GEOLOGY TEACHER: "Name the constituents of quartz."

STAR PUPIL: "Pints."

•

The little girl was visiting her aunt. It was the first time she had been away from home and after the first two days the novelty had worn off and she began to cry.

"You aren't homesick, are you?" her aunt chided gently.

"No," was the tearful response, "I'm here sick."

•

MAMA'S GUEST: "When did you live in New York?"

PRECOCIOUS: "When I was twins."

MAMMA'S GUEST: "When you were twins?"

PRECOCIOUS: "Yeah, my mother has a picture of me when I was two."

"Are any colors discernible to the touch?" asked the teacher.

"I have often felt blue," replied the boy at the head of the class.

•

Fox: "Say, Beavy, they tell me you can cut down any size tree."

Beaver: "Well, I've never been stumped yet."

•

Tot: "There are two kinds of goats, aren't there?"

Mom: "What are they?"

Tot: "Billy goats and holy goats."

•

Teacher: "What is an octopus?"

Small Boy: "It's an eight-sided cat."

•

Papa: "See that dog chasing his tail?"

Precocious: "Poor little pup. He is trying to make both ends meet."

"Well, Son, what did you learn in Sunday school today?"

"We learned all about a cross-eyed bear named Gladly."

"About a what?"

"Yes, Daddy. We learned a song about him: all about 'Gladly, the cross I'd bear.'"

●

TEACHER: "We do not keep all kinds of birds in captivity; some wouldn't live. Now, what kind do we keep behind bars?"

CHILD: "Jail birds."

●

LITTLE ETHEL: "Don't you like to play with paper dolls any more?"

LITTLE WILLIE: "Gee, I cut them out long ago."

●

"Hey, Pop," called little David, "remember that dog you named Ben? It just had puppies, so I renamed it Ben Hur."

●

"What's the matter, dear," Bobby's hostess asked. "You look mournful."

"That's what's the matter—I'm more 'n full."

SUNDAY SCHOOL TEACHER: "Can you tell something about Good Friday, James?"
JAMES: "Yes'm; he was the fellow that did the housework for Robinson Crusoe."

"Mother sent me to get a package of diapers for the new baby."

"Here's the package," said the storekeeper. "That'll be fifty cents for the diapers and two cents for the tax."

"Never mind the tacks," said the boy. "Mother uses safety pins."

SUNDAY SCHOOL SPEAKER: "And now, children, what shall I talk about?"

LITTLE WILL: "Talk about a minute and then sit down."

●

"Bill, you young scamp, if you had your due, you'd get a good whipping."

"I know it, Daddy; but bills are not always paid when due."

●

JOHNNY: "Your brother said he was quite cool when the mad dog ran after him."

DONNIE: "I'll say! Why, his teeth were chattering!"

●

TEACHER: "What's the use of the reindeer?"

CECIL (happily): "To make the flowers grow."

Brat-worst
Variety

INTERESTED RELATIVE: "I suppose your baby reigns as king in your family."
TIRED NEW FATHER: "No—Prince of Wails."

●

YOUNGEST BROTHER: "What's a pauper?"
ELDEST BROTHER: "The guy who married Mama."

DIAPERS: Changeable seat covers.

●

ARTY: "What did the protoplasm say to the amoeba?"
SMARTY: "Don't bacilli."

●

TEACHER: "Who can give me a sentence using the word 'Amazon?' "
WILLIE: "You can pay for the eggs but the amazon me."

●

Someone sent an adding machine to Farmer Brown after the birth of his seventeenth child and followed it up with a visit.

"Why don't you throw some rocks at the darn stork and chase him away?" the friend asked.

"Aw, he ain't doin' much harm," said Farmer Brown. "He's just kiddin' around."

SONNY: "Mother, Dolly is using fearful swear-words."
MOTHER: "What did she say?"
SONNY: "She said she wouldn't wear those darned stockings any more."

●

OLD LADY, sympathetically: "There, there, little boy. I wouldn't cry like that if I were you."
THE YOUNGSTER: "You cry your way, Ma'am, and I'll cry mine."

●

KID (greeting Mrs. Von Nosinair): "I heard my father say you were stuck up. How much did they get?"

●

SON (eating an apple): "Yipe! I just swallowed a worm."
MOM: "Come right in the house and I'll give you something for it."
SON: "Nope, I'll just let it starve."

●

Ill-bred children always display their pest manners.

●

DOPEY DAN thinks a kindergarten teacher is one who knows how to make the little things count.

●

NEIGHBOR: "Ah, your baby looks very pretty in that dress. Where are you taking her?"
MOTHER: "To her grandmother's house for a general overmauling."

Maybe healthy babies should be a delicate pink, but you usually find they're robust yellers.

The music teacher was very surprised, one day in class, to hear little Jackie's private interpretation of Stephen Foster's "Oh, Susanna":

> "I come from Alabama
> With a bandaid on my knee."

GEOGRAPHY TEACHER: "Did you ever see the Catskill Mountains?"

WILLING FARMBOY: "No, sir; but I've seen them kill mice."

•

When Papa Dionne found that he had quintuplets, he could hardly believe his own census.

Party Punegyrics

PROPER PRUDENCE knows it is not generally considered in really good taste for the hostess to wear a T-shirt while serving tea.

●

PROPER PRUDENCE is also aware of the fact that you must never break your bread or roll in the soup.

PUNCTUAL: "Wonder what time it is? I'm invited to dinner at 8:30 and my watch isn't going."

FUNCTIONAL: "Why? Wasn't your watch invited?"

•

MRS. KATISH, to her maid, (making final arrangements for an elaborate celebration: "Now Nancy, for the first half-hour I want you to stand at the door and call the guests' names as they arrive."

NANCY (her face lighting up): "Oh thank you, Ma'am. I've been wanting to do that to some of your friends for the last 20 years."

•

GROGGY: "Did *we* throw a big party in our basement last night!"

FOGGY: "Was your Uncle John there?"

GROGGY: "Was he? *He* was the big party we threw in the basement."

•

MRS. HIGHHAT: "Yes, we are having a big dinner and a dance next Wednesday. You see, my daughter Beatrice is 'coming out.' "

MRS. LOWSHOES: "I don't blame you, making a fuss of the poor girl; by the way, what was she in for?"

•

MIXER: "Did you ever have a party soda?"

PLAIN: "Party soda? What's that?"

MIXER: "Well, last night we had a party so da landlady trew us out."

INDIGNANT: "That's no way to insult my guests."
INSOLENT: "Do you know a better way?"

●

MRS. LAST-AS-USUAL: "I beg your pardon for coming so late."
COOL HOSTESS: "No pardons are needed, my dear. You can *never* come too late."

Dress Reversals

CELIA: "He is so fat in shorts he looks like a chiffonier."
DELIA: "What's that?"
CELIA: "A big thing with drawers."

HARRY: "Raising rabbits for ladies' fur coats is quite a job. They don't live long. You know, here today and gone tomorrow."

BARRY: "You mean—hare today and mink tomorrow."

●

JERRY: "I should have been a songwriter—I have a squeaking shoe."

PERRY: "What has a squeaking shoe got to do with being a songwriter?"

JERRY: "I've got music in my sole."

●

SAGE SAM says the best way to make a coat last is to make the vest and trousers first.

●

SAGE SAM thinks that a dressmaker is one who knows the seamy side of life.

●

FIGURE-ATIVE: "May I try on that dress in the window?"

LITERAL: "Well, don't you think it would be better to use the dressing room?"

●

TAILOR: "How do you like the fit?"

FUSSY: "Fit? It's a convulsion."

●

WILLY: "We were so poor I didn't have pants to wear."

NILLY: "Not even jeans?"

WILLY: "Hers wouldn't fit me."

DANNY: "Why do you run around with your stockings full of holes like that?"
ANNIE: "I don't give a darn."

The girl was sounding out the soldier as to his bravery.

"Would you come to me in distress?" she asked.

"Babe," he answered, "it wouldn't make any difference to me what you were wearing."

Bustling into his tailor's, Jones handed him a pair of pants. "Here's the last pair of trousers you made for me," he said. "I want them reseated. You know, I sit a lot."

The tailor looked at him dejectedly. "I had hoped," he replied mournfully, "that you had brought me a check. You know, I've stood a lot."

•

PETE: "You certainly look cute in that gown."
SWEET: "Oh, this? I wear it to teas."
PETE: "To tease whom?"

•

JASON: "Your pants look rather sad today."
MASON: "What do you mean?"
JASON: "Sort of depressed."

•

ROB: "Do you make blouses?"
BOB: "Shirtainly!"

•

BROWN: "Young Dudel's body has been recovered."
GREEN: "Why, I didn't know he had been drowned!"
BROWN: "He hasn't. He merely bought a new suit of clothes."

•

PROSPECT: "I want some winter underwear."
RESPECT: "How long, sir?"
PROSPECT: "How long? I don't want to rent 'em—I want to buy 'em."

MOLLY: "That fur coat looks terrible."

POLLY: "This is my insomnia coat."

MOLLY: "What do you mean, insomnia coat?"

POLLY: "It hasn't had a nap for three years."

●

FLO: "Emma wears the worst clothes when she is riding horseback. Look at her now!"

FRED: "That certainly is one of her bad habits."

●

BERT: "Roses are red—violets are white . . ."

CURT: "Violets are blue, you sap."

BERT: "Violet's are white—I saw them on the line this morning."

Stuffing
Nonsense

ST. PETER: "How did you get here?"
LATEST ARRIVAL: "Flu!"

WISE WILFRED warns, "No matter how high an awning may be suspended, it is only a shade above the street."

•

"That," said the loaf, pointing to the oven, "is where I was bred."

•

ANGRY AGNES sputters, "Every time I get on a ferry boat it makes me cross."

•

EDUCATED EDDIE explains: "The reason they call a sensational report a canard is because one canardly believe it."

•

SHAWN: "If a woman could change her sex, what would her religion be?"
DAWN: "She would be a he-then, of course."

•

"Ha, ha, the yolks on me," said the Swedish gal, as she dropped an egg on the front of her dress.

•

JOLLY JIM statistics: More than five million American women are overweight. These, of course, are round figures.

•

INTELLECTUAL: "Wasn't it Porter who said 'Take no quarter from the enemy?' "
FACTUAL: "No. No porter ever said that."

BROWN: I've been digging over my garden, and I'm all worn out."

GREEN: "Ah! A new variety of earthen-ware, eh?"

She was fond of flowers and especially liked the salvia, but was never very reliable in getting the names right. She was giving directions to her gardener. "On this side of the walk," she said, "I want you to put some salivas. Now what would you suggest for the other side?"

"Well, madam," answered the gardener solemnly, "maybe it would be a good idea to put some spittoonias there."

INANE: "Is there anything I can get you?"
INSANE: "Yes, I'd like a watch that tells time."
INANE: "Doesn't your watch tell time?"
INSANE: "No, I have to look at it."

●

EDITOR, picking up phone: *"City desk speaking."*
ASTONISHED CALLER: "Yeah? What drawer?"

●

CURIOUS CARL wants to know why a pantomimist can not tickle nine Esquimaux.
WISE WILFRED replies it's because he can gesticulate.

●

FASTIDIOUS: "Shall I put chlorine in the water?"
PUGNACIOUS: "Sure—put her in if she needs a bath."

●

LAZY LOU says half a loaf is better than no vacation at all.

●

CYNIC: "Can you show me the road to heaven?"
BISHOP: "Turn to the right and keep straight ahead."

●

SHAM: "Do you know why that bald man's head is like Alaska?"
SAM: "I'm sure I don't know."
SHAM: "Because it's a great white bear place."

●

RAY: "My ancestors spring from a long line of peers."
FAY: "Well, I had an uncle that jumped off a dock."

Sᴜᴇ (doing in a friend) : "Has he ever tried to tell you about his forbears?"

Pʀᴜᴇ: "Really? Don't tell me he's also an animal trainer!"

CYNICAL CYRUS complains: "You can't win either way. As a rule, rich relatives are either distant or close."

●

Whereupon CYNICAL CYNTHIA contends that while all men are not homeless, some are home less than others.

●

He spent a thousand dollars to have his family tree looked up, and found out he was a sap.

●

CURIOUS CARL wonders if a boy is a lad and he has a step-father, is the boy a step-ladder?

●

ALARM CLOCK: A convenient device if you like that sort of thing.

●

A cockroach was running at great speed across the top of an unopened cracker box, and another one was trying to keep up with him.

"Why are we in such a hurry?" the second one asked.

"Can't you see the sign?" said the other. "It says, 'Tear along the dotted line.'"

●

"Is the proprietor in?" asked the carpenter over the telephone, to the building supply store. "I want to order some doors."

"He's around somewhere," replied the smart clerk, "but I think he's out of doors."

ARNY: "How do you spell sense?"

BARNEY: "Money or brains?"

ARNY: "I don't know. I only want to tell my girl I've had indigestion sense Friday."

•

"Do I bore you?" asked the mosquito, politely, as he sunk a half-inch shaft into a man's leg.

"Not at all," replied the man, squashing him with a book. "How do I strike you?"

•

Said the house painter, as he fell off the ladder:

"Well, I'm going down with flying colors, anyhow."

Word-y Causes

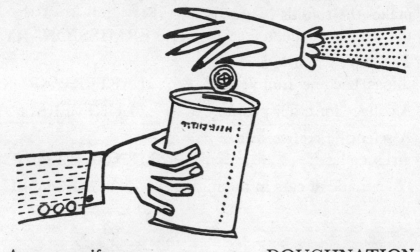

A money gift:............... DOUGHNATION

Something they very sel-
dom are on babies:.................. DRYPERS

Financial reverberations:.......... ECONOMICS

To recognize by sight:........... EYEDENTIFY

A door for men only:............. GENTRANCE

What a sailor should never
make himself:.................. GOBNOXIOUS

An inaccurate appraisal:........ GUESSTIMATE

The only thing a rooster
has to offer:............. HENTERTAINMENT

What a girl always needs
to capture a man:.............HEQUIPMENT

A Salvation Army girl who
makes the rounds between
the acts in a theater:......INTERMISSIONARY

The time when lots of
things become funny:.........LAFTERWARDS

A college for crazy people:........LUNIVERSITY

A scientific course in a
girl's college:...............MENGINEERING

A serenade of cats in the night:........MEOWSIC

A good month to make fun
of things:......................MOCKTOBER

What he or she is when he
or she is the one and only:........ONEDERFUL
What a fellow is when
he's frightened:....................SCAREFUL
Doing away with oneself by
jumping into a manhole:..........SEWERCIDE
What you get when lovers
stop talking:......................SIGHLENCE
What a suitcase is to a
grab-and-run thief:................SNATCHEL
A wonderful party:..........SWELLEBRATION

What a giant redwood
usually is:......................TREMENDOUS

What lovers always want
to be:.........................TWOGETHER

What a discussion some-
times turns into:...............WARGUMENT

Limber-licks

A major, with wonderful force,
Called out in Hyde Park for a horse.
    All the flowers looked round,
    But no horse could be found;
So he just rhododendron, of course.

A maiden at college, Miss Breeze,
Weighed down by B.A.'s and Litt. D.'s,
        Collapsed from the strain.
        Said her doctor, "It's plain
You are killing yourself—by degrees!"

●

An indolent vicar of Bray,
His roses allowed to decay;
        His wife, more alert,
        Bought a powerful squirt,
And said to her spouse, "Let us spray."

●

There was a young lady named Banker,
Who slept while the ship lay at anchor;
        She awoke in dismay
        When she heard the mate say:
"Now hoist up the topsheet, and spanker!"

●

There once was a man from Nantucket
Who kept all his cash in a bucket;
        But his daughter, named Nan,
        Ran away with a man,
And as for the bucket, Nantucket.
But he followed the pair to Pawtucket—
The man and the girl with the bucket;
        And he said to the man
        He was welcome to Nan,
But as for the bucket, Pawtucket.

The Sultan was peeved with his harem,
And cooked up a scheme for to scare 'em.
    He caught a big mouse
    Which he loosed in the house.
(Such confusion is called harem-scarem).

Shoplaughing

OLD LADY: "Are you really a doctor, young man?"
SODA JERK: "No, I'm not. They probably call me 'Doc' because because I'm a fizzician."

●

MOE: "So you are going to start a bakery?"
JOE: "If I can raise the dough."

BUTCHER: "Round steak, madam?"

NEW BRIDE: "The shape doesn't matter, so long as it's tender."

●

An old fellow brought his small radio into a repair shop. "What's wrong with it?" asked the mechanic. "Dunno. It's just outta commotion."

●

MUGGS: "I'll take a cake of soap."

DRUGS: "Scented or unscented?"

MUGGS: "I'll take it with me."

●

CUSS: "Is the color fast?"

TOMER: "Why don't you chase it and see?"

●

The man told the pharmacist: "I want some consecrated lye."

"You mean concentrated?"

"It does nutmeg any difference. You know what I camphor. How much does it sulphur?"

"I never cinnamon with so much wit," said the druggist, entering into the spirit of the conversation.

●

Pity the poor clock-maker. He never gets any extra pay, and yet every day he works overtime.

●

SWEET: "Why is a manicurist bound to get rich?"

SIXTEEN: "She makes money hand over fist."

155

"Do I look like this picture?" he demanded. "The thing's an outrage. You've given me an awful squint and made me look like a prize fighter. Now answer me, and no nonsense about it. Do you call that a good likeness?"

The photographer took the print, studied it carefully, looked at his customer, and then said: "The answer is in the negative."

●

Ack to Emma, while looking at two wigs in a store window: "They're as alike as toupees."

●

In some ways a doughnut retailer is really in the hole-sale business.

●

A backwoodser came into a drug store and walked up to a clerk.

"I want one of them plasters you stick on your back."

"Okay," said the clerk. "You mean one of our porous plasters?"

"No! Of course not! I don't want one of your *porous* plasters, I want the *best* one you got!"

●

PAWNBROKER: One who lives on the flat of the land.

●

CYNICAL CYRUS claims: "A barber is a clip-joint operator."

SAGE SAM says that pleasant-faced people are generally the most welcome, but the auctioneer is always pleased to see a man whose countenance is for bidding.

●

MRS. LOOK-IN-EVERYTHING: "I'm not going to buy any luggage right now. I'm only looking for a friend."
WEARY SALESLADY: "I'd be glad to let you look in this last trunk if you think she's in it."

●

CURIOUS ONLOOKER: "Why did you pick the grocer to play the bass drum in your band?"
OBLIGING CONDUCTOR: "Because he's an honest fellow and gives full weight to every pound."

MERCHANT, polite but firm: "Sir, your account has been standing for two years. I must have it settled immediately."

CUSTOMER, equally so: "Sir, things usually do settle by standing. I regret that my account is an exception. If it has been standing too long, suppose you let it run a little."

•

FORLORN: "I used to go to barber college."

SHORN: "You mean you never graduated!"

FORLORN: "I was a shear leader . . . but they threw me out for cutting a class."

•

ROSIE: "You should see what that extravagant Clara bought at an auction sale today. A Ming vase, no less!"

JOSIE: "Maybe she wants it because it goes with her ming coat."

•

CUSTOMER: "My goodness, eggs are high!"

GROCER: "Sure, part of the war program."

CUSTOMER: "How?"

GROCER: "All the hens are busy making shells."

Admiral
General-ities

A sailor was washed overboard in a storm and the captain saw him swallowed by a whale. The resourceful officer took after the whale in a rowboat and, by judicious handling of an oar, managed to beat the tar out of him.

The parachute troops were being instructed on the use of their life-savers.

"What if it doesn't open?" asked one.

"That, my friend," said the instructor, "is known as jumping to a conclusion."

●

MOPE: "So you got kicked out of the army. Why?"
DOPE: "I took a furlong."
MOPE: "You mean furlough, don't you?"
DOPE: "No. I went too fur and stayed too long."

●

When asked to furnish his school and college affiliations, a New England job applicant paused briefly, then wrote, "Korea, Clash of 1952."

●

ARLENE: "My brother went to West Point for only two years. So he's just a half soldier."
DARLENE: "Is that so? *My* brother is a wholesaler."

●

An old beggar accosted a colonel, declaring that he was a veteran.

"You don't look it," said the colonel bluntly, and barked, "Attention! Eyes right! Eyes front! Now, what comes next?"

"Present alms," was the instant rejoinder.

●

COPORAL: "Squad's right!"
REAR RANK: "After all these years he admits it."

POLITE CIVILIAN: "How do you like life on the high seas?"

BORED SAILOR: "It's simply the knots!"

●

SALTY: "Have you weighed anchor?"

FLEDGLING: "Yes. It hasn't gained an ounce since we left Shanghai."

●

An ex-private was seeking employment from his former general.

HIS LATE SUPERIOR (shouting with laughter upon seeing him): "Where the deuce, my good fellow, did you lose your nose?"

THE PRIVATE: "I lost it, General, in the battle in which you lost your head."

●

TEACHER: "Can anyone tell me what happened after Napoleon mustered his army?"

PUPIL: "Yes, sir, he peppered the enemy and took the citadel by assault."

TEACHER: "Sit down, my lad. I'll have no sauce from you."

●

FIRST ROOKIE: "What do you think of the sergeant?"

SECOND ROOKIE: "The way he behaves they should spell it 'Snarlgeant.' "

●

G.I., in the South Pacific: "Long time no she."

SOLDIER: An army man who is first drawn and then quartered.

•

ADMIRAL (watching enemy ship sink): "Who fired that shot?"
MATE: "The ship's cook, sir. He got the range and stove in her side."

•

TEACHER: "Yes, children, when the war broke out all the able-bodied men who could leave their families enlisted in the army. Now can any of you tell what motives took them to the front?"
BRIGHT BOY: "Locomotives."

•

LOVESICK G.I.: "I can see, darling, that I am only a little pebble on the beach of your life."
PRETTY GIRL: "Well, go on. Be a little boulder."

•

KINDLY SERGEANT: "Private Perkins, is it true what Private Patterson tells me: that you have a wife and four children at home and have never seen one of them?"
PRIVATE PERKINS: "Quite true, sir."
KINDLY SERGEANT: "But how can that *be?* It's impossible!"
PRIVATE PERKINS: "Well, no, sir—it really isn't: you see, the one I've never seen was born after I left for here."

WAVES: Sailors who go down to the sea in slips.

●

A dinner guest of Lincoln's once told him he couldn't beat the Confederates. "They'll retreat into the Southern swamps and bayous along with the fishes and crocodiles," he said. "You haven't got the fish-nets made that'll catch 'em."

"Look here," said Abe. "We've got just the nets for 'em, in the bayous or anywhere."

"What nets?" asked the guest.

"Bayounets!" answered Abe.

Lawn Order

JUDGE: "Have you ever been up before me?"
PRISONER: "What time do you get up, Judge?"

●

DOUR JUDGE: "Your impudence forces me to increase
your fine $10. What do you think of that?"
CHEERY CHARLIE: "I think that's extra fine!"

DAWN: "Why do they call it a libel suit?"

JAWN: "Because you're liable to win and you're liable to lose."

●

"Pedestrians are prone to carelessness," advises SAGE SAM. "And after they have been careless they are certainly prone."

●

MAGISTRATE: "Where were you born?"

SLIPPERY ONE: "New Jersey."

MAGISTRATE: "And were you brought up there?"

SLIPPERY ONE: "Yes, but only two or three times."

●

BRUCE: "And so on account of one little paragraph in the contract you are going to confiscate all my property?"

DRUCE: "That's right. It's simply a matter of clause and effects."

●

JUDGE: "Order, order in the court!"

PRISONER: "I'll take a ham sandwich on rye with beer."

●

JUDGE: "Take the chair!"

WITNESS: "What for? I got plenty of furniture now."

●

Once more her uncle is with the F.B.I.—they finally caught up with him.

DOPEY: "What floor is this, your Honor?"
JUDGE: "The fifth floor."
DOPEY: "I'm going upstairs."
JUDGE: "What for?"
DOPEY: "I want to be tried in a higher court."

●

MANNY: "How did you get on at the police court yesterday?"
MOE: "Fine."

●

TRUANT OFFICER, outside the movies: "Have you missed school lately?"
ERRING SCHOOLBOY: "Not a bit."

●

JEEVES: "I was walking along with my friend David, and a man came up and handed me this big piece of paper."
REEVES: "Affidavit?"
JEEVES: "No, after *me*."

●

MAGISTRATE: "You have been sentenced eight times, and this makes the ninth. You ought to be thoroughly ashamed of yourself."
PRISONER: "I say, your Honor, no man ought to be ashamed of his convictions."

●

DOPEY DIANA'S uncle is now in prison and very popular. He's the lifer of the party.

DOPEY DIANA remembers her father's always being bothered by flat feet. They kept giving him tickets for speeding.

●

JUDGE: "The sentence is twenty years' penal servitude."

AGED PRISONER (in tears): "Sir, I shall not live long enough to serve the sentence."

JUDGE (in kindly tone): "Don't worry, do what you can."

Gliberal Education

TEACHER (trying hard to unfasten coat for a little pupil): "Did your mother hook this coat for you?"
LITTLE PUPIL: "No, ma'am! She *bought* it."

TEACHER: "What was the former ruler of Russia called?"
CLASS: "Tsar."
TEACHER: "Yes. And what was his wife called?"
CLASS: "Tsarina."
TEACHER: "What were the Tsar's children called?" There was a pause. Then, said Susie triumphantly, "Tsardines!"

●

CYNICAL CYRUS says a college boy's definition of a male parent is: "the kin you love to touch."

●

PROF: "Take this sentence: 'Let the cow be taken out of the lot.' What mood?"
FROSH: "The cow."

●

PROFESSOR: "Give the most important fact about nitrates."
STUDENT: "They're cheaper than the day rates."

●

PROF: "Muddle, I'm sure you can tell us who wrote the CRITIQUE OF PURE REASON."
MUDDLE, admitting sadly: "I. Kant."
PROF: "Amazing, this is the first correct answer you have given me in your five years as a freshman!"

●

PROF: "What are the Phoenicians noted for?"
STUDENT: "Blinds."

TEACHER: "Can you explain to me how matches are made?"

SCHOLAR (sympathetically): "No, ma'am, I'm sorry I don't know. I'd love to be able to tell you."

TEACHER (a little surprised): "Why, what do you mean?"

SCHOLAR: "Well, I've heard mother say you have been trying hard to make a match these last half-dozen years."

●

ENGLISH TEACHER: "Who will define 'unaware?'"

LITTLE JOE: "It's the last thing I take off at night."

●

TEACHER: "Give me a sentence with a direct object."

WISE ALREADY: "Teacher, everybody thinks you are beautiful."

TEACHER: "Why, thank you, but what is the direct object?"

WISE ALREADY: "A good report card next month."

●

"You call yourself a kind father and yet you haven't sent me a check for a month," wrote the college sophomore.

"That's unremitting kindness," his dad replied.

●

TEACHER: "Spell 'weather,' Jimmie."

JIMMIE: "W-e-t-h-i-r."

TEACHER: "Hmm. That's just about the worst spell of weather we've had around here for several years."

DICK: "The class has a head and the class has a foot. Now what's in between?"

SHUNARY: "The student body."

•

TEACHER: "Susie, if I write 'n-e-w' on the blackboard, what does that spell?"

"New."

"Now, I'll put a 'k' in front of it and what have we?"

"Canoe, of course."

•

TEACHER: "An anecdote is a tale. Now Sidney, use it in a sentence."

SIDNEY: "I tied a tin can to the dog's anecdote."

•

JOE: "Tell me the story of the police raiding your fraternity."

COLLEGE: "Oh, that's a closed chapter now."

•

JOLLY JIM says, "a chorus girl gets her education by stages—a college girl by degrees."

•

GIL: "What do they mean by adolescence?"

BERT: "Well, you add a lesson here and you add a lesson there, and by and by you learn something."

•

DRAMATICS TEACHER: "What is a plagiarist?"

STUDENT: "A plagiarist is a person who writes plays."

TEACHER (in chemistry class): "What is the formula for water?"
STUDENT: "H-I-J-K-L-M-N-O."

"Who ever told you that?" shouted the exasperated professor.
STUDENT: "*You* did, sir. You told me it was H to O."

•

EDUCATED EDDIE knew that even Mason and Dixon had to draw the line some place.

•

TEACHER: "What is the line opposite the right angle in a right-angled triangle?"
JOHNNIE: "The hippopotamus."

In-sign-ity

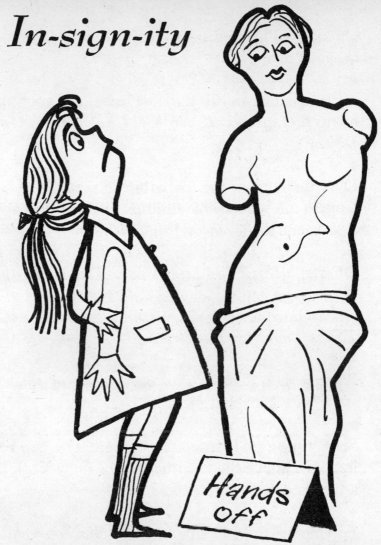

At the art museum the sign *Hands Off* was conspicuously displayed before a statue of Venus of Milo.
A little girl looked from the sign to the statue.
"Anybody can see *that*," she said, puzzled.

Outside a Phoenix auto repair shop: *"May we have the next dents?"*

●

A blood bank ran this sign: "Please keep your appointments promptly. *Let's Not Get Caught With Our Pints Down."*

●

Over the door of the log cabin retreat of the superintendent of schools of Phillips, Wisconsin, appeared this legend: *"Bored of Education."*

●

Offer of a furrier—*"Ladies own skins made up."*

●

On a Galveston, Texas, bathing beach: *"A Coat of Tan is Yours for the Basking."*

●

Battery shop sign: *"The only place in town where everybody can* charge *it."*

●

Some time ago, before an unimaginative cop removed it, a sign above the entrance to the New York morgue advertised: *"Remains to be seen."*

●

For motorists in Connecticut: *"Give our children a brake."*

●

On the wall of a diner along Route 101: *"What foods these morsels be!"*

By a chicken incubator in Vermont: *"Cheepers by the dozen."*

●

A tailor's window contained a pair of the bluest trousers ever beheld, enlivened with a wide pink stripe. Adjacent was this sign: *"These pants were uncalled for."*

●

Notice in a dry-cleaning establishment:

> *"Ladies who drop off their clothes here as they go by can be assured of prompt and individual attention."*

●

A sign in the library at Amarillo, Texas, reads: *"Low Conversation Permitted."*

Sign in roadside eating place on a Maryland highway:

SOME PAY BEFORE DUE
SOME PAY WHEN DUE
SOME PAY WHEN PAST DUE
SOME NEVER DO
HOW DO YOU DO?

●

A Kentucky electrical dealer who sells washing machines has the following sign in his window:

"Don't kill your wife. Let our washing machines do the dirty work."

●

Sign seen over local dairy:

"You can't beat our milk, but you can whip our cream."

●

Offered by a dry-goods emporium in Allentown, Pennsylvania:

"Bath towels for the whole damp family."

●

At Wellesley, a bright miss hung over a dormitory bathtub the reminder:

"Don't forget your ring."

●

Sign in a hatter's window—*"My felt hats fit so well that they cannot be felt."*

●

Popular desk motto: "THINK—OR THWIM."

Travel-errs

ALI: "Does your family live here in Arabia?"

BABA: "No. My father makes suitcases in Iraq."

ALI: "Oh—a bag-dad!"

•

FLO: "I spent last summer in a very pretty city in Switzerland."

JOE: "Berne?"

FLO: "No, I almost froze."

FIRST TURK: "I think we've met somewhere before, don't you?"
SECOND TURK: "I can't remember your name, but your fez seems familiar."

●

DOPEY DAN, just back from Europe, is still so dumb he thinks a fjord is a Norwegian automobile.

●

REX: "While I was in Europe I saw a bed twenty feet long and ten feet wide."
TEX: "Sounds like a lot of bunk."

●

A Los Angeles fellow travels only to Kansas City, believing that Missouri loves company.

●

Inspecting a pair of trousers in his shop in Athens, a tailor queried: "Euripides?"
CUSTOMER: "Yah, Eumenides."

●

AL: "How come you know so much about railroads?"
PAL: "Well, it did take a lot of training."

●

SAM (in their stateroom): "They put the trunks down the hatchway."
PAM: "Huh?"
SAM: "I said, they put the trunks down the hatchway. Don't you know what a hatchway is?"
PAM: "Sure—that's where baby chickens are born."

MARK: "What do you call all the little rivers that run into the Nile?"
ETT: "The Juveniles!"

●

EGYPTIAN GUIDE (with great pride): "Yes, ma'am, it took two thousand years to build these pyramids."
POMPOUS MADAM from 5th Avenue: "I can quite believe it. Builders at home are every bit as indolent."

●

WORLD TRAVELER, lecturing: "There are certain spectacles one never forgets."
SWEET OLD THING: "Can you tell me where I can buy a pair of those, please? I'm always forgetting mine."

●

GUIDE, on tour: "Gentlemen, we are now passing one of the oldest taverns in England."
GENTLEMEN, in chorus: "Why?"

●

The street car conductor opened the door to the front platform to collect his fares. He encountered five policemen riding home from work.

"Five coppers," remarked the conductor, "and not a nickel in the bunch."

●

SOUR: "I went to a hotel for a change and a rest."
PUSS: "Did you get it?"
SOUR: "The bellboy got the change and the hotel got the rest."

179

Pro-verb-ial Pun

A rolling stone gathers no boss.

●

When you are climbing a mountain, don't talk; silence gives ascent.

ROBERT JONES BURDETTE

●

The female of the speeches is more deadly than the male.

HARRY HERSHFIELD

The more waist, the less speed.

OLIVER HEREFORD

●

None but the brave desert the fair.

ADDISON MIZNER

●

It's a wise child that owes his own father.

CAROLYN WELLS

●

A bachelor never quite gets over the idea that he is a thing of beauty and a boy forever.

HELEN ROWLAND

●

Levity is the soul of wit.

MELVILLE D. LANDON

●

One man's Mede is another man's Persian.

GEORGE S. KAUFMAN

●

A fool and her money are soon courted.

HELEN ROWLAND

●

"Tough luck," said the egg in the monastery. "Out of the frying pan into the friar."

OLIVER HEREFORD

●

There is no time like the pleasant.

OLIVER HEREFORD

Eat, drink, and be merry, for tomorrow ye diet.

WILLIAM GILMORE BEYMER

Circumstances alter faces.

CAROLYN WELLS

A woman is never too old to yearn.

ADDISON MIZNER

Great aches from little toe corns grow.

No man is a hero to his wallet.

As ye sew, so shall ye rip.

No thyself.

Misprints in the Sands of Time

A fish story from the *Northwest Organizer* ended with this startling statement: "For sheer tricks, fight, and stamina, give me a small-mouthed lass at sundown, any time."

When, on the death of President McKinley, Theodore Roosevelt succeeded to the highest office, a New York editor desired to contrast the event with a recent coronation in Europe. But, the compositor, coming to the word "oath" in the manuscript, struck a wrong key and the sentence appeared, "For sheer democratic dignity, nothing could exceed the moment when, surrounded by the cabinet, Mr. Roosevelt took a simple bath as President of the United States."

●

A western paper ran an item stating that "The departing Mr. Smithers was a member of the defective bureau of the police force."

The chief of police made a strong protest, whereupon the paper published an apology as follows: "Our announcement should have read "The detective branch of the police farce."

●

England is suffering from a plague of aunts. In many houses these have visited rooms on the second floor. —MONTPELIER (VT.) paper.

●

The Garden Club will meet Wednesday at 2:30 P.M. The subject will be "Conservation of Native Pants." — TIPTONVILLE (TENN.) paper.

●

Send-a-Dame Chain Letters Deluge City; Interest Keen. —Headline in KINGSPORT (TENN.) paper.

OFFICER CONVICTED OF ACCEPTING BRIDE.
　　　　—Headline in RALEIGH NEWS AND OBSERVER.

Widows made to order. Send us your specifications.
　　　　—Ad in an EL PASO paper.

Miss Chalmers is a boy and arrow enthusiast and hopes
to make a mark for herself in the sport.

HELP WANTED: Busy lawyer seeks alert young woman
to act as deceptionist.

Better let us flush your cooing system and fill it with the
proper amount of antifreeze.

CAR — CARESS — CARELESS — CARLESS. —
　　　　Headline in THE LONDON DAILY HERALD.

"See here," said the angry visitor to the reporter, "what do you mean by inserting the derisive expression 'applesauce' in parenthesis in my speech?"

" 'Applesauce?' Great scott, man. I wrote 'Applause.' "

●

A Thanksgiving dinner was served at the home of Mr. and Mrs.——, after the wedding of their daughter.

POUGHKEEPSIE paper.

●

A rural poet indited a sonnet to his sweetheart, entitled "I kissed her sub rosa." The compositor set it up, "I kissed her snub nosa."

●

Sprinkle on the shelves a mixture of half borax and half sugar. This will poison every aunt that finds it.

NORWICH (CONN.) BULLETIN

●

Wanted—Farm mule. Must be reasonable.

—Ad in the BIRMINGHAM AGE HERALD

●

An ad in an ALABAMA weekly reads:

"Anybody found prowling around my chicken house in the night will be found still there the next morning.

●

One chaste longe and other furniture. —Ad in a

MOBILE paper.

For sale: To a kind master, full grown, domesticated tigress, goes daily walk untied, and eats flesh from the hand. —Ad in a CALCUTTA paper.

•

The bride was gowned in white lace. The bridesmaids' gowns were punk. The whole color scheme of the decoration was punk. —New York paper, according to the WEST VIRGINIA MOUNTAINEER.

•

Dr. S——, one of our most eligible bachelors, is retiring from practice. Hale and hearty at 65, Doc says all he wants is a little peach and quiet.

—WICHITA (KAN.) EAGLE.

Oh, Bring Back My Anatomy!

RAFE: "These marks on my nose were made by glasses."

LAFE: "How many glasses?"

•

GLAND: The only thing secretive about a woman.

•

"Don't high-hat me," said one bit of protoplasm to another. "I remember when we were cell-mates."

MISSIONARY IN AFRICA: "Ah, my dear friends, if every one of you were to turn around and look at yourselves squarely in the eyes and ask yourselves what you needed first of all, what would be your answers?"
CURLY-HAIRED YOUTH: "Sir, we should want first of all a neck like the giraffes."

●

MED. STUDE: "I wonder what it must be like to remove a thyroid."
MORE STUDE: "It really must be a gland and goreious feeling."

●

The skin men love to touch is the skin girls love to retouch.

●

SVEN (to doctor): "I tink I sprain my uncle because I got veak niece."
DOCTOR: "Well, I'm sure we'll be able to fix you up in a relatively short time."

●

LEGS: Beautiful legs are sometimes without equal, but bow-legs are always without parallel.

●

Garry Moore once asked Jimmy Durante about a girl they both knew. "In the true language of blood, Jimmy, is she vein?"

"Don't talk like that, Garry. She's varicose to my hearteries."

BILL: "When is a girl's cheek not a cheek?"
WILL: "When it's a little pail (pale)."

●

MACK: "She thinks I've got a crazy cat."
MICK: "How come?"
MACK: "Someone told her I had a silly puss."

●

SAGE SAM says that a mustache is the one thing that keeps many a man from being a bare-faced liar.

●

The lecturer on physiology addressed the student nurses.

"We will take up the heart, kidneys, lung, and liver in that order."

"Oh dear, another organ recital," whispered one nurse to the other.

Woman Here to Slay

TELLER

BANK TELLER, sadly, to man at window: "Sorry, Sir, your wife beat you to the draw."

●

WISE WILFRED says: "When women start to get rich, demure they get, demure they want."

LAZY LOU is truly a modern male—he will stand for anything but a woman in a streetcar. He also thinks modern women are those who try to imitate men and make perfect fools of themselves.

•

PROPER PRUDENCE thinks Romantic Rena isn't as bad as she is painted—but that she certainly *is* painted.

•

CATTY KITTY purrs: "Dopey Diana wore her hair over her shoulder—she should have worn it on her head. And the way she keeps her eyebrows certainly takes a lot of pluck."

•

CAT: "She has a head like a doorknob."
PAT: "How come?"
CAT: "Any man can turn it."

•

MITTY: "She certainly is polished, don't you think?"
KITTY: "Yeah. Everything she says casts a reflection on someone."

•

BERT: "He concedes that he is a self-made man."
BART: "Maybe, but his wife is the power behind the drone."

•

NEIGHBOR: "Your wife is delightfully outspoken, isn't she?"
JONES: "By whom?"

CYNICAL CYRUS: "Women remind me of angels. They're always up in the air and harping on something."

●

BLAKE: "Do you believe in clubs for women?"
JAKE: "If everything else fails."

●

WISE WILFRED says: "Give a woman an inch and she thinks she's the ruler."

●

CYNICAL CYRUS knows that when a woman gets a man on the spot she usually takes him to the cleaners.

●

SAGE SAM defines womanhood as one of the louder figures of speech.

●

And everyone knows that a myth is a woman who hasn't got a husband.

●

CYNICAL CYRUS thinks women are very biased—"buy us this" and "buy us that."

●

P. S. But then CYNICAL CYNTHIA thinks men are like kites—wind and pull raised them where they are.

Tattle Titles

ARTICLES
"Bringing Things to a Berle"

GILBERT MILLSTEIN
(in an article about
MILTON BERLE)

BOOKS

"From Bed to Worse"

ROBERT BENCHLEY

"Westward Ha!"

S. J. PERELMAN

"It's Still Maloney"

RUSSELL MALONEY

"Jest What the Doctor Ordered"

DR. FRANCIS LEO GOLDEN

"Enchanted Aisles"

ALEXANDER WOOLLCOTT

OTHER PIECES

"Game of No Mythstakes"

from THE FAMILY BOOK OF HUMOR

"Bulletin Boredom"

RICHARD ARMOUR

"Shelf Esteem"

RICHARD ARMOUR

"No Arm Done"

LEWIS COPELAND

CHAPTER HEADINGS

"Juries and Other Injuries"
"The Ties that Blind"
"Police To Meet You"
"You Gotta Have Wile Power"
"Jestice of the Peace"

by FRANCIS LEO GOLDEN

SOME HEADINGS

"Reigning Cats and Dogs"

Marilyn, We Roll Along"
(on MARILYN MONROE)

by BENNETT CERF

"Guided Muscles"

"The Pun-American Conference"

Pun
and Games

LILY: "I knew you were on the football team—on account of your mustache."

BILLY: "How could you tell by my mustache?"

LILY: "I could see the first down on your upper lip."

Rob: "Did you go around the golf course in eighty-one?"

Bob: "What?"

Rob: "I said, I heard you went around the golf course in eighty-one."

Bob: "Gosh, no! I wasn't *born* in eighty-one."

●

Some fisticuffers make great price fighters.

●

Mavis: "Do you like cycling with a party?"

Davis: "No, I prefer to cyclone."

●

Older Student: "Don't you know what drama is?"

Little Bobby: "Oh sure—baby talk—my drama lives in the country and we go to visit her every Christmas."

●

"I am being trey-deuced!" George S. Kaufman once cried out in a poker game.

●

Stoic: "When I was your age I thought nothing of a ten-mile walk."

Slowic: "Well, I don't think much of it either."

●

Wise Wilfred knows a golf ball is a golf ball . . . no matter how you putt it.

●

Card: "Did you see the Straight of Magellan?"

Shark: "Yeah. But he beat me. I only had two pair."

A famous jockey was taken suddenly ill, and the trainer advised him to visit a doctor in the town.

"He'll put you right in a jiffy," he said.
The same evening he found Benjamin lying curled up in the stables, kicking his legs about in agony.

"Well, Benny! Haven't you been to the doctor?"
"Yes."

"Well, didn't he do you any good?"

"I didn't go in. When I got to his home there was a brass plate over the door: 'Dr. Kurem. Ten to one.' I wasn't going to monkey with a long shot like that!"

DOUG: "If you find you're losing the fight just start singing and we'll call it off."

PUG: "Well, if I'm out of tune, you'll know he knocked me flat."

•

CYNICAL CYRUS says, "Any man who marries a girl with a substantial check attached may very properly be said to have been check-mated."

•

A New York foursome has beaten a London foursome at bridge. London Bridge is falling down.

•

CLARENCE: "The Sing Sing football team wants to play the West Point team."

ALOYSIUS: "I wonder why Sing Sing wants to play the army."

CLARENCE: "They probably want to prove the pen is mightier than the sword."

•

BLUE: "I suppose when you were in the army you often saw a picket fence?"

GREY: "Yes, but it was a more common sight to see a sentry box."

EDUCATED EDDIE tells us that Magellan went around the world in 1521—not too many strokes when you consider the distance.

•

MAJOR MOPPUS defines a kibitzer as a guy who'll bet your shirt on somebody else's hand.

•

"Fore!" yelled the golfer, ready to play. But the woman on the course paid no attention.

"Fore!" he shouted again with no effect.

"Ah," suggested his opponent in disgust, "try her once with three-ninety-eight."

•

TUTTI: "I lost a big wad."

FRUTTI: "Next time don't bet chewing gum."

•

LAZY LOU was the cream of fighters . . . he got whipped.

•

ANGRY AGNES moans: "I've been skating for hours on end. Maybe I ought to take lessons."

•

During a tennis tournament a fellow sat down beside a girl.

"Whose game?" he asked.

"I am," she said.

Tee-hee
Spuns

Greta Garbo is rumored to have dreamed one night that she sprinkled six boxes of grass seed in her hair. She awakened moaning, "I vant to be a lawn."

An eccentric millionaire decided to build a log house entirely of knot-holes. He was explaining it to an even more eccentric friend.

"See?" said the first. "These are all knot-holes."

"Perhaps," said the second. "But they look like real holes to me."

•

A young man wanted to buy a gift for his girl friend, and he asked her if she was interested in book ends.

"Yes," she answered, "that's the part I always read first."

•

SQUARE PEG: "This coconut juice is real crazy, man, real crazy!"

ROUND HOLE: "That's probably why it comes in a padded shell."

•

MOVIE PRODUCER: The man who thanks his lucky stars.

•

CRIT: "His stuff is so bad he must be using a tripe-writer."

ICK: "Or recording it on a dictaphony."

•

The moron stuck his head in the oven because he wanted a baked bean.

•

America's nocturnal theme song: "You Ferment for Me."

203

Look at the punny characters in Peter De Vries' novel, *The Tunnel of Love*. One thinks a seersucker is a man who spends all his money on fortune-tellers. A second keeps asking his analyst, "Have I told you about my abberation?" A third calls his place Moot Point (because there's a legal difficulty about the right of way).

●

Definitions:
One woman talking . . . a manologue.
Two women talking . . . a cat-a-logue.

●

JOLLY JIM describes light housekeeping as just one canned thing after another.

●

"This is so sodden!" said the recently married husband as he graciously accepted another proof of his wife's good cooking.

●

ANDY: "My father was Sir Andrew, Knight of the Garter, Golden Fleece, Pearly Teeth . . ."
RANDY: "Shake hands. My father was a duke, my grandfather was a duke, my great-grandfather was a duke . . ."
ANDY: "Oh, you're looking for an argument!"
RANDY: "I'll match my ancestry with yours any time."
ANDY: "All right, put up your dukes!"

●

An actor's motto: Better a small role than a long loaf.

EDGAR: "Do you know Poe's Raven?"
ALLAN: "No, what's he mad about?"

•

TEASING DAN (about a rival suitor): "His family goes back to the early Boones."
IMPRESSED NAN: "Well! I didn't know he came from the *Boones!*"
TEASING DAN: "Sure—his grandfather was a 'baboon.' "

•

KING ARTHUR: "How much'll you take for this armor, Lance?"
SIR LANCELOT: "Four cents an ounce, that's first-class mail."

KIM: "Well, all right then, since you won't lend me the money, I'll haunt you when I die."
TIM: "You can't."
KIM: "Why not?"
TIM: "You haven't got a haunting license."

●

JOLLY JIM reminds us that many men smoke but Fu Manchu.

●

AUNT HETTY: "Sakes alive! I don't believe *no* woman could ever be so fat."
UNCLE HIRAM: "What y' readin' now, Hetty?"
AUNT HETTY: "Why this paper tells about an English woman who lost two thousand pounds."

●

MILLIE: "Was *Uncle Tom's Cabin* written by a female hand?"
TILLIE: "No, by Harriet Beecher's toe."

●

ASTRID: "I love to browse in a library."
INGEBORG: "High browse or low browse?"

●

E. W. HORNUNG, CONAN DOYLE'S BROTHER-IN-LAW:
 "Tho' he might be more humble,
 "There's no Police like Holmes."

●

Dinner in an insane asylum: Simply a matter of serving soup to nuts.

A farmhand, who had suffered a black eye and multiple contusions at the hands of the belle at the square dance, admitted that he had been struck by the beauty of the place.

A high Soviet commissar named Rudolph Mozoltoff was walking down a Moscow street with two friends— a man and his wife—when a drop of moisture settled on his blouse.

"It's raining," he announced through his beard.

"You're wrong," said the wife. "It's snowing."

"Oh, no," insisted her husband. "Rudolph, the Red, knows rain, dear."

The telephone rang. "What is it?" asked the moron.

"It's a long distance from New York," replied the operator.

"I know it is," said the moron and went back to bed.

•

PEN: "Why did you call the hero of your story 'Adam'?"

PAL: "You said to write it in the first person."

•

SAGE SAM says, "We are told 'General Sherman was always the coolest when on the point of attack.' Most people are hottest when on the point of a tack."

•

"And," the press agent went on enthusiastically, "our show at the Palace has a chorus of fifty."

"Well," said the newspaper critic, "from where I sat, they certainly looked it."

•

CAUTIOUS CATHIE warns, "some people do odd things to get even."

•

ALEX: "Who is that man over there? He annoys me."

ALIX: "He's my cousin—once removed."

ALEX: "Well, remove him again."

•

BARNEY: "Why did they hang that picture?"

BLARNEY: "Because they couldn't find the artist."

MOTHER: "What did you have for lunch today?"
RETURNING SCHOOLBOY: "Three guesses."
MOTHER: "No wonder you are so hungry."

•

CLARIBEL: "I hear that your fiance is doing settlement work."
ANNABELLE: "Yes, his creditors finally caught up with him."

•

MANNA: "Do you file your nails?"
CURIST: "No, I cut them off and throw them away."

•

PH.D: "The human anatomy is a wonderful bit of mechanism."
MISS: "Yes. Pat a man on the back and you'll make his head swell."

PHIL: "Are you going to take the subway home?"

BILL: "No, my wife would only make me take it back."

●

WISE WILFRED'S wife knows that a mother's life is one darned stocking after another.

●

A great big strapping he-looking man was talking to a much-impressed-looking girl at a party. Said the Tarzan:

"What I do for a living takes a lot of guts."

Just then a lad who knew them both passed by.

"The feller's right," said the newcomer; "he strings tennis racquets."

●

STANLEY: "I understand your mother-in-law is visiting you?"

THROCKMORTON: "Yep, another mouth to heed."

●

ALVIN: "My instructor in English told me not to say 'hair-cut.'"

CALVIN: "How's that?"

ALVIN: "He said it was a barbarism."

●

George went to see his girl, and she called down from upstairs that she was not dressed.

"Can't you slip on something and come down?" he called. So she slipped on the top step and came down.

🙰 🙰

ROCKY: "What is untold wealth?"

FELLER: "That which does not appear on income tax reports."

●

CO-ED: "Her hair looks terrible and she's too fat. She should diet."

HER ROOMMATE: "She's going to, but can't make up her mind what color."

●

Critic Jack O'Brian upon hearing that the famous Dublin poet, George Russell (who wrote under the pseudonym "AE") had lost his temper in a debate, wrote, "You mean that AE's Irish rose."

●

"I'm afraid our six-foot bed is not long enough for you," said the landlord to a seven-foot guest.

"Never mind," he replied; "I'll add two more feet to it when I get in."

RIDDLES

RIDDLES

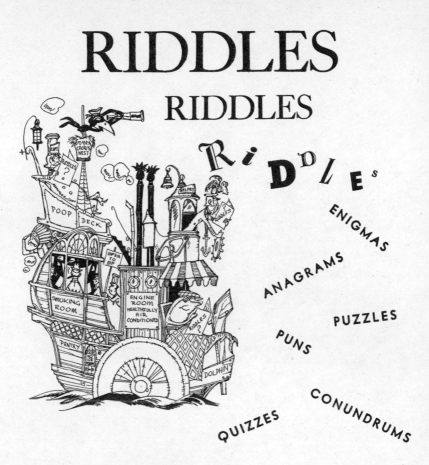

RIDDLES

ENIGMAS

ANAGRAMS

PUZZLES

PUNS

CONUNDRUMS

QUIZZES

Edited by JOSEPH LEEMING

Illustrated by SHANE MILLER

WHAT'S
WHAT?

1   **What kind of shoes are made out of banana skins?**
    Slippers.

2   **What makes the Tower of Pisa lean?**
    It never eats.

3   **What colors would you paint the sun and the wind?**
    The sun rose and the wind blue.

4   **What would happen if a girl should swallow her teaspoon?**
    She wouldn't be able to stir.

5   **What is the easiest thing for a stingy man to part with?**
    A comb.

6   **What is the most difficult train to catch?**
    The 12:50, because it's 10 to 1 if you catch it.

3

7   **What most resembles half a cheese?**
    The other half.

8   **What is never of any use unless it is in a tight place?**
    A cork.

9   **What, besides a good rule, works both ways?**
    A ferry boat.

10 **What ship has two mates but no captain?**
    Courtship.

11 **What do all ships weigh, regardless of their size?**
    Their anchors.

12 **What man's business is best when things are dullest?**
    A knife-sharpener.

13 **What is always filled when it is used and empty when at rest?**
    A shoe.

14 **What becomes higher when the head is off?**
    A pillow.

15 **What is sure to go out the tighter it is locked in?**
    A fire.

16 **What coat is put on only when it is wet?**
    A coat of paint.

17 **What can be a speaking likeness and yet is dumb?**
    A photograph.

18 **What man can raise things without lifting them?**
A farmer.

19 **To what man does everyone always take off his hat?**
The barber.

20 **What tongue can wag and yet never utter a word?**
The tongue of your shoe.

21 **What does everyone take off last when going to bed?**
His feet from the floor.

22 **What may have wings, yet not fly?**
A house.

23 **What kind of boat is like a knife?**
A cutter.

24 **What musical instrument has the best character?**
A piano, because it may be grand, upright or square.

25 **What keeps the moon in place?**
Its beams.

26 **What liquid is like the load a freight ship carries?**
Gasoline, because it makes the car go.

27 **Why is the Senate like a book?**
Because it has so many pages.

28 **What time is it when a pie is divided among four hungry boys?**
A quarter to one.

29 What cord is always full of knots, not one of which can be untied?

A cord of wood.

30 What kind of clothing lasts the longest?

Underwear, because it is never worn out.

31 What is the keynote of good manners?

B natural.

32 What kind of noise annoys an oyster?

A noisy noise annoys an oyster.

33 What is the right kind of lumber for castles in the air?

Sunbeams.

34 What is the highest pleasure you can think of?

Riding in an airplane.

35 What is smaller than an ant's mouth?

What the ant eats.

36 What American has had the largest family?

George Washington, who was the "father of his country."

37 What insect does a blacksmith manufacture?

He makes the fire-fly.

38 What did the blind man say to the policeman when the policeman said he would arrest him if he didn't move on?

I'd just like to see you do it.

39 **What do you call a boy who eats all the apples he can get, whether they are green or old?**

He is what we might call a pains-taking youngster.

40 **What is the smallest bridge in the world?**

The bridge of a nose.

41 **What is the highest building in New York?**

The Public Library has the most stories.

42 **What does a hen do when it stands on one leg?**

Lifts up the other leg.

43 **What is the most indigestible meal you can eat?**

Bolt the door and tuck in the sheets.

44 **What part of a fish weighs the most?**

The scales.

45 **What is the best way to keep goats from smelling?**

Cut off their noses.

46 **What man has eyes in the back of his head?**

The man whose hindsight is better than his foresight.

47 **What do you think is the greatest feat of eating ever known?**

The one in which the man began by bolting a door, threw up a window, and then sat down and swallowed a story whole.

48 **What game do the waves like to play?**

Pitch and toss.

49 What geometrical figure represents a lost parrot?
Polygon (polly gone).

50 What is the best thing to make in a hurry?
Haste.

51 What should you do if you split your sides laughing?
Run fast until you get a stitch in them.

52 What kind of money do girls like the most?
Matrimony.

53 What is the most difficult key to turn?
A donkey.

54 What is there about a yardstick that is very remarkable?
Though it has no head nor tail, it has a foot at each end
and another foot in the middle.

55 What good quality does the North Pole remind you of?
Justice (just ice).

56 What makes the ocean angry?
It has been crossed so many times.

57 What is the best thing to put into pies?
Your teeth.

58 What makes more noise than a pig caught under a fence?
Two pigs.

59 What is worse than finding a worm in an apple?
Finding half a worm.

60 What great benefit is there in a paper of pins?
It has a lot of good points.

61 What word is usually pronounced wrong, even by the best of scholars?
Wrong, of course.

62 What question is it to which you positively must answer yes?
What does Y-E-S spell?

63 What roof never keeps out the wet?
The roof of your mouth.

64 What wind does a hungry sailor like the most?
A wind that blows foul (fowl) and chops about.

65 What is the most contradictory sign seen in a library?
To speak aloud is not allowed (aloud).

66 What is the most disagreeable month for soldiers?
A long March.

67 What is a sure sign of an early spring?
A cat with her back up, watching a hole in the wall.

68 What is the best way to make time go fast?
Use the spur of the moment.

69 **What is a well-known put-up job?**
The paper on the wall.

70 **What is the only thing you can break when you say its name?**
Silence.

71 **What question can never be answered by "Yes"?**
Are you asleep?

72 **What relation is the doorstep to the doormat?**
A step-father (farther).

73 **What is most like a hen stealin'?**
A cock robin.

74 **What salad is best for newlyweds?**
Lettuce alone.

75 **What is the largest room in the world?**
Room for improvement.

76 **What is the oldest piece of furniture in the world?**
The multiplication table.

77 **What walks over the water and under the water, yet does not touch the water?**
A woman crossing a bridge over a river with a pail of water on her head.

78 **What does a calf become after it is one year old?**
Two years old.

79 What is the best thing to take when you are run down?
The number of the car that hit you.

80 What pets make stirring music?
Trumpets.

81 What is the coldest place in a theater?
Z row (zero).

82 What fishes have eyes nearest together?
The smallest fishes.

83 What does a person usually grow in a garden if he works hard?
Tired.

84 What happens to a cat when it crosses a desert on Christmas Day?
It gets sandy claws (Santa Claus).

85 What did the big firecracker say to the little firecracker?
"My pop's bigger than your pop."

86 What is the hardest thing about learning to ride a bicycle?
The pavement.

87 What is the end of everything?
The letter G.

88 What room can no one enter?
A mushroom.

89 What driver never gets arrested?
A screwdriver

90 What is there in your house that ought to be looked into?
A mirror.

91 What coin is double its value when half is deducted?
Half a dollar.

92 What is the surest way to double your money?
Fold it.

93 What is the best and cheapest light?
Daylight.

94 What goes through a door, but never goes in or comes out?
A keyhole.

95 What did Paul Revere say when he finished his famous ride?
"Whoa."

96 What fish may be said to be out of place?
A perch in a bird cage.

97 What has a hand but can't scratch itself?
A clock.

98 What sort of necktie would a smart pig choose?
A pig's tie (pigsty).

99 What intelligent insect do you find in schoolrooms?
Spelling bees.

100 **What flies up but still is down?**
A feather.

101 **What is the richest country in the world?**
Ireland, because its capital is always Dublin.

102 **What does the garden say when it laughs?**
"Hoe, hoe, hoe!"

103 **What would you call a man who is always wiring for money?**
An electrician.

104 **What letter in the Dutch alphabet will name a titled lady?**
A Dutch-ess.

105 **What musical instrument should we never believe?**
A lyre.

106 **What soap is the hardest?**
Castile (cast steel).

107 **What are the most difficult ships to conquer?**
Hardships.

108 **What is a hot time?**
A clock in an oven.

109 **What is the worst weather for rats and mice?**
When it rains cats and dogs.

HOW MANY FISH CAN YOU CATCH?

Here are thirty well-known fish, with a good clue given for each one. How many of them can you catch?

1 What is a struggling fish?

2 What is a cheating fish given to sharp practices?

3 What is a fish of precious metal?

4 What fish is man's best friend?

5 What fish is a royal fish?

6 What is a heavenly fish?

7 What fish is in the band?

8 What fish is an animal that is almost extinct?

9 What fish is an ugly old witch?

10 What fish is a household pet?

11 What fish do you find in a bird cage?

12 What fish is good with hot biscuits?

13 What fish is a sharp-pointed weapon that soldiers used in Robin Hood's time?

14 What fish is a member of a barber shop quartet?

15 What fish is a deep guttural sound?

16 What fish is used on certain boats?

17 What fish is very useful in hot weather?

18 What fish is used by a fencer?

19 What fish is seen at night?

20 What poor fish is always ailing?

21 What fish makes a good sandwich?

22 What fish is a very evil fish?

23 What fish is a very dark color?

24 What fish floats through the air?

25 What fish is a favorite with dairy farmers?

26 What fish is a rosy biter?

27 What fish represents three letters used by stores delivering goods you buy?

28 What fish represents a process used in refining metals?

29 What is a gloomy, down-in-the-mouth fish?

30 What fish warms the earth?

1 Flounder   2 Shark   3 Goldfish   4 Dogfish
5 Kingfish 6 Angelfish 7 Drumfish 8 Buffalo fish
9 Hagfish   10 Catfish   11 Perch   12 Butterfish
13 Pike   14 Bass   15 Grunt   16 Sailfish
17 Fantail 18 Swordfish 19 Starfish 20 Weakfish
21 Jellyfish   22 Devilfish   23 Blackfish
24 Balloon fish   25 Cowfish   26 Red snapper
27 Cod (C.O.D.) 28 Smelt 29 Bluefish 30 Sunfish

? 16

PLEASE
TELL
ME
WHY?

1 **Why should you never tell secrets in a cornfield?**
Because corn has ears and is bound to be shocked.

2 **Why do you always make a mistake when you put on a shoe?**
Because you put your foot in it.

3 **Why does Santa Claus like to go down the chimney?**
Because it suits (soots) him.

4 **Why do white sheep eat more than black ones?**
Because there are more of them in the world.

5 **Why is a ship one of the most polite things on earth?**
Because it always advances with a bow.

6 **Why is the snow different from Sunday?**
Because it can fall on any day of the week.

7   **Why is a good student always on the run?**
Because he is always pursuing his studies.

8   **Why does a man who has just shaved look like a wild animal?**
Because he has a bear face.

9   **Why should watermelon be a good name for a newspaper?**
Because we're sure it is red on the inside.

10   **Why is it vulgar to sing and play by yourself?**
Because such a performance is so low (solo).

11   **Why can't it rain for two days continually?**
Because there is always a night in between.

12   **Why does an Indian wear feathers in his hair?**
To keep his wigwam.

13   **Why is your nose in the middle of your face?**
Because it is a scenter (center).

14   **Why should fish be well educated?**
Because they are so often found in schools.

15   **Why would you expect a fisherman to be more honest than a shepherd?**
Because a fisherman lives by hook and a shepherd
lives by crook.

16   **Why is your sense of touch impaired when you are ill?**
Because you don't feel well.

17 **Why do carpenters believe there is no such thing as glass?**
Because they never saw it.

18 **Why should a lost traveler never starve in the middle of a desert?**
Because of the sand which is (sandwiches) there.

19 **Why are photographers the most progressive of men?**
Because they are always developing.

20 **Why is coffee like a dull knife?**
Because it has to be ground before it can be used.

21 **Why is tennis such a noisy game?**
Because each player raises a racket.

22 **Why should everyone go to sleep immediately after drinking a cup of tea?**
Because when the T is gone, night is nigh.

23 **Why is an orange like a church belfry?**
Because we get a peel (peal) from it.

24 **Why are weary people like automobile wheels?**
Because they are tired.

25 **Why is a river rich?**
Because it always has two banks.

26 **Why does the tightrope dancer always have to repeat his performance?**
Because he is always on cord (encored).

27 Why do we all go to bed?
Because the bed won't come to us.

28 Why can't a tugboat in New York Harbor go in a straight line?
Because some tow (toe) in, and others tow out.

29 Why should taxicab drivers be brave men?
Because "none but the brave deserve the fair" (fare).

30 Why does a chicken cross the road?
To get to the other side.

31 Why does a coat get bigger when you take it out of a suitcase?
Because you will find it increases (in creases).

32 Why do we buy clothes?
Because we can't get them for nothing.

33 Why is coal the most contradictory thing that is bought and sold?
Because when it is bought, instead of going to the buyer, it goes to the cellar.

34 Why is it that every man's trousers are too short?
Because his legs always stick out two feet.

35 Why should a doctor never be seasick?
Because he is so accustomed to sea (see) sickness.

36 Why does a tall man eat less than a short man?
Because he makes a little go a long way.

37 Why is a doctor the meanest man on earth?

Because he treats you and then makes you pay for it.

38 Why doesn't a steam locomotive like to sit down?

Because it has a tender behind.

39 Why are fat men sad?

Because they are men of sighs (size).

40 Why are fishermen such wonderful correspondents?

Because they always like to drop a line.

41 Why is a fly one of the grocer's best customers?

Because when he comes for sugar, he settles on the spot.

42 Why is a gardener the most extraordinary man in the world?

Because he has more business on earth than any other man; he has good grounds for what he does; he is master of the mint; he sets his own time (thyme); he has more bows (boughs) than the President of the United States; and better still, he can raise his own salary (celery) every year.

43 Why are tall people always the laziest?

Because they are longer in bed than short people.

44 Why does lightning shock people?

Because it doesn't know how to conduct itself.

45 Why is it impossible for a person who lisps to believe in the existence of young ladies?

Because with him every miss is a myth.

46 Why is it that when you are looking for something you always find it in the last place you look?

Because you always stop looking when you find it.

47 Why don't women become bald as soon as men?

Because they wear their hair longer.

48 Why is paper money more valuable than coins?

When you put it in your pocket you double it, and when you take it out you find it still in creases.

49 Why can a bride hide nothing?

Because somebody always gives her away.

50 Why is it useless to send a telegram to Washington today?

Because he is dead.

51 Why should a fisherman always be wealthy?

Because all his business is net profit.

52 Why is life the hardest riddle?

Because everybody has to give it up.

53 Why is a heavy fall of snow easy to understand?

Because you can always see the drift of it.

54 Why does a bald-headed man have no use for keys?

Because he has lost his locks.

55 Why should you never swim in the River Seine, at Paris?

Because, if you did, you would be insane (in Seine).

56 Why should you expect a fire in a circus to be very destructive?
Because it is intense (in tents).

57 Why should a dishonest man always stay indoors?
So no one will ever find him out.

58 Why should a spider make a good outfielder?
Because it is always catching flies.

59 Why can hens lay eggs only during the day?
Because at night they become roosters.

60 Why should you be careful about telling secrets in the country?
Because the corn has ears, the potatoes have eyes, and
the beans talk (beanstalk).

61 Why is handwriting in ink like a dead pig?
Because it is done with a pen.

62 Why does a Model-T Ford remind you of a schoolroom?
Because it has a lot of little nuts, with a crank up front.

63 Why does time fly?
Because so many people are trying to kill it.

64 Why is a hungry man willing to be a martyr?
Because he is more than ready to go to the stake (steak).

65 Why did Babe Ruth make so much money?
Because a good batter always makes good dough.

66   **Why is a pig the most unusual animal in the world?**
Because he is killed before he is cured.

67   **Why did Bill's mother knit him three stockings when he was in the army?**
Because Bill wrote her he had gotten so tall he had grown another foot.

68   **Why is the inside of everything so mysterious?**
Because we can't make it out.

69   **Why should ladies who wish to remain slender avoid the letter C?**
Because it makes fat a fact.

70   **Why do children object to the absence of Santa Claus?**
Because they prefer his presence (presents).

71   **Why does a warm day give an icicle a bad reputation?**
Because it turns it into an eavesdropper.

72   **Why does the Statue of Liberty stand in New York Harbor?**
Because it can't sit down.

73   **Why is autumn the best time for a lazy person to read a book?**
Because autumn turns the leaves for him.

74   **Why is a policeman the strongest man in the world?**
Because he can hold up automobiles with one hand.

75   **Why did John tiptoe past the medicine chest?**
Because he was afraid he'd awaken the sleeping pills.

?

76 Why is a tailor a very fine lover?
Because he is an expert at pressing a suit.

77 Why did the jelly roll?
It saw the apple turnover.

78 Why is your nose not twelve inches long?
Because then it would be a foot.

79 Why is the position of President of the United States like a back tooth?
Because it is hard to fill.

80 Why is an empty purse always the same?
Because there is never any change in it.

81 Why are passengers in airplanes so polite to each other?
For fear of falling out.

82 Why is a crown prince like a cloudy day?
Because he is likely to reign.

83 Why would a barber rather shave six men from New York than one from Kokomo?
Because he would get six times as much money.

84 Why does a cook wear a high white hat?
To cover his head.

85 Why is an empty matchbox superior to all others?
Because it is matchless.

86 **Why is a coward like a leaky faucet?**

Because they both run.

87 **Why can you call a horse the most negative of all the animals?**

Because he always neighs (nays).

88 **Why does a cat look first to one side and then to the other when it enters a room?**

Because it can't see both sides at once.

89 **Why is the tongue like an unhappy girl?**

Because they are both down in the mouth.

WHAT
AM I?

1   I am something that never asks any questions, but I demand a great many answers. What am I?

A doorbell.

2   I am something that can run and whistle, but can neither walk nor talk. What am I?

A railroad engine.

3   I am something that can be heard and caught, but never seen. What am I?

A remark.

4   I am something everybody tends to overlook no matter how careful he is. What am I?

Your nose.

5   I am something that is lighter than a feather, and yet harder to hold. What am I?

Your breath.

6   I am something that is often found where I don't exist. What am I?

Fault.

7   I am something that always increases the more I am shared with others. What am I?

Happiness.

8   I am something that is too much for one, enough for two, but nothing at all for three. What am I?

A secret.

9   Use me well, I'm everybody; scratch my back, and I'm nobody. What am I?

A mirror.

10 I am taken from a mine and shut up in a wooden case from which I am never released, and yet I am used by nearly everybody. What am I?

The lead in a pencil.

11 Take away my first letter; take away my second letter; take away all my letters, and I remain the same. What am I?

The postman.

12 Those who have me not, do not wish for me. Those who have me do not wish to lose me. Those who win me have me no longer. What am I?

A lawsuit.

13 I am forever, and yet was never. What am I?

Eternity.

14   I'm a part of a chain. Change my first letter and I become a color. Change my first letter again and I am a place where people go to skate. Change my first letter again and I am an entanglement. Change it again and I become a fur-bearing animal. Give me a different first letter and I am found in the kitchen. Change my first letter again and I am a motion of the eye. What am I?

Link, pink, rink, kink, mink, sink, wink.

15   I occur once in every minute, twice in every moment, and yet not once in a hundred thousand years. What am I?

The letter M.

16   You can hang me on the wall, but if you take me down, you can't hang me up again. What am I?

Wallpaper.

17   I am something that everyone holds once in a while, but hardly anyone touches me. What am I?

The tongue.

18   I am something that always weighs the same, whether I am larger or smaller. What am I?

A hole.

19   I am something that makes everything visible, but am myself unseen. What am I?

Light.

20   I am something that always goes around a button. What am I?

A goat. A goat always goes around a-buttin'.

21 I am something that is known all over the world, and I have a name of three letters. Strangely enough, when two of my letters are taken away, I still have the same name. What am I?

Tea.

22 I am something that comes with a train, goes with a train, is of no use to the train, and yet the train can't go without me. What am I?

Noise.

23 I am something that has never been felt, seen, nor heard; never existed; and yet I have a name. What am I?

Nothing.

24 I am something that has four legs and only one foot. What am I?

A bed.

25 I am something that one man can carry, but a hundred men can't stand on end. What am I?

A rope.

26 I am something that can run but can't walk. What am I?

Water.

27 I am something that has form and size and can be seen, yet I cannot be felt, and I have neither substance nor weight. What am I?

A shadow.

28   I am something that every living person has seen, but no one will ever see me again. What am I?

Yesterday.

29   I am something that a girl often looks for, but always hopes she won't find. What am I?

A run in her stocking.

30   I am something that is full of holes and yet can hold water. What am I?

A sponge.

31   I am something that is filled every morning and emptied every night, except once a year when I am filled at night and emptied in the morning. What am I?

A stocking.

32   I am something that no man wants, yet no man wants to lose. What am I?

A bald head.

33   I am something that has teeth, but can't eat. What am I?

A comb.

34   I am something that no one has ever seen, but many have heard me, and I won't speak unless I'm spoken to. What am I?

An echo.

35   I am something that grows stronger, instead of weaker, the older I get. What am I?

Butter.

36 I am something that has three feet and yet I am unable to walk. What am I?

A yardstick.

37 I am something that has a head and a tail, but no body. What am I?

A penny.

THE RIDDLE OF THE SPHINX

The Riddle of the Sphinx is probably the oldest of all riddles. It appears in ancient Greek mythology.

The Sphinx, a monster with a human head and the body of a beast, sat on a high rock by the roadside near the city of Thebes, in Egypt. To everyone who passed by she asked the following riddle:

"What is it that has but one voice, and goes first on four feet, then on two, and lastly on three?"

All who could not solve the riddle were strangled by the Sphinx and then thrown down from the high rock. For a long time nobody could guess the answer, and a great many people were killed.

Finally, Oedipus, the son of the king of Thebes, came along the road and was stopped by the Sphinx. The Sphinx asked him the famous riddle.

Said Oedipus, "The answer to your riddle is 'a man.' "

"What makes you think that?" demanded the Sphinx.

"Because a man crawls on all fours as an infant, then walks erect on two feet, and in his old age uses a staff or a cane," Oedipus replied.

33 ?

This was indeed the right answer. The Sphinx was so furious when her riddle was solved that she threw herself down from the high rock and perished. But her riddle has lasted throughout the centuries, and still puzzles a lot of people, even today.

SOME
(SHAGGY)
DOG
RIDDLES

1 **Why does a dog turn around three times before lying down?**
Because one good turn deserves another.

2 **Plant a puppy and what would come up?**
Why, dogwood (dog would), doggone it.

3 **What is the difference between a dog's tail and a rich man?**
One keeps a waggin' (wagon), and the other keeps two or three big automobiles.

4 **Why is a dog's tail like the heart of a tree?**
Because it's farthest from the bark.

5 **Why is a hill like a lazy dog?**
Because a hill is an inclined plane; an inclined plane is a slope up (slow pup); and a slow pup is a lazy dog.

35 ?

6 Why is a dog longer in the morning than in the evening?

Because he is let out in the morning and taken in in the evening.

7 A mother asked her daughter one day, "Susie, why is Rover like a religious creed?"

Susie was no dope. She was a pretty smart kid and answered right back, "Because he's a dog, Ma (dogma)."

8 When the doctor looks at a dog's lungs with an X-ray, what do you think he finds?

The seat of his pants.

9 When you look into a dog's mouth, what do you sometimes find?

The seat of someone else's pants.

10 Why does a dog wear more clothes in summer than in winter?

Because in winter he wears a coat, but in summer he wears a coat, and pants too.

11 When is a dog's tail not a dog's tail?

When it's a wagon (waggin').

12 Why is a dog biting his own tail like a good manager?

Because he makes both ends meet.

13 When is a dog most like a human being?

When he's between a man and a boy.

14 Why is a dog with a lame leg like a schoolboy adding six and seven?

Because he puts down three and carries one.

15 **What does a dog have that nothing else has?**
Puppies.

16 **Why is a dainty little lapdog like a galloping hyena?**
Because a hyena is a fast, hideous (fastidious) beast.

17 **What makes a pet dog wag his tail when he sees his master?**
Because he's got one to wag.

18 **What makes a coach dog spotted?**
His spots.

19 **When is a black dog not a black dog?**
When he is a greyhound (some greyhounds are black).

20 **Why is a dog like a tree?**
Because they both produce a bark.

21 **When does a black-and-tan dog change his color?**
When he turns to bay.

22 **What is the difference between a dog losing his hair and a man painting a small building?**
One is shedding his coat, and the other is coating his shed.

23 **What garment does a dog put on for fast trips?**
Pants.

24 **What dog keeps the best time?**
A watch dog.

25 What is more wonderful than a dog that can count?
A spelling bee.

26 Why are a shaggy dog and a tree alike?
Because they both lose their bark when they die.

27 When is a shaggy dog most likely to enter a house?
When the door is open.

HOW'S
YOUR
GEOGRAPHY?

1 **What would you do if you found Chicago Ill?**
Get a Baltimore MD.

2 **When do you get like a well-known South American country?**
When you are Chile.

3 **Why is Massachusetts like an egg?**
Because it has a Hol-yoke.

4 **What New York river asks a question, and what Vermont river answers it?**
Hoo-sick? Pa-sum-sick.

5 **Why is a barefoot boy like an Alaskan Eskimo?**
Because he wears no shoes (wears snow shoes).

6 **Why doesn't Sweden have to send abroad for cattle?**
Because she keeps a good Stockholm (stock home).

7 **If Mississ Ippi should lend Miss Ouri her New Jersey, what would Dela Ware?**
Al-ask-a (I'll ask her).

8 **What was the greatest feat of strength ever performed in the United States?**
Wheeling West Virginia.

9 **What state is round at both ends and high in the middle?**
Ohio.

10 **What is the happiest state?**
Merryland (Maryland).

11 **Why is the isthmus of Suez like the first U in cucumber?**
Because it's between two seas (C's).

12 **What did Tennessee?**
The same thing that Arkansas.

13 **What did Tennessee the next time it looked?**
It saw Ida hoe (Idaho).

14 **If Iowa month's rent, what does Ohio?**
Money for taxes (Texas).

15 **Which was the largest island before Australia was discovered?**
It was Australia, just the same.

16 **What sea would you like to be in on a wet, rainy day?**
Adriatic (a dry attic).

17 Why do some people think that Noah was born in New Jersey?
Because he was a New-ark man.

18 Why is the Mississippi the most talkative of rivers?
Because it has a dozen mouths.

19 Why do so many of the Chinese travel on foot?
Because there is only one Cochin-China (coach in China).

20 Which of the West Indian islands does a maker of preserved fruits resemble?
Jamaica (jam-maker).

21 What is it that is found in the very center of America and Australia?
The letter R.

22 Why is the leaning tower of Pisa like Greenland?
Because it is oblique (so bleak).

23 Why is a trip to Egypt fit only for very old gentlemen?
Because it's a see-Nile (senile) thing to do.

24 Why is a man hurrying to rescue Hannah from drowning like a man journeying to a well-known southern city?
Because he is going to save Hannah (Savannah).

25 If Ireland should sink, what would float?
Cork.

26 What part of London is in France?

The letter N.

27 What continent do you see when you look in the mirror in the morning?

You see Europe (you're up).

SOME
DIFFICULT
FEATS
(FEETS)

1 What is a foot to get for a barefoot boy?

2 What foot tells you that someone is right behind you?

3 What foot do you find on a page?

4 What foot do you find on a stage?

5 What is a foot that steals things?

6 What foot do you feel after a long walk?

7 What foot is a servant in a castle?

8 What foot does grandma like to have in the living room?

9 What foot is free and a roamer?

10 What foot is an exciting outdoor game?

1 Footwear 2 Footfall 3 Footnote 4 Footlight 5 Footpad
6 Footsore 7 Footman 8 Footstool 9 Footloose 10 Football

WHICH
IS
WHICH?

1 **Which is the strongest day of the week?**

Sunday, because all the rest are weak days.

2 **Which can move faster, heat or cold?**

Heat, because you can catch cold.

3 **Which is correct: The white of the eggs is yellow, or the white of the eggs are yellow?**

Neither. The whites are never yellow.

4 **Which takes less time to get ready for a trip—an elephant or a rooster?**

The rooster. He takes only his comb, while the elephant has to take a whole trunk.

5 **Which is better—complete happiness or a bread-and-butter sandwich?**

A bread-and-butter sandwich. Nothing is better than complete happiness, and a bread-and-butter sandwich is much better than nothing.

45 **?**

6 Which has more legs—a horse or no horse?

No horse. No horse has five or more legs. A horse has just four legs.

7 Which candles burn longer—wax candles or tallow candles?

Neither. They both burn shorter.

8 Which is heavier, milk or cream?

Milk is, because cream rises to the surface.

9 Which would you rather have—a lion eat you or a tiger?

Thanks, I'd rather have the lion eat the tiger.

10 Which is the most dangerous bat that flies in the air?

A brickbat.

11 Which has more legs, a cow or no cow?

Well, no cow has eight legs, and that is more than most cows have.

12 Which member of Congress wears the largest hat?

The one with the largest head.

13 Which is the left side of a round plum pudding?

The part that isn't eaten.

14 Which tree is the most suggestive of romance?

Yew, dear.

15 **Which is heavier, a half or a full moon?**

The half, because the full moon is as light again as the half moon.

16 **Which of the heavenly bodies has the most small change in it pockets?**

The moon, because it is always changing quarters.

17 **Which is the laziest plant, and which the most active?**

The creeper and the running vine.

18 **Which of your parents is your nearest relative?**

Your mother, because your other parent is always father (farther).

19 **Which of the four seasons is the most literary?**

Autumn, because then the leaves are turned and are red (read).

20 **Which of the stars should be made to obey the game laws?**

The shooting stars.

21 **Which is the only tool that grows sharper with use?**

The tongue.

22 **Which is heavier, a pound of gold or a pound of feathers?**

A pound of feathers, because it weighs an avoirdupois pound, or sixteen ounces, while a pound of gold weighs a pound troy, or twelve ounces.

23 **Which of your relatives are dependent upon you, whether you know it or not, for their existence?**

Your uncles, aunts and cousins, because without U they couldn't exist.

24 **Which is easier to spell—fiddle-de-dee or fiddle-de-dum?**

Fiddle-de-dee, because it is spelled with more ease (E's).

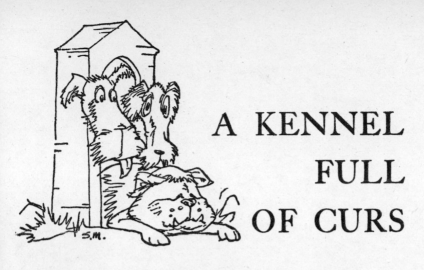

A KENNEL
FULL
OF CURS

1   What cur do you find at the edge of a street?

2   What cur tolls at nighttime?

3   What cur is a religious one?

4   What cur is a healer?

5   What cur is a person in charge of a museum?

6   What cur is full of electricity?

7   What cur is good for making jelly?

8   What cur is the most inquisitive one?

9   What cur hangs at the window?

10 What cur can you spend?

11 What cur is a bird?

12 What cur belongs to a baseball pitcher?

1 Curb 2 Curfew 3 Curate 4 Cure 5 Curator 6 Current
7 Currant 8 Curiosity 9 Curtain 10 Currency 11 Curlew
12 Curve

LOTS
OF
LETTUCE
(LETTERS)

1 **Why is the letter E always discontented?**

Because, while it is never out of health or pocket, it never appears in good spirits.

2 **Why is the letter A like honeysuckle?**

Because a B (bee) is always after it.

3 **Why is the letter D like a bad boy?**

Because it makes ma mad.

4 **Why is O the noisiest of the vowels?**

Because all the other vowels (A, E, I, U) are inaudible (in "audible").

5 **Why do you think B comes before C?**

Because we must be (B) before we can see (C).

6   **What starts with a T, ends with a T, and is full of T?**
A teapot.

7   **What helpful thing does the letter A do for a deaf woman?**
It makes her hear.

8   **What is always invisible yet never out of sight?**
The letters I and S.

9   **Why is the letter F like death?**
Because it makes all fall.

10   **Why is a false friend like the letter P?**
Because he is the first in pity, but the last in help.

11   **Tommy Tucker took two strings and tied two turtles to two tall trees. How many T's are there in that?**
To be perfectly frank, there are only two T's in "that."

12   **What word of only three syllables contains twenty-six letters?**
Alphabet.

13   **Why is a sewing machine like the letter S?**
Because it makes needles needless.

14   **Why is the letter E so unfortunate?**
Because it is always out of cash and always in debt and great danger.

15   **Which two letters of the alphabet have nothing between them?**
N and P have O (nothing) between them.

?

16 **What letter of the alphabet separates Europe from Africa?**

C (sea).

17 **What four letters of the alphabet would scare off a burglar?**

O, I C U (Oh, I see you).

18 **What is it that every pauper possesses that others have not?**

The letter P.

19 **What is the most important thing in the world?**

The letter E, because it is first in everybody and everything.

20 **What letter is always nine inches long?**

The letter Y, which is always one-fourth of a yard.

21 **What letter is never found in the alphabet?**

The one you mail.

22 **What letter in the alphabet can travel the greatest distance?**

The letter D, because it goes to the end of the world.

23 **If all the letters of the alphabet were invited to a luncheon party, what six letters would fail to arrive on time?**

The letters U, V, W, X, Y and Z, because they come only after T (tea).

24 **What always has at least ten letters in it and may have tens of thousands of letters?**

A post office.

25 **In what way are the letter O and a neatly kept house alike?**
Both are always in order.

26 **In what way are the letter A and high noon alike?**
Both are in the middle of day.

27 **What letter is a drink?**
T.

28 **What letter is a vegetable?**
P.

29 **What letter is an insect?**
B.

30 **What letter is a part of the head?**
I.

31 **Why is U the jolliest letter?**
Because it is always in the midst of fun.

32 **Why is I the happiest of the vowels?**
Because it alone is in bliss, while E is in hell and all the other vowels are in purgatory.

33 **What three letters make a man of a boy?**
A—G—E.

34 **Why should boys and men avoid the letter A?**
Because it makes men mean.

35 **What letter makes pies inquisitive?**

The letter S will turn them into spies.

36 **Why is a poker and shovel manufacturer the most likely person to make money by causing the alphabet to quarrel?**

Because he makes A poke R and shove L, and gets paid for doing it.

37 **Why is the letter P like one of the Roman emperors?**

Because it is near O (Nero).

38 **Can you list ten ways of spelling the sound O?**

1. O as in go. 2. Ough as in dough. 3. Owe as in owe. 4. Oh as in oh. 5. Ot as in jabot. 6. Ow as in snow. 7. Ew as in sew. 8. Eau as in beau. 9. Oe as in toe. 10. Oa as in boat.

39 **Why are the letters C and S in the word "cloves," although separated, closely attached?**

Because there is love between them.

40 **Why is the letter I in Cicero like Arabia?**

Because it is between two seas (C's).

41 **Why is the letter E like London?**

Because it is the capital of England.

42 **Why is the letter T like an island?**

Because it is in the midst of water.

43 **What letter will set one of the heavenly bodies in motion?**

T, because it will make a star start.

44   When can the alphabet be shortened?

When U and I are one.

45   Why is the letter F like a cow's tail?

Because it is at the end of beef.

46   Why is the letter R absolutely necessary to friendship?

Because without it your friends would be fiends.

47   Why is the letter B like fire?

Because it makes oil boil.

48   Why should a housekeeper never put the letter M in her refrigerator?

Because it will change ice into mice.

49   When is a man like the letter B?

When he is in bed.

50   Why is the letter D like a sailor?

Because it follows the C (sea).

51   Why is the letter G like the sun?

Because it is the center of light.

52   If all the letters of the alphabet were on top of a mountain. which letter would leave first?

D would always start descent.

53   What one letter in the alphabet will spell the word "potatoes"?

The letter O. Put them down one at a time until you have put eight O's (potatoes).

54 Why is making fun of people like the letter D on horseback?

Because it is deriding (D riding).

55 Which are the most sensible letters?

The Y's (wise).

56 Which letters are the hardest workers?

The B's (bees).

57 Why is a glassblower the most likely person to set the alphabet off at a gallop?

Because he can make a D canter (decanter).

58 What does the letter B do for boys as they grow up?

As they grow older it makes them bolder.

59 How can the letter W be used to bring music up to date?

By changing sing to swing.

60 Why is the letter O like a pain?

Because it makes man moan.

GIRLS
ARE
ALWAYS
RIDDLES

1 **When is a pretty girl like a ship?**

When she's attached to a boy (buoy).

2 **How can a girl best keep a boy's affection?**

By not returning it.

3 **How would it work if all the post offices were in the charge of pretty girls?**

It would work so well that the mails (males) would arrive and depart every hour of the day.

4 **If a pretty girl fell into a well, why couldn't her brother help her out?**

How could he be a brother and assist her (a sister) too?

5 **In what month do girls talk the least?**

In February, because it is the shortest month.

6 **How can you tell a girl named Ellen that she is delightful, in eight letters?**

U-R-A-B-U-T-L-N (You are a beauty, Ellen).

7 **What is the difference between a soldier and a pretty girl?**

One faces the powder, and the other powders the face.

8 **Why is a nice but inelegant girl like brown sugar?**

Because she's sweet but unrefined.

9 **Why do girls like to look at the moon?**

Because there's a man in it.

10 **Why is a proud girl like a music book?**

Because she is full of airs.

11 **One boy calls his girl-friend "Postscript." What do you think her real name is?**

Adeline Moore (Add a line more).

12 **What two beaus can every girl always have near at hand?**

Elbows.

13 **Why are girls like hinges?**

Because they are things to a door (adore).

14 **Why are girls like their own watches?**

Because they are pretty to look at, have delicate faces and hands, but are sometimes difficult to regulate when once they get going.

15 **What girl is always making blunders?**

Miss Take (mistake).

16   **What girls are they whose days are always unlucky?**
Miss Chance, Miss Fortune and Miss Hap.

17   **What girls have especially jealous tempers?**
Miss Give and Miss Trust.

18   **What are the three quickest ways of spreading the news?**
Telegraph, telephone, and tell a girl.

19   **Why should a group of pretty girls squeezing wet clothes remind us of going to church?**
Because the belles (bells) are wringing (ringing).

20   **Why do girls make good post-office clerks?**
Because they know how to manage the mails (males).

21   **Why should girls not learn French?**
Because one tongue is enough for any girl.

22   **Which is the favorite word with girls?**
The last one.

23   **Why are some girls like facts?**
Because they are stubborn things.

24   **Why are some girls like salad?**
Because they need a lot of dressing.

25   **Why is a bright girl's thought like the telegraph?**
Because it's so much quicker than the mail (male) intelligence.

26 If there were only three girls in the world, what do you think they would talk about?

Two of them would get together and talk about the other one.

27 Why are some girls very much like teakettles?

Because they sing away pleasantly and then all at once boil over.

28 What is the difference between a girl and a parasol?

You can shut up the parasol.

29 When is a girl not a girl?

When she is a bell (belle) or a deer (dear).

30 What is the best way to find a mysterious girl out?

Go around to her house when she isn't in.

31 Why do girls like sunset and twilight so much?

Because they are daughters of Eve.

32 Why is a melancholy girl the most pleasant of all companions?

Because she is always a-musing (amusing).

33 Why is a fashionable school for girls like a flower garden?

Because it's a place of haughty culture (horticulture).

34 Why should girls always set a good example?

Because boys are so apt to follow them.

35 When is a girl's cheek not a cheek?

When it's a little pail (pale).

36 **Why are girls so extravagant about their clothes?**

Because when they get a new dress, they wear it out the first day.

37 **When is a girl not sorry to lose her hair?**

When she has it cut.

38 **Why are girls like umbrellas?**

Because they are made out of ribs; you have to dress them in silk to make them look their best; at the least bit of a storm they go right up in the air; it is often your best friend who takes them away from you; and they are accustomed to reign (rain).

WHERE
IN THE
WORLD?

1 **Where are you likely to go when you are fourteen years old?**
   Into your fifteenth year.

2 **Where are the largest diamonds in New York City kept?**
   In the baseball fields.

3 **Where are the kings of England usually crowned?**
   On the head.

4 **Where can everyone always find money when he looks for it?**
   In the dictionary.

5 **Where will you find the center of gravity?**
   At the letter V.

6 **Where is the best place to get fat?**
   At the butcher shop.

7   **Where did Noah strike the first nail he put in the ark?**

On the head.

8   **Where is the best place to have a very painful boil?**

On someone else.

9   **Where do you have the longest view in the world?**

By a roadside where there are telephone poles, because
there you can see from pole to pole.

WHAT IF?

1 **If a father gives fifteen cents to his son and a dime to his daughter, what time of day is it?**

A quarter to two.

2 **If a pencil and a piece of paper had a race, which would win?**

The pencil, because the paper would always remain stationary (stationery).

3 **If ten sparrows were on a roof and you shot one, how many would remain?**

None, because they would all fly away.

4 **If a chicken could talk, what kind of language would it speak?**

Foul (fowl) language, I'm afraid.

5 **If your uncle's sister is not your aunt, just what relation is she to you?**

She is your mother.

?

6 **If you saw a counterfeit dollar bill on the sidewalk and walked by without picking it up, why should you be arrested?**

Because you passed counterfeit money.

7 **If a pretty girl wanted her father to take her rowing on a lake, what person in Greek mythology would she name?**

Europa (You row, pa).

8 **If butter is fifty cents a pound in Chicago, what are window panes in Detroit?**

Glass.

9 **If you add a syllable to a certain word it becomes shorter. What is the word?**

Short.

10 **If you add to it, it becomes smaller. If you don't add to it, it becomes larger. What is it?**

A hole in your stocking. If you add thread to it, it becomes smaller.

11 **If I were in the sun and you were out of it, what would the sun become?**

Sin.

12 **If a man can mow a lawn a hundred feet square in two hours, how long will it take him to mow a lawn fifty feet square, if he mows at the same rate of speed?**

Half an hour. The second lawn is one-quarter as big as the first one.

13 **If a two-wheeled conveyance is a bicycle, and a three-wheeled**

? 68

conveyance is a tricycle, what is a five-wheeled conveyance?

A V-hicle.

14　If an acrobat fell off his trapeze, what would he fall against?

Against his inclination.

15　If a boy wears his pants out, what will he do next?

Wear them in again.

16　If a burglar got into the cellar, would the coal shoot (chute)?

No, but the kindling would (wood).

17　If a little chicken could speak, and found an orange in its nest, what do you think it would say?

Oh, look at the orange marmalade (mama laid).

18　If a man gets up on a donkey, where do you think he should get down?

From a goose.

19　If you were invited out to dinner, and found nothing on the table but a beet, what would you say?

Well, that beets all!

20　If the eyes and nose of a boy with a cold were to run a race, which would win?

The eyes, for the nose would be blown, while the eyes would run till they dropped.

21　If a man tries to jump across a ditch and falls, why is he likely to miss seeing the beauties of summer?

Because the Fall follows right after the Spring.

22 If a church should catch on fire, what part could not be saved?

The organ, because the hose couldn't play on it.

23 If you were fishing in a harbor and a hostile warship came into sight, what would be the best thing to do?

Pull up your line and sinker (sink her).

24 If a man shot at two frogs and killed one, what do you think the other frog would do?

Croak.

25 If a goat should swallow a rabbit, what would be the result?

A hare (hair) in the butter.

26 If a biscuit is a soda cracker, what is an ice pick?

A water cracker.

27 If one man carries a sack of flour and another man carries two sacks, which has the heavier load?

The one with a sack of flour, because a sack of flour is heavier than two (empty) sacks.

28 If I walk into a room full of people and put a new penny on the table in full view of everybody, what does the penny do?

It looks 'round.

29 If you lose a dollar today, why would it be a good plan to lose another tomorrow?

So as to make your loss a gain (again).

30 **If a general should ask in vain for some martial music, what word would express his feelings?**

Conundrum (Can none drum)?

31 **If I were to bite off the end of your nose, what would the magistrate compel me to do?**

Keep the peace (piece).

32 **If Dick's father is Tom's son, what relation is Dick to Tom?**

Tom is Dick's grandfather.

33 **If you call a sheep's tail a leg, how many legs will he have?**

He'll still have only four.

34 **If a dog should lose his tail, where could he get another?**

In a department store, where everything is retailed.

35 **If a thief were engaged to sing in a chorus, what part would be most suitable for him?**

The base (bass) part.

36 **If you throw a white stone into the Red Sea, what will it become?**

It will become wet.

37 **If two postal telegraph operators were married in San Francisco, what would they make?**

A Western Union.

38 **If a postmaster went to the circus and a lion ate him, what time would it be?**

Eight (ate) P.M.

71 ?

39   If a tree were to break the panes of a window, what would the window panes say?

Tree, mend us (tremendous)!

40   If a farmer can raise two hundred bushels of corn in dry weather, what can he raise in wet weather?

An umbrella.

41   If you saw a bird sitting on a twig and you wanted to get the twig without disturbing the bird, what would you do?

Wait until the bird flew away.

42   If a man sent his son to college and paid a thousand dollars a year to put him through, how much change might he get back?

He might get a quarterback.

43   If a man smashed a clock, could he be accused of killing time?

Not if the clock struck first.

44   If you had a box of candles and no matches, how would you light them?

Just take one candle out of the box and then it will be a candle-lighter.

45   If one horse is shut up in a paddock and one is running loose down the road, which horse is singing, "Don't fence me in"?

Neither horse. Horses can't sing.

46   If you were locked in a room that had in it only a bed and a calendar, what would you do for food?

Get water from the bed springs and dates from the calendar.

? 72

47 **If your neighbor quarreled with you and called you an insect, would he be wrong?**

Yes, an insect has six legs.

48 **If two is company, and three is a crowd, what are four and five?**

Nine.

49 **If I had an apple and you had only a bite, what would you do?**

Scratch the bite.

50 **If twelve makes a dozen, how many make a million?**

Not very many.

GHOSTLY GUESSERS

If you lived in a graveyard:

1 **With what would you open the gate?**
   With a skeleton key.

2 **What would you do if you got a bad cold that settled in your throat?**
   Start coffin (coughin').

3 **How would you identify in three letters a poem written for someone who had passed on?**
   L-E-G (elegy).

4 **What kind of jewels would you wear?**
   Tombstones.

5 **Where would you keep them?**
   In a casket.

6 What would you do if you were getting ready for a play?
Rehearse.

7 What would protect you from the sun?
The shades.

8 Supposing a woman told you she was going to call?
You would 'specter (expect her).

9 What would be your disposition?
Grave.

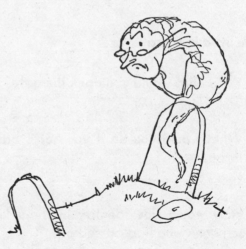

HORSE
LAUGHS

1   **How can you make a slow horse fast?**
   Don't give him anything to eat for a while.

2   **How can you put a good horse on his mettle?**
   Shoe him. That will put him on his metal.

3   **Barnum, the great circus man, had in his museum ten horses that had only twenty-four feet in all, yet they trotted about as well as other horses. How was this possible?**
   The ten horses had twenty fore-feet.

4   **Why is a horse the most unusual feeder of all the animals?**
   Because he eats best when there isn't a bit in his mouth.

5   **Why is a horse like the letter O?**
   Because Gee (G) makes it GO.

6 Why is a wild young horse like an egg?

It must be broken before it can be used.

7 Why are horses such great gossips?

Because they are always tale bearers.

8 Why is a well-trained horse like a kindhearted man?

Because he always stops at the sound of whoa (woe).

9 Why does tying a slow horse to a post make him a better racer?

Because it makes him fast.

10 What do you think is the principal part of a horse?

His mane part.

11 How can it be proved that a horse has six legs?

Because he has forelegs (four legs) in front and two legs behind.

12 Why is even a good-natured hunting horse likely to get angry unexpectedly?

Because the better tempered he is, the easier he takes a fence (offense).

13 What horse sees as much in the rear as he does in the front?

A blind horse.

14 What is wrong about describing a horse as a cart-horse?

Because this description puts the cart before the horse.

WHAT'S THE DIFFERENCE?

1   **What is the difference between an old penny and a new dime?**

Nine cents.

2   **What is the difference between some people you know and a mirror?**

Some people you know talk without reflecting, while a mirror reflects without talking.

3   **What is the difference between a cloud and a boy getting a spanking?**

The cloud pours with rain and the boy roars with pain.

4   **What is the difference between a pianist and sixteen ounces of lead?**

The pianist pounds away and the lead weighs a pound.

5   **What difference is there among a piano, a ship on a stormy sea, and you?**

The piano makes music. The ship makes you sick, and you make me sick. (Better be careful who you try this on!)

79 **?**

6 What is the difference between a naughty boy and a postage stamp?

You lick one with a stick, and you stick the other with a lick.

7 What is the difference between a cat and a comma?

The cat has claws at the end of its paws, while the comma has its pause at the end of its clause.

8 What is the difference between a mouse and a beautiful girl?

The mouse harms the cheese, and the girl charms the he's.

9 What is the difference between a man going to the second floor and a man looking upstairs?

One is stepping upstairs, and the other is staring up steps.

10 What is the difference between an undersized witch and a deer trying to escape from a hunter?

One is a stunted hag, and the other is a hunted stag.

11 What is the difference between a bottle of medicine and a bad boy?

One is well shaken before taken, and the other should be taken and well shaken.

12 What is the difference between a moneyless man and a feather bed?

One is hard up and the other is soft down.

13 What is the difference between a sailor and six broken clocks?

The sailor goes to sea, and the clocks cease to go.

14 **What is the difference between a man who has eaten a hearty meal and a man who has signed his will?**

One is dined and sated, and the other has signed and dated.

15 **What is the difference between Christopher Columbus and the lid of a dish?**

One is a discoverer, and the other is a dish coverer.

16 **What is the difference between a book of fiction and the rear light of a car?**

One is a light tale, and the other is a tail light.

17 **What is the difference between a glutton and a hungry man?**

One eats too long, and the other longs to eat.

18 **What is the difference between a china shop and a furniture store?**

One sells tea sets, while the other sells settees.

19 **What is the difference between a crazy hare and a counterfeit coin?**

One is a mad bunny, and the other is bad money.

20 **What is the difference between a barber and a woman with a lot of children?**

One has razors to shave, and the other has shavers to raise.

21 **What is the difference between an organist and a cold in the head?**

One knows the stops, and the other stops the nose.

22 **What is the difference between a book and a talkative bore?**

You can shut up the book.

23 **What is the difference between a man taking an oath of office and a suit of cast-off clothes?**

One is sworn in, and the other is worn out.

24 **What is the difference between a tailor and a groom?**

One mends a tear, and the other tends a mare.

25 **What is the difference between a weather forecaster and a watch key?**

One watches the wind, while the other winds the watch.

26 **What is the difference between a milkmaid and a seagull?**

One skims milk, and the other skims water.

27 **What is the difference between a postage stamp and a girl?**

One is a mail fee, and the other is a female.

28 **What is the difference between one yard and two yards?**

Usually a fence.

29 **What is the difference between a fisherman and a lazy schoolboy?**

One baits his hook, while the other hates his book.

30 **What is the difference between a person who is late for a train and a teacher in a girls' school?**

One misses the train, and the other trains the misses.

31 **What difference is there among a gardener, a billiard player, a precise man, and a church janitor?**

The gardener minds his peas; the billiard player, his cues; the precise man, his p's and q's; and the church janitor, his keys and pews.

32 **What is the difference between a beached ship and an airplane?**

One grounds on the land, and the other lands on the ground.

33 **What is the difference between a man struck with amazement and a leopard's tail?**

One is rooted to the spot, while the other is spotted to the root.

34 **What is the difference between an auction sale and seasickness?**

One is a sale of effects, and the other, the effects of a sail.

35 **What is the difference between a baby and a shipwrecked sailor?**

One clings to his ma, and the other clings to his spar (his pa).

36 **What is the difference between a bee and a donkey?**

One gets all the honey, and the other gets all the whacks (wax).

37 **What is the difference between a piece of honeycomb and a black eye?**

One is produced by a laboring bee, and the other by a be-laboring.

38 What is the difference between a bell and an organ?

One rings when it is told (tolled), but the other will
be blowed first.

39 What is the difference between a blind man and a disabled sailor?

One can't see to go, and the other can't go to sea.

40 What is the difference between a millionaire and a prizefighter?

One makes money hand over fist, and the other makes
his fist hand over money.

41 What is the difference between a prizefighter and a man with a cold?

One knows his blows, and the other blows his nose.

42 What is the difference between a boy who is twelve years old and a man taking a nap?

One is twelve, and the other is a-dozin' (dozen).

43 What is the difference between a school boy studying his lessons and a farmer watching his cows?

One is stocking his mind, and the other is minding his
stock.

44 What is the difference between an elephant and a flea?

An elephant can have fleas, but a flea can't have
elephants.

45 What is the difference between a jug of water and a man throwing his wife into the river?

One is water in the pitcher, and the other is pitch her
in the water.

46 What is the difference between a chicken who can't hold up his head and seven days?

One is a weak one, and the other is one week.

47 What is the difference between an oak tree and a tight shoe?

One makes acorns, and the other makes corns ache.

48 What is the difference between a light in a cave and a dance in an inn?

One is a taper in a cavern, and the other is a caper in a tavern.

49 What difference is there among a rooster, Uncle Sam, and an old maid?

The rooster says "Cock-a-doodle-doo"; Uncle Sam says "Yankee Doodle Doo"; and the old maid says "Any dude'll do."

50 What is the difference between a locomotive engineer and a schoolteacher?

One minds the train, while the other trains the mind.

51 What is the difference between a farmer and a seamstress?

One gathers what he sows, and the other sews what she gathers.

52 What is the difference between a new sponge and a fashionably dressed man?

If you wet one it makes it swell, but if you wet the other it takes all the swell out of him.

53 What is the difference between a hill and a pill?

One is hard to get up, while the other is hard to get down.

85 **?**

54 What is the difference between a hunting dog and a locomotive?

One is trained to run, and the other runs a train.

55 What is the difference between a man with an unnatural voice and one with unnatural teeth?

One has a falsetto voice, and the other has a false set-o'-teeth.

56 What is the difference between a professional violinist and the person who goes to hear him?

One plays for his pay, and the other pays for his play.

57 What is the difference between perseverance and obstinacy?

One arises from a strong "will," and the other from a strong "won't."

58 What is the difference between photographers and the whooping cough?

One makes facsimiles, and the other makes sick families.

59 What is the difference between a church bell and a pickpocket?

One peals from the steeple, and the other steals from the people.

60 What is the difference among a king's son, a monkey's mother, a bald head, and an orphan?

A king's son is an heir apparent, a monkey's mother is a hairy parent, a bald head has no hair apparent, and an orphan has nary a parent.

? 86

61 **What is the difference between the Milky Way and a room full of great-grandfathers?**

One is a lot of pale stars, and the other is a lot of stale pas.

62 **What is the difference between a bright boy in school and shoe polish?**

One shines at the head of the class, and the other shines at the foot.

63 **What is the difference between a skilled marksman and the man who tends the targets?**

One hits the mark, and the other marks the hits.

64 **What is the difference between a grocer selling a pound of sugar and a druggist with a pestle and mortar?**

One weighs a pound, and the other pounds away.

65 **What is the difference between reckless speculation and some slices of bacon?**

One is rash, and the other is a rasher.

66 **What is the difference between the rising and the setting sun?**

All the difference in the world.

67 **What is the difference between the sun and bread?**

The sun rises in the east, and the bread rises with the (y)east in it.

68 **What is the difference between the manager of a theater and a sailor?**

A sailor likes to see a lighthouse and the manager doesn't.

87 **?**

69 What is the difference between truth and eggs?

Truth crushed to earth will rise again, but eggs won't.

70 What is the difference between an honest and a dishonest laundress?

One irons your clothes, and the other steels (steals) them.

71 What is the difference between the land and the ocean?

One is dirt-y, and the other is tidy (tide-y).

72 What is the difference between a man and a banana peel?

Sometimes a man throws a banana peel in the gutter, and sometimes a banana peel throws a man in the gutter.

73 What is the difference between here and there?

The letter T.

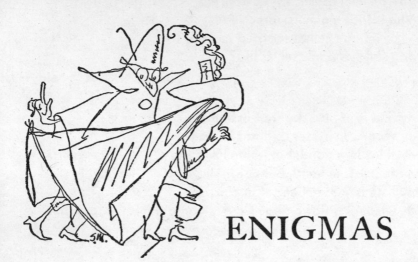

ENIGMAS

Enigmas are riddles, often in verse form, in which there is a hidden meaning imaginatively described.

1   I'm not in earth, nor the sun, nor the moon.
You may search all the sky—I'm not there.
In the morning and evening—though not in the noon—
You may plainly perceive me, for, like a balloon,
I am midway suspended in air.
Though disease may possess me, and sickness and pain,
I am never in sorrow nor gloom;
Though in wit and in wisdom
I equally reign,
I'm the heart of all sin and have long lived in vain;
Yet I ne'er shall be found in the tomb.

The letter I.
(This is a famous enigma written by Lord Byron.)

2 Pray tell me, ladies, if you can,
Who is that highly favored man,
Who, though he has married many a wife,
May still live single all his life?

A clergyman.

3 My first is in pork, but not in ham;
My second in oyster, but not in clam;
My third is in pond, but not in lake;
My fourth is in hand, but not in shake;
My fifth is in eye, but not in pink;
My whole is a flower, you'll guess if you think.

Peony.

4 The beginning of eternity,
The end of time and space,
The beginning of every end,
The end of every place.

The letter E.

5 Two heads I have and strange as it may be,
I can be found in every big army.
I'm always still except when roughly used,
But I can be noisy when beat or abused.
Soldiers of all nations rely on me,
So I can be useful, as you can see.

A drum.

6 A headless man had a letter to write;
It was read by one who had no sight;
The dumb repeated it word for word,

?

And he that was deaf both listened and heard.
What was written?

The letter O, or nothing.

7   I am a caller at every home that you may meet,
For daily I make my way along each street;
Take one letter from me and still you will see
I'm the same as before, as I always will be;
Take two letters from me, or three or four,
I'll still be the same as I was before.
In fact, I'll say that all my letters you may take,
Yet of me nothing else you'll make.

A postman.

8   We are familiar little creatures,
Each has different forms and features.
One of us in a glass is set,
Another you will find in jet;
A third you'll find if you look in tin,
A fourth, a beautiful box within;
And the fifth, if you pursue,
It will never fly from you.

The vowels—A, E, I, O and U.

9   Just equal are my head and tail,
My middle slender as can be,
Whether I stand on head or heel,
'Tis all the same to you or me.
But if my head should be cut off,
The matter's true, although 'tis strange,
My head and body, severed thus,
Immediately to nothing change.

The figure 8.

10   I have wings yet never fly,
I have sails yet never go,
I can't keep still if I try,
Yet forever stand just so.

A windmill.

11   I go but never stir,
I count but never write,
I measure and divide and, sir,
You'll find my measures right.
I run but never walk,
I strike but never wound,
I tell you much but never talk
In all my daily round.

A clock.

12   Three-fourths of me an act display,
Three-fourths a bed for man;
Three-fourths have legs that cannot stray,
Three-fourths have legs that can.
I have a back without a spine,
An arm without a bone is mine.

A coat. Three-fourths of its letters spell act, cot (the bed with legs that cannot stray), and cat (with legs that can)

SAY
WHEN!

1 **When does a boat show affection?**
  When it hugs the shore.

2 **When does the sun get the best of an argument with the dew?**
  When it makes it dry up.

3 **When does a chair dislike you?**
  When it is broken and can't bear you.

4 **When does a farmer have the best chance to see his pigs?**
  When he has a sty on his eye.

5 **When is a door not a door?**
  When it is a jar (ajar).

6 **When is a lady not a lady?**
  When she turns into a drug store.

?

7 When does a leopard change his spots?
When he moves.

8 When does a man never fail to keep his word?
When no one will take it.

9 When the clock strikes thirteen, what time is it?
Time to have the clock fixed.

10 When is an artist very unhappy?
When he draws a long face.

11 When is a trunk emotional?
When it is empty and easily moved.

12 When is a doctor like an angry man?
When he loses his patience (patients).

13 When is it a good time for everyone to lose his temper?
When it becomes bad.

14 When is a blow on the head like a piece of fabric?
When it is felt.

15 When is a department store like a boat?
When it has sales (sails).

16 When is a bill like an old chair that is repaired?
When it is receipted (re-seated).

17 When is roast beef highest in price?
When it is rarest.

18 **When do 2 and 2 make more than 4?**
When they make 22.

19 **When does a brave heart turn to stone?**
When it becomes a little bolder (boulder).

20 **When is a hat not a hat?**
When it becomes a girl.

21 **When is a man like a pony?**
When he is a little hoarse (horse).

22 **When is a chair like a kind of material?**
When it is sat in (satin).

23 **When is a man in love like a tailor?**
When he is pressing his suit.

24 **When is a soldier not a complete soldier?**
When he is in quarters.

25 **When is a ship at sea not on water?**
When it is on fire.

26 **When is a man where he never is and never could be?**
When he is beside himself.

27 **When a boy falls into the water, what is the first thing he does?**
Gets wet.

28 **When is money damp?**

When it's due (dew) in the morning and it's missed (mist) at night.

29 **When is a window like a star?**

When it is a skylight.

30 **When are two apples alike?**

When they are paired (pared).

31 **When is a baby like a china cup?**

When it's a-teething (a tea thing).

32 **When is a bald-headed man most likely to be reminded of his youth?**

When he thinks of his top.

33 **When is a boat like a heap of snow?**

When it's adrift (a drift).

34 **When do broken bones begin to make themselves useful?**

When they begin to knit.

35 **When are houses like books?**

When they have stories in them.

36 **When is a boy not a boy?**

When he's a bed (abed).

37 **When does a candle get angry?**

When it is put out or when it flares up.

?

38 When was beef the highest it has ever been?

When the cow jumped over the moon.

39 When does a cow change places with her keeper?

When she bellows, because then she is a cowherd
(cow heard).

40 When is a chair treated most spitefully?

When you have it caned simply because it can't bear you.

41 When is a chicken's neck like a bell?

When it's rung (wrung) for dinner.

42 When is a man both hospitable and a cheat at the same time?

When he takes you in.

43 When is a chicken a glutton?

When he takes a peck at a time.

44 When is a clock on the stairs dangerous?

When it runs down and strikes one.

45 When can your coat pocket be empty and yet have something in it?

When it has a hole in it.

46 When is coffee like the surface of the earth?

When it is ground.

47 When has a man the right to scold his coffee?

When he has more than sufficient grounds.

48 When are cooks most cruel?

When they beat the eggs and whip the cream.

49 When does a cook break the game laws?

When she poaches some eggs.

50 When is corn like a question?

When you are popping it.

51 When a man complains that his coffee is cold, what does his wife do?

She makes it hot for him.

52 When is an elevator not an elevator?

When it is going down.

53 When does a man shave himself with copper?

When he cuts off his hair (heir) with a penny.

54 When are eyes not eyes?

When the wind makes them water.

55 When a lady faints, what number will restore her?

You must bring her 2.

56 When does a farmer perform miracles?

When he turns his horse to grass and turns his cows to pasture.

57 When does a farmer act with cruelty to his corn?

When he pulls its ears.

58 **When is a woman dressed like an Indian war chief in all his feathers?**
When she is dressed to kill.

59 **When are you most nearly related to a fish?**
When your grandmother is a dear old soul (sole).

60 **When are oysters like fretful people?**
When they're in a stew.

61 **When is a fruit stalk like a strong swimmer?**
When it stems the currants (currents).

62 **When is an apple not an apple?**
When it's a crab.

63 **When can you be said to have four hands?**
When you double your fists.

64 **When is your hair like a stick of wood?**
When it's knotted.

65 **When is a man like frozen rain?**
When he is hail (hale).

66 **When is a bright idea like a clock?**
When it strikes one.

67 **When is a girl's arm not an arm?**
When it's a little bare (bear).

68 When is a lawyer like a crow?

When he wishes his cause (caws) to be heard and gets raving (raven) mad about it.

69 When does a ship tell a falsehood?

When she lies at the wharf.

70 When did the lobster blush?

When it saw the salad dressing.

71 When is music like an icy pavement?

When you will B flat if you don't C sharp.

72 When is music like vegetables?

When there are two beats (beets) to a measure.

73 When is a nose not a nose?

When it is a little radish (reddish).

74 When is the water in the ocean most likely to escape?

When it's only half-tied (half-tide).

75 When can you say that a public speaker is a thief of lumber?

When he takes the floor.

76 When is a plant like a pig?

When it begins to root.

77 When does the hotel boy become a porter?

When he reaches the lugg-age.

78 When does a joke become a father?
When the catch line becomes apparent (a parent).

79 When does the rain become too familiar to a lady?
When it begins to pat her (patter) on the back.

80 When is a rope like a boy at school?
When it is taut (taught).

81 When is a piece of wood like a queen?
When it is made into a ruler.

82 When is a schoolboy like a postage stamp?
When he is licked and put in a corner to make him stick to his letters.

83 When is a sailor not a sailor?
When he's a board (aboard).

84 When is a ship in love?
When she seeks a mate.

85 When is a Scotchman like a donkey?
When he strolls along his banks and braes (brays).

86 When a shoemaker is ready to make a shoe, what is the first thing he looks for?
The last.

87 When is a shoemaker like a doctor?
When he is heeling (healing).

88 When is silence likely to get wet?

When it reigns (rains).

89 When you go to a store for ten cents' worth of very sharp tacks, for what do you want them?

For ten cents.

90 When is a sick man a contradiction?

When he is an impatient patient.

91 When are you not yourself?

When you are a little pale (pail).

92 When does a man sneeze seven times?

When he can't help it.

93 When a small boy gets his stockings on wrong side out, what surprising thing does his mother do?

She turns the hose on him.

94 When are tailors and house agents both in the same business?

When they gather the rents.

95 When does a tailor serve his customers both well and ill?

When he gives them fits.

96 When do your teeth take over the functions of your tongue?

When they start to chatter.

97 When is a man greatly tickled but doesn't laugh?

When a fly lights on his nose.

98 **When a tree is chopped down, why has it no reason to complain?**

Because it was axed (asked).

99 **When is a trunk like two letters of the alphabet?**

When it is empty (MT).

100 **When are potatoes used for mending clothes?**

When they are put in patches.

101 **When is a loaded express wagon like a forest?**

When it is full of trunks.

102 **When is a wall like a fish?**

When it is scaled.

103 **When is it socially correct to serve milk in a saucer?**

When you give it to a cat.

104 **When is a restaurant like a woodshed?**

When it is a chop-house.

105 **When do elephants have eight feet?**

When there are two of them.

106 **When butter is worth twenty cents a pound, what will a ton of coal come to?**

Ashes.

107 **When is a river like the letter T?**

When it must be crossed.

108 **When is the wind like a woodchopper?**
When it is cutting.

109 **When does an automobile go exactly as fast as a train?**
When it is on the train.

110 **When may we say a student is very hungry?**
When he devours his books.

111 **When does a bather capture a large bird?**
When he takes a duck in the water.

112 **When is an altered dress like a secret?**
When it is let out.

113 **When is a house like a crow?**
When it has wings.

114 **When is the time on a clock like the whistle on a train?**
When it's two to two (toot-toot-too).

115 **When you look around you on a cold winter morning, what do you see on every hand?**
A glove.

116 **When should any pig be able to write?**
When he has been turned into a pen.

117 **When is a piece of string like a stick of wood?**
When it has knots in it.

118 **When is a horse like a house?**
When it has blinds on.

NAME THE NATIONS

1 **What country suggests a straw hat?**
   Panama.

2 **What country expresses anger?**
   Ireland.

3 **What country mourns?**
   Wales.

4 **What country has a good appetite?**
   Hungary.

5 **What country is popular on Thanksgiving Day?**
   Turkey.

6 **What country is a coin?**
   Guinea.

7   **What country does the cook use?**
    Greece.

8   **What country is good for skaters?**
    Iceland.

9   **What country is useful at mealtime?**
    China.

BIBLE
RIDDLES

1   **When were automobiles mentioned in the Bible?**
When Elijah went up on high.

2   **Who was the most successful doctor in the Bible?**
Job, because he had the most patients (patience).

3   **Who was the most popular actor in the Bible?**
Samson. He brought down the house.

4   **When is money first mentioned in the Bible?**
When the dove brought the "green" back to the ark.

5   **When is high finance first mentioned in the Bible?**
When Pharaoh's daughter took a little profit (prophet)
from the bulrushes.

6   **At what time of day was Adam created?**
A little before Eve.

7 When was radio first mentioned in the Bible?

When the Lord took a rib from Adam and made it into a loud speaker (Eve).

8 What evidence does the Bible give to show that Adam and Eve were rather noisy?

They raised Cain.

9 Why couldn't Eve have the measles?

Because she'd Adam (had 'em).

10 What animal took the most baggage into the ark, and what animals the least?

The elephant took his trunk, but the fox and the rooster took only a brush and a comb between them.

11 What did the cat say when the ark landed?

Is that Ararat?

12 What simple affliction caused the death of Samson?

He died of fallen arches.

13 Who was the best financier in the Bible?

Noah. He floated his stock (animals) while the whole world was in liquidation.

14 What man in the Bible had no parents?

Joshua, the son of Nun.

15 Why should we be encouraged by the story of Jonah and the whale?

Because Jonah was down in the mouth, but came out all right.

16 **Who was the straightest man in the Bible?**
Joseph, because Pharaoh made a ruler out of him.

17 **Who is the smallest man mentioned in the Bible?**
Bildad, the Shuhite (shoe-height).

18 **Why was Lot's wife turned into a pillar of salt?**
Because she was dissatisfied with her Lot.

19 **What was it that Adam and Eve never had and yet they gave to their children?**
Parents.

20 **What was the longest day in the Bible?**
When there was no Eve in it.

21 **Did Eve ever have a date with Adam?**
No; it was an apple.

22 **How long did Cain hate his brother?**
As long as he was Abel.

23 **Who in the Bible was the champion runner of all time?**
Adam. He was the first in the human race.

24 **What did the Egyptians do when it got dark?**
They turned on the Israelites.

25 **Who in the Bible was the first and the largest guardian of another person?**
The whale. He brought up Jonah.

26 **What did they use to do arithmetic with in Bible times?**
The Lord told them to multiply on the face of the earth.

27 **When was tennis first mentioned in the Bible?**
When Joseph served in Pharaoh's court.

28 **What was the first theatrical venture in the Bible?**
When Eve appeared for Adam's benefit.

29 **When was the first meat mentioned in the Bible?**
Noah took Ham into the ark.

30 **When was medicine first mentioned in the Bible?**
When the Lord gave Moses two tablets.

31 **What was the first gift mentioned in the Bible?**
Eve presented Adam with a cane (Cain).

32 **Why did Adam bite the apple?**
Because he didn't have a knife.

33 **How do we know that Noah was preceded from the ark by at least three other people?**
Because the Bible says that Noah came forth (fourth).

34 **Why was the giant Goliath very much astonished when David hit him with a stone?**
Because such a thing had never before entered his head.

35 **What sentence of three words which read the same backward and forward did Adam use when he introduced himself to Eve?**
"Madam, I'm Adam."

36 Do you know about the baseball game in the Bible?

Eve stole first; Adam stole second; Rebecca walked to the well with the pitcher; then Gideon rattled the pitchers; Goliath was put out by David; and the prodigal son made a home run.

37 Why didn't Noah catch more fish than he did during the voyage of the ark?

Because he had only two worms.

38 How were the Egyptians paid for the goods taken by the Israelites when they fled from Egypt?

The Egyptians received a check on the Bank of the Red Sea.

39 Where was Noah when the light went out?

In d-ark.

40 How was Ruth rude to Boaz?

She pulled his ears and trod on his corn.

41 Who was the strongest man in the Bible?

Jonah, because the whale couldn't hold him even after he got him down.

42 What proof have we that there was sewing in the time of David?

He was hemmed in on all sides.

43 In what place did a rooster in the Bible crow where all the people in the world could hear him?

In the ark.

44 **What reason is there to think that Moses wore a wig?**

Because he was sometimes seen with Aaron (hair on), and sometimes without.

45 **Which are the two smallest things mentioned in the Bible?**

The widow's mite and the wicked flee (flea).

46 **Who was the older, David or Goliath?**

David must have been, because he rocked Goliath to sleep.

HISTORY'S
A MYSTERY

1   **Why are the Middle Ages called the Dark Ages?**
Because there were so many Knights (nights) in them.

2   **What famous ruler of ancient Greece would you mention when asking someone to put some coal on the fire?**
Philip the Great (Fill up the grate).

3   **Why did Henry VIII differ from other husbands?**
Because he married his wives first and asked (axed) them afterwards.

4   **What is history's favorite fruit?**
Dates.

5   **Why was the death of John Huss, who was burned at the stake, preferable to that of King Charles I, who was beheaded?**
Because a hot steak is better than a cold chop.

6 **What letter of the alphabet is most like a Roman emperor?**

The C's are (Caesar).

7 **Why did William Tell shudder when he shot the apple from his son's head?**

Because it was an arrow (a narrow) escape for his son.

8 **Why is the history of England like a wet season?**

Because it is so full of rains (reigns).

9 **When could the British Empire be purchased for the smallest amount?**

When King Richard III offered his kingdom for a horse.

SECRETS OF THE SEAS

1 What is the most insurgent sea?

2 What is a sea that is good and safe?

3 What is the calmest sea?

4 What is a very old sea?

5 What sea shows an orderly sequence of events?

6 What sea is always prim and precise?

7 What sea adds a nice flavor to food?

8 What sea is it that has nearly finished its schooling?

9 What sea is it that breaks away?

10 What sea is very choosy?

11 What sea shuts itself apart from the world?

12 What sea follows as a result of something that has gone before?

13 What sea is very harsh and stern?

1 Sedition   2 Security   3 Serenity   4 Senility   5 Series
6 Sedate 7 Seasoning 8 Senior 9 Secession 10 Selectivity
11 Seclusion   12 Sequence   13 Severity

HOW
CAN
THIS
BE?

1   **Sam Patch always goes up to the tallest trees, takes off his boots and jumps over them. How can this be?**

He just jumps over his boots.

2   **Down south, it is said, the mosquitoes are so large that a good many of them weigh a pound, and they sit on the logs and bark when people go by. How can this be?**

A good many of them taken together <u>would</u> weigh a pound, and they sit on the bark (of trees).

3   **A doctor had a brother who went out West. But the man who went out West had no brother. How can this be?**

The doctor was a lady doctor.

4   **Two men, with their two wives and two sons, are related to each other as follows: The men are each other's fathers and sons, their wives' fathers and husbands, and their children's fathers**

117 ?

and grandfathers. The women are the children's mothers and sisters; and the boys are uncles to each other. How can this be?

The two men had been widowers, and married each other's daughters.

5   A train ran off a big bridge recently and no one was killed or injured. How can this be?

It ran off the bridge at one end as usual and went on its way along the tracks.

6   Three men are under an umbrella, but none of them gets wet. How can this be?

It isn't raining.

7   There was a carpenter who made a cupboard door which proved to be too big. He cut it, and unfortunately then he cut it too little. He thereupon cut it again and made it fit beautifully. How can this be?

He didn't cut it enough the first time. He cut it too little.

8   The schoolteacher and his daughter, the minister's wife and the minister, are out walking in the woods. They find a bird's nest with four eggs in it. Each of them takes out an egg and yet one egg is left in the nest. How can this be?

There were only three people, because the minister's wife was the schoolteacher's daughter.

ANIMAL CRACKERS

1 **What animal are you when you have a cold?**
Horse.

2 **What animals are in all banks?**
Doe and bucks.

3 **What animal is on every legal document?**
A seal.

4 **What animal is in every baseball game?**
A bat. (Yes, a bat is an animal.)

5 **What animal needs clothing, poor thing?**
Bear (bare).

6 **What animal never plays fair?**
Cheetah (cheater).

7   **What animal is nearest to your brain?**
    Hare (hair).

8   **What animal do you need when you are driving a car?**
    A good steer.

9   **What animal is your girl-friend?**
    Deer.

10 **What animal is tiresomely talkative?**
    Boar.

11 **What animal has the most brains of any?**
    A hog, because he has a hogshead full of them.

12 **Why is the camel so easily angered?**
    Because he always has his back up.

13 **When is a donkey spelled with one letter?**
    When it's U, dear.

14 **What two animals go with you everywhere?**
    Your calves.

15 **What animals do you find in the clouds?**
    Reindeer (rain, dear).

16 **What animal would you like to be on a very cold day?**
    A little otter (hotter).

17 **What farm animal is very much like a cannibal?**
    A cow, because it always wants to eat its fodder (father).

18 Which animal is the heaviest in all creation?

A led (lead) horse.

19 What well-known animal drives an automobile?

A road hog.

?

WHAT
IS IT?

1 **What is it that has eyes but can't see?**
A potato.

2 **What is it that grows larger the more you take away from it?**
A hole.

3 **What is it that everybody gives but few take?**
Advice.

4 **What is it that is always behind time?**
The back of a watch.

5 **What is it that passes in front of the sun yet casts no shadow?**
The wind.

6 **What is it that is bought by the yard but worn by the foot?**
A carpet.

?

7 As I was going through the woods, I found something, picked it up and couldn't find it, ran home, looked for it, found it, didn't want it and threw it away. What was it?

A thorn in my foot.

8 What is it that is black and white and red all over?

A book.

9 What is it that has a tongue but cannot talk?

A shoe.

10 What valuable thing that he never had and never will have does a man give a woman?

A husband.

11 What is it that has legs but can't walk?

A table or a chair.

12 What is it that lives in winter, dies in summer, and grows with its roots upward?

An icicle.

13 What is it that contains more feet in winter than in summer?

An outdoor skating rink.

14 What is it that you ought to keep after you have given it to someone else?

A promise.

15 What is it that can and does speak in every known language and yet never went to school?

An echo.

16   What is it that will go up a chimney down, but won't go down the chimney up?

An umbrella.

17   What is it that goes all the way from New York to San Francisco without moving an inch?

The road.

18   What is it that everyone in the world is doing at the same time?

Growing older.

19   What is it that is always cracked when it is heard?

A joke.

20   What is it that has two heads, six feet, one tail and four ears?

A man on horseback.

21   What is it that goes farther the slower it goes?

Your money.

22   What is it that may be lost yet at the same time its location may be known?

A needle in a haystack.

23   What is it that never has anything to say, but its action is always directly to the point?

A wasp.

24   What is it that everyone has to catch before he can sing?

His breath.

25 What is it that though dark has done most to enlighten the world?

Ink.

26 What is it that is alive and has only one foot?

A leg.

27 What is it that is always coming but never arrives?

Tomorrow. When it arrives, it is today.

28 What is it that can be broken without being hit or dropped?

Silence.

29 What is it that you need most in the long run?

Your breath.

30 What is it that gets less tired the farther it goes?

An auto wheel.

31 What is it that everybody wants, and yet wants to get rid of as soon as possible?

A good appetite.

32 What is it that works when it plays and plays when it is working?

A fountain.

33 What is it that a man can be that a woman can't?

The father of a family.

34 What is it that always walks with its head downward?

A nail in your shoe.

? 126

35 **What is it that, while it is yours alone, is used much more by other people than by yourself?**

Your name.

36 **What is it that becomes too young the longer it exists?**

A portrait of a person.

37 **What is it that is often given to you, but which you never have, and yet often have to give up?**

A conundrum.

38 **What is it that goes around the house in daytime and lies in a corner at night?**

A broom.

39 **What is it that we never borrow but often return?**

Thanks.

40 **What is it that grows longer the more it is cut?**

A ditch.

41 **What is it we all say we will do, tell others to do, and yet no one has ever done it?**

Stop a minute.

42 **What is it that everyone can divide, but no one can see the place at which it has been divided?**

Water.

43 **What is it that, supposing its greatest length to be nine inches, width four inches, and depth three inches, still contains a solid foot?**

A shoe.

44 **What is it that has eight feet and can sing?**
A quartet.

45 **What is it that goes all day, comes in at night, and stands with its tongue out?**
A wagon.

46 **What is it that we have in December that we don't have in any other month?**
The letter D.

47 **What is it that goes up and never goes down?**
Your age.

48 **What is it that falls often but never gets hurt?**
Snow.

49 **What is it that has eighteen legs and catches flies?**
A baseball team.

50 **What is it that, when once lost, you can never find again?**
Time.

51 **What is it that stays hot in a refrigerator?**
Mustard.

52 **What is it that you cannot see, but is always before you?**
The future.

53 **What is it that runs in and out of town all day and night?**
The road.

WHY
ARE
THEY
ALIKE?

1 Why are authors and chickens alike?
Because both have to scratch for a living.

2 Why are a railroad engine and the family wash alike?
Because both of them go on a line.

3 Why are a bad boy and a dirty rug alike?
Because both of them need a beating.

4 Why are a bruise and a bubble alike?
Because both are caused by a blow.

5 Why are clouds and horseback riders alike?
Because they both hold the rains (reins).

6 Why is a vote in Congress like a cold?
Because sometimes the ayes have it, and sometimes the noes.

Why is the head chef of a big hotel like a man on top of the Washington Monument?

Because they are both in a high culinary (high, cool and airy) situation.

8 Why is a coward like a leaky faucet?

Because both of them run.

9 Why is a steel trap like the measles?

Because it's catching.

10 Why is a bad joke like an unsharpened pencil?

Because it has no point.

11 Why is a baseball umpire like a dog?

Because he wears a muzzle, snaps at flies, and is always chasing fouls (fowls).

12 Why are weathervanes like loafers?

Because they both go around doing nothing.

13 Why is a letter like a bottle of perfume?

Because both are sent (scent).

14 Why is a hat on the head like a bucket full of water?

Because they are both filled to the brim.

15 Why are a hobo and a balloon alike?

Because both are without any visible means of support.

16 Why are a river and a clock alike?

Because neither of them runs without winding.

17 **Why are money and a secret alike?**
Because both of them are hard to keep.

18 **Why are talkative people and male pigs alike?**
Because after a while both of them become bores (boars).

19 **Why are the posts of a gate and vegetable seeds alike?**
Because they both prop-a-gate.

20 **Why is a mouse like hay?**
Because the cat'll (cattle) eat it.

21 **Why is a good architect like a popular actor?**
Because they both draw good houses.

22 **Why is a defeated baseball team like wool?**
Because it is worsted.

23 **Why is a large tree like a trip around the world?**
Because its root (route) is a long one.

24 **Why is riding in an airplane like falling down stairs?**
Because it makes you soar (sore).

25 **Why are some children like flannel?**
Because they shrink from washing.

26 **Why is a sleepless person like a worn piece of cloth?**
Because he has no nap.

27　**Why are sticks of candy like horses?**

Because the more you lick them the faster they go.

28　**Why is a dog biting its tail like a good manager?**

Because he is making both ends meet.

29　**Why is bread like the sun?**

Because it isn't light before it rises.

30　**Why is an empty room like a room full of married people?**

Because there isn't a single person in it.

31　**Why is a bowl of flowers on a table like a speech made on the deck of a ship?**

Because it is a decoration (deck oration).

32　**Why is a bad cold like a great humiliation?**

Because it brings the proudest man to his sneeze (his knees).

33　**Why is a dilapidated house like old age?**

Because its gate (gait) is feeble and its locks are few.

34　**Why is a nail fast in the wall like an old man?**

Because it is in firm (infirm).

35　**Why is a person with rheumatism like a window?**

Because he is full of pains (panes).

36　**Why is greediness like a bad memory?**

Because it is always forgetting (for getting).

? 　132

37 **Why are a blacksmith and a safe, gentle horse alike?**
Because one is a horse-shoer and the other is a sure horse.

38 **Why is a duke like a book?**
Because he has a title.

39 **Why is a loaf of bread four weeks old like a mouse running into a hole in the wall?**
Because you can see its tail (it's stale).

40 **Why is a cat going up three flights of stairs like a high hill?**
Because she's a-mountin' (a mountain).

41 **Why is a plum pudding like the ocean?**
Because it is full of currants (currents).

42 **Why is a crash of thunder like a jeweler?**
Because both make the ear ring.

43 **Why is a baseball game like a pancake?**
Because its success depends on the batter.

44 **Why is a windy orator like a whale?**
Because he often rises to spout.

45 **Why is a healthy boy like the United States?**
Because he has a good constitution.

CAN YOU
FIGURE
THESE OUT?

1   **Why is the figure 9 like a peacock?**
    Because without a tail it is nothing (0).

2   **What figure increases its value by one-half when turned upside down?**
    The figure 6.

3   **Why is an account book like a model agency?**
    Because it is full of figures.

4   **Why should the number 288 never be mentioned in polite company?**
    Because it is too gross (two gross).

5   **Why is twice ten like two times eleven?**
    Because twice ten is twenty, and two times eleven is twenty too (twenty-two).

6   **From what number can you take half and leave nothing?**
    The number 8. Take away the top half and 0 is left.

7   **Add half a score to nothing and what animal does it make?**
    O and X (10) added together make ox.

8   **Add two figures to 19 and make it less than 20.**
    19½.

9   **If a cork and a bottle cost $2.10, and the bottle costs $2.00 more than the cork, what does the cork cost?**
    The cork costs $.05, and the bottle costs $2.05.

10 **What is the difference between 100 and 1,000?**
    Nothing (0).

11 **See if you can put three sixes together so as to make seven.**
    6 6/6.

12 **What fraction, if you turn it upside down, will have exactly the same value as before you turned it upside down?**
    6/9.

13 **What is the difference between twice twenty-two and twice two and twenty?**
    The first is 44, and the second is 24.

14 **What two numbers multiplied together will give you seven?**
    Few people ever seem to think of these two numbers.
    They are 7 and 1.

15   Can you show that eight 8's added together add up to 1,000?

$$\begin{array}{r} 888 \\ 88 \\ 8 \\ 8 \\ 8 \\ \hline 1,000 \end{array}$$

16   Two women went shopping. One spent $10.00 more than the other, and together they spent $40.00. How much money did each of them spend?

One spent $15.00 and the other spent $25.00.

17   If you double a number between 1 and 10, the result will be the same as if you added 2 to it. What is the number?

2.

18   How many times can 19 be subtracted from 190?

Only once, because any later subtractions wouldn't be from 190, but from a smaller number.

19   What three figures multiplied by 4 give 5?

1.25 (1¼).

CATS! CATS! CATS!

1   What cat is fuzzy and looks like a worm?

2   What cat is a cat that flies?

3   What cat is a quiz cat?

4   What cat is a tree?

5   What cat is a wild cat?

6   What cat is a bad cat for the eyes?

7   What cat is a shooting cat?

8   What cat gives you a cold in the head?

9   What cat is a very calamitous cat?

10   What cat is a very violent and destructive cat?

11   What cat is a tool of a scheming person?

12   What cat is a rancher's cat?

13   What cat is a fisherman's cat?

14 What cat is found in a library?
15 What cat is a loud, harsh cry?
16 What cat is a violinist's cat?
17 What cat is a church cat?
18 What cat is a classification?
19 What cat is a waterfall?

1 Caterpillar   2 Catbird   3 Catechism   4 Catalpa
5 Catamount   6 Cataract   7 Catapult   8 Catarrh
9 Catastrophe   10 Cataclysm   11 Catspaw   12 Cattle
13 Catfish   14 Catalogue   15 Caterwaul   16 Catgut
17 Cathedral   18 Category   19 Cataract

RIDDLE
ME
THIS

1 **What amount of money can be divided fifty-fifty between two persons, giving one person a hundred times more than the other?**

Fifty dollars and fifty cents.

2 **There is one thing that no one knows any more about no matter how much it is looked into. What is it?**

A mirror.

3 **A tree, a horn, tongues and laces have to do with something we wear. What is it?**

Shoes.

4 **A man bought two fishes and had three when he got home. How did this happen?**

He had two fishes—and one smelt.

?

5   On which side of a church does a yew tree grow?

On the outside.

6   **The first part of an odd number is removed and it becomes even. What number is it?**

(S)even.

7   **At what time of life does everyone weigh the most?**

When he is the heaviest.

8   **What two vegetables begin and end with the same two letters in the same order?**

Tomato and onion.

9   **Can you name eight different subjects taught in school or college that end in _ics_?**

Economics, ethics, mathematics, physics, mechanics, dramatics, civics, calisthenics.

10 **Soldiers mark time with their feet. What does the same thing with its hands?**

A watch.

11 **Sisters and brothers have I none, but that man's father is my father's son. Who am I looking at?**

My own son.

12 **What miracle happened when Mr. Stone and Mr. Wood stood on a corner and a pretty girl passed by?**

Stone turned to Wood and Wood turned to Stone. Then they both turned to look. The girl turned into a beauty shop.

?

13 Suppose there was a cat in each corner of the room; a cat sitting opposite each cat; a cat looking at each cat; and a cat sitting on each cat's tail. How many cats would there be?

Four. Each cat was sitting on its own tail.

14 A girl had an aunt who was in love. She sent her an animal whose name urged the aunt to run away and get married. The aunt sent her back a fruit that brought the message that this was impossible. What was the animal and what was the fruit?

Antelope (aunt, elope) and canteloupe (can't elope).

15 What are two of the greatest modern miracles?

The deaf-mute who picked up a wheel and spoke, and the blind man who picked up a hammer and saw.

16 A duck, a frog and a skunk went to the circus. Each had to have a dollar to get in. Which got in, and which didn't?

The duck got in because she had a bill. The frog got in on his green-back. But the poor old skunk couldn't get in because he had only a cent (scent), and it was a bad one.

17 Abraham Lincoln was asked how long a man's legs should be to be the most serviceable. What was his answer?

Long enough to reach the ground.

18 Can you tell me of what parentage Napoleon I was?

Of course I can (of Corsican).

19 What is it that stands aloft and regulates our daily program, yet feels no interest in our concerns; directs us when to go and when to come, yet cares not about our actions; often strikes a

143 **?**

heavy blow to urge us on, and we feel no resentment when this reproof is given?

A clock.

20 The king's fool offended him and was condemned to death. The king said: "You have been a good fool, so I will let you choose the manner of your death." What manner of death did the fool choose?

To die of old age.

21 How many eggs can a man eat on an empty stomach?

None. As soon as he begins to eat even one bite of an egg, his stomach is no longer empty.

22 On a clear winter's day, what are the best fishes to fasten together?

Skates, soles and (h)eels.

23 An old woman in a red cloak was crossing a field in which there was a goat. What strange transformations suddenly took place?

The goat turned to butter (butt her) and the old woman became a scarlet runner.

24 Speaking of milk, said the milk bottle, have you heard of the strange case of the Boston baby brought up on elephant's milk?

It was the elephant's baby.

25 Can you spell "blind pig" with two letters?

Pg (pig without an eye).

26 Do you know the difference between a bicycle and a sewing machine?

If you don't, you'd better be careful the next time you go
to buy a bicycle, or they may sell you a sewing machine.

27   **Tell me the name of the oldest whistler in the world, and what tune he whistled?**

The wind, whistling "Over the hills and far away."

28   **How can you tie a cross to a monkey and turn him into a point?**

Add X to ape, and it becomes "apex."

29   **Can you make sense out of the following:**
Yy u r yy u b
I c u r yy 4 me.

Too wise you are, too wise you be,
I see you are too wise for me.

30   **How can you divide seventeen apples absolutely equally among eleven small boys?**

Make the apples into applesauce, and measure it out
very carefully.

31   **There were sixteen ears of corn in a barrel. A rabbit came each night and carried away three ears. How long did it take him to empty the barrel?**

It took him sixteen nights, because each night he carried
away one ear of corn and his own two ears. This made
three ears each night.

32   **Smith bet that he could eat more oysters than Jones. Smith ate ninety in a week, and Jones ate a hundred and one. How many more did Jones eat than Smith?**

Ten. He ate a hundred and won.

33 There is a girl in a candy store in Denver who is 6 feet 6 inches tall, has a waist measure of 42 inches, and wears number 12 shoes. What do you think she weighs?

She weighs candy.

34 Write down VOLIX, and ask a friend how to pronounce it.

Volume nine (Vol. IX).

35 Mr. Brown said: "I could make a success in my business only by reversing the usual rule. I had to start at the top and work down." What is Mr. Brown's business?

He is a paperhanger.

36 How might you be completely sleepless for seven days and still not lack any rest?

By sleeping nights.

37 How can you make fifteen bushels of corn from one bushel?

By popping it.

38 How can you make sense out of the following sentence: "It was and I said not but"?

"It was AND, I said, not BUT."

39 If a carpenter receives twenty-five cents for sawing a board into two lengths, how much should he receive for sawing the board into four lengths?

Seventy-five cents, because it takes only three saw-cuts.

40 Each of the Flapdoodle brothers has as many sisters as he has brothers. But each of the Flapdoodle sisters has twice as many

brothers as she has sisters. How many brothers and sisters are there in the Flapdoodle family?

Four brothers and three sisters.

41 Can you make the following make sense:

Stand	take	to	world
I	you	throw	the

I understand you undertake to overthrow the underworld.

42 Down on our farm we had a hen that laid an egg six inches long. Can you beat that?

Yes, with an eggbeater.

43 Do you believe in clubs for young people?

Only when kindness fails.

44 What relation is that child to its father who is not its father's own son?

His daughter.

45 Name a carpenter's tool you can spell forward and backward the same way.

Level.

46 "Railroad crossing,
Look out for the cars";
Can you spell it without any R's?

I—t spells "it."

47 Two Indians are standing on a hill, and one is the father of the other's son. What relation are the two Indians to each other?

Husband and wife.

48 Under what circumstances are a builder and a newspaper reporter equally likely to fail?

When they make up stories without foundations.

WHO IN THE WORLD?

1 **Who are the best acrobats in your house?**
The pitchers and the tumblers.

2 **Who is the most painstaking professional man?**
The dentist.

3 **Who in Shakespeare's plays killed the greatest number of chickens?**
Hamlet's uncle, because he "did murder most foul."

4 **Who are the best bookkeepers?**
The people who never return the books you lend them.

5 **Who always has a number of movements on foot for making money?**
A dancing teacher.

6 **Who handles more letters in a day than the busiest of Uncle Sam's postmen?**

A hard-working typesetter.

7 **Who is a man who always finds things dull?**

A scissors grinder.

8 **Who dares to sit before the Queen of England with his hat on?**

Her chauffeur.

9 **Who always goes to bed with his shoes on?**

A horse.

CHARADE RIDDLES

Written charades are very much like those you act out when you play the game of charades at a party. The answer to each is a word, and the charade itself describes each syllable of the word. The word "charade" comes from the Spanish <u>charrada</u>, which means the speech of a clown. Charades are composed in both prose and verse. Here are some prose ones for you to try:

1 My first is company; my second is a veiled lady who shuns company; my third assembles company; and my whole amuses company.

Co-nun-drum.

2 My first is a number; my second is found in the head; my third is what my second does; and my whole is an American state.

Tennessee (ten-eye-see).

3 My first is something you should do; my second is an

exclamation; my third is a great crowd of people; my fourth is a wormlike fish; and my whole is something you ride in.

Automobile (ought-oh-mob-eel).

4 Without my first, my second could never have existed, and my whole is as old as creation.

Sun-day.

5 My first is used in driving a horse; my second is needy; my third is a boy's name; and my whole is a bird.

Whip-poor-will.

6 My first means equality; my second inferiority; and my whole superiority.

Match-less.

7 In my first, my second sat; my third and fourth I ate.

In-sat-i-ate.

8 My first is a pronoun; my second is used at weddings; and my whole is a fish.

Her-ring.

9 My first is a farm animal; my second is another animal. My second worried my first, and thus proved himself to be my whole.

Bull-dog.

10 My first is a vehicle; my second is a preposition; and my whole is a cozy part of a ship.

Cab-in.

11 My first is a kitchen utensil; my second is a big body of water; and my whole is a well-known flower.

Pansy (pan-sea).

12 My first is a vehicle; my second is what the United States is; and my whole is a flower.

Car-nation.

13 My first is a pronoun; my second is not high; my third we all must do; my fourth is a plural pronoun; and my whole is musical.

Melodious—me-low-die-us.

14 My first is found in every country of the globe; my second is what we all should be; and my whole is the same as my first.

Man-kind.

RHYMED
CHARADES

1   My first some gladly take
  Entirely for my second's sake;
  But few, indeed, will ever care
  Both together ever to bear.

  Misfortune (Miss-fortune).

2   My first is a tool,
  My second a coin;
  My whole is speech that's sometimes annoying.

  Accent (Ax-cent).

3   My first is what you're doing now,
  My second is obtained from stone;
  Before my whole you often stand,
  But mostly when you're all alone.

  Looking-glass.

4 My first's an ugly insect,
   My second, an ugly brute;
   My whole's an ugly phantom,
   Which nought can please or suit.

   Bug-bear.

5 My first is what,
   My second is not,
   And my whole you put in a corner.

   A whatnot.

6 My number, definite and known,
   Is ten times ten, told ten times o'er;
   Though half of me is one alone,
   And half exceeds all count and score.

   Thou-sand.

7 My first of anything is half,
   My second is complete;
   And so remains until once more
   My first and second meet.

   Semi-circle.

8 My first I hope you are,
   My second I see you are,
   My whole I know you are.

   Wel-come.

9 Without my first you'd look very strange,
   My second we all want to be;
   My whole is what many a lady has worn
   At a dance or a party or tea.

   Nose-gay.

? 156

10 My first is myself in a short little word,
    My second's a plaything, and you are my third.

    Idol (I-doll).

11 My first is a circle, my second a cross,
    If you meet with my whole, look out for a toss.

    Ox.

12 My first is a part of the day,
    My last a conductor of light;
    My whole to take measure of time
    Is useful by day and by night.

    Hour-glass.

HOW
COME?

1 **How many girls would it take, standing in single file, to reach from Fort Worth to Dallas, which is about thirty miles?**

About thirty girls, because a miss is as good as a mile.

2 **How far can you go into the woods?**

As far as the middle. After that, you will be going out.

3 **How can five people divide five cookies so that each gets a cookie and yet one cookie remains on the plate?**

The last person takes the plate with the cookie.

4 **How would you most easily swallow a door?**

By bolting it.

5 **How does the fireplace feel when you fill it with coal?**

Grateful (grate full).

6 **How can we know that a lion has whiskers?**
Because he is so often bearded in his den.

7 **How would you most easily increase the speed of a slow boat?**
By making it fast to the dock.

8 **How can bookkeeping be taught in a lesson of three words?**
Never lend them.

9 **How can you keep a rooster from crowing on Sunday?**
By getting him stuffed on Saturday night.

10 **How can you make a thin child fat?**
Throw him into the air and he'll come down plump.

11 **How can you make a coat last?**
Make the trousers and vest first.

12 **How do we know that a dentist is unhappy in his work?**
Because he looks down in the mouth.

13 **How would you say in one word that you had just encountered a doctor?**
Met-a-physician.

14 **How do locomotives hear?**
Through their engineers (engine-ears).

15 **How can a place be lighted by a thousand fires, yet give no warmth, neither can we put them out?**
When it is lighted by fireflies.

?

16 How many bushel baskets full of earth can you take out of a hole that is three feet square and three feet deep?

None. The earth has already been taken out.

17 How can you shoot one hundred and twenty hares at one shot?

Fire at a wig.

18 How can hunters best find their game in the woods?

By listening to the bark of the trees.

19 How can you best learn the value of money?

By trying to borrow some.

20 How many of his relations live on a landlord's property?

His ten aunts (tenants).

21 How can you always have what you please?

By always being pleased with what you have.

22 How does a boy feel who has been kept after school for bad spelling?

Simply spell-bound.

23 How would you speak of a tailor when you couldn't remember his name?

As Mr. So-and-so (Sew-and-sew).

24 How can you make a tall man short?

By borrowing a lot of money from him.

25 How can a man with false teeth have a new set of teeth inserted free of charge?

By kicking a bulldog. The bulldog will quickly insert his teeth.

26   How can you change a pumpkin into a squash?

Throw it up high and it will come down a squash.

27   How long will an eight-day clock run without winding?

It won't run at all without winding.

28   How is it possible to get up late in the day and yet rise when the rays of the sun first come through the window?

By sleeping in a bedroom facing the west.

29   How does a sailor know there is a man in the moon?

Because he has been to see (sea).

30   How many sticks go to the building of a crow's nest?

None. They are all carried.

31   How long is a string?

Just twice as long as half its length.

32   How can a cat go into a cellar with four feet and come out with eight?

It catches a mouse.

MISS TREES
(MYSTERIES)

1 **What tree does everyone carry in his hand?**
Palm.

2 **What tree is a kind of grasshopper?**
Locust.

3 **What tree is an inlet of the sea?**
Bay.

4 **What tree is like an old joke?**
Chestnut.

5 **What tree is always very sad?**
Weeping willow.

6 **What tree is a good-looking girl?**
Peach.

7   What tree is a carpenter's tool?
    Plane.

8   What tree grows at the seaside?
    Beech.

9   What is the most important of all the trees in history?
    Date.

10 What tree always has a neat appearance?
    Spruce.

11 What tree goes into ladies' winter coats?
    Fir (fur).

12 What tree is always longing for someone?
    Pine.

13 What tree is one of your parents?
    Pawpaw (Papa).

14 What trees are nice to kiss?
    Tulip (trees).

15 What tree is always in high favor?
    Poplar (popular).

16 What trees are left behind after a fire?
    Ashes.

17 What tree is often found in bottles?
    Cork.

18 **What tree is it that is made of stone?**
Lime.

19 **What tree always is two people?**
Pear (pair).

20 **What tree is a fish?**
Bass(wood).

21 **What tree is the straightest tree that grows?**
Plum (plumb).

22 **What tree is older than most other trees?**
Elder.

23 **What tree is often found in people's mouths?**
Gum.

24 **What tree runs over the meadows and pastures?**
Yew (ewe).

25 **What tree is an awful grouch?**
Crab.

26 **What tree is worn in the Orient?**
Sandal (wood).

27 **What tree suggests a color?**
Redwood.

28 **What tree suggests a fabric?**
Cotton(wood).

DICTIONARY NATIONS

1 What nation is a fortune-telling nation?

2 What nation is tough on rats?

3 What nation is a fanciful nation?

4 What nation is dreaded by schoolboys?

5 What nation is a religious nation?

6 What nation is one of the most resolute nations?

7 What nation is a dramatic nation?

8 What nation is one that has come to an end?

9 What nation is a crazy nation?

10 What nation is a political nation?

11 What nation is a bewildered nation?

12 What nation is one that travelers often want?

13 What nation is a disliked nation?

?

14 What nation is a teacher's nation?

15 What nation is a very bright nation?

16 What nation is a leaning nation?

17 What nation produces the greatest number of marriages?

18 What nation scatters things far and wide?

19 What nation is a tyrant?

20 What is a very unfair nation?

21 What nation is a scheming nation?

22 What nation is at the peak?

23 What nation is a lazy nation?

24 What nation is a disrespectful nation?

1 Divination	2 Extermination	3 Imagination
4 Examination	5 Denomination	6 Determination
7 Impersonation	8 Termination	9 Hallucination
10 Nomination	11 Consternation	12 Destination
13 Abomination	14 Explanation	15 Illumination
16 Inclination	17 Fascination	18 Dissemination
19 Domination	20 Discrimination	21 Machination
22 Culmination	23 Procrastination	24 Insubordination

SEE
ANY
RESEMBLANCE?

1 **Why do good resolutions resemble ladies who faint in church?**
Because the sooner they are carried out the better.

2 **Why does the Fourth of July resemble an oyster stew?**
Because we enjoy it most with crackers.

3 **Why does a good gardener resemble a detective-story writer?**
Because he works hard at his plot.

4 **Why does a hat resemble a king?**
Because it has a crown.

5 **Why do laws resemble the ocean?**
Because the most trouble is caused by the breakers.

6 **Why does opening a letter resemble a strange way of entering a room?**
Because it is breaking through the ceiling (sealing).

?

7   Why does a young man trying to raise a moustache resemble a cow's tail?

Because he is growing down.

8   Why does a love of the ocean resemble curiosity?

Because it has sent many a boy to sea (see).

9   Why does a pig in a parlor resemble a fire?

Because the sooner it's put out the better.

10   Why does a farmer guiding a plow resemble an ocean liner?

Because one sees the plow, and the other plows the sea.

11   Why does a postage stamp resemble an obstinate donkey?

Because the more you lick it the more it sticks.

12   Why does a New Year's resolution resemble an egg?

Because it is so easily broken.

13   Why does a man riding swiftly uphill resemble one who gives a young dog to his girl-friend?

Because he gives a gallop up (gives a gal a pup).

14   Why does a person with his eyes closed resemble a bad schoolteacher?

Because he keeps his pupils in darkness.

15   Why does your shadow resemble a false friend?

Because it only follows you in sunshine, and deserts you when you're under a cloud.

?

16　**Why does a bootblack resemble the sun?**
Because he shines for all.

17　**Why does an old man's head resemble a song sung by a very bad singer?**
Because it is often terribly bawled (bald).

18　**Why does snow resemble a maple tree?**
Because it leaves in the early Spring.

19　**Why do sentries resemble day and night?**
Because when one comes the other goes.

20　**Why does an opera singer resemble a drugstore soda jerker?**
Because she gives out high screams (ice creams).

21　**Why do the fixed stars resemble paper?**
Because they are stationary (stationery).

22　**Why do stars resemble an old barn?**
Because there are R-A-T-S in both of them.

23　**Why does sympathy resemble a game of blindman's buff?**
Because it is a fellow feeling for a fellow mortal.

24　**Why does an oyster resemble a man of good sense?**
Because it knows how to keep its mouth shut.

HEADS
I WIN

1 What is a head that glows?

2 What is a head that is bound to have its own way?

3 What is a head that every football player knows?

4 What is a head that pains?

5 What is a head that makes progress?

6 What is a head that's good to eat?

7 What is a head that chases after people to do them no good?

8 What is a head that you see in newspapers?

9 What is a head that is the center of operations?

10 What is a head that seats you in a hotel dining room?

11 What is a head that flows rapidly?

12 What is a head that Indians like to wear?

1 Headlight 2 Headstrong 3 Headgear 4 Headache
5 Headway 6 Headcheese 7 Headhunter 8 Headlines
9 Headquarters   10 Head waiter   11 Headwater
12 Headdress

DOWN
THE
GARDEN
PATH

1 **What vegetable is measured like diamonds?**
   Carrots (carats).

2 **What fruit is never found singly?**
   A pear (pair).

3 **What vegetable hurts when you step on it?**
   Corn.

4 **What fruit will shock you if you touch it?**
   Currant (current).

5 **What vegetable do you find in crowded streetcars and buses?**
   Squash.

6 **What vegetable makes up the alphabet?**
   Lettuce (letters).

?

7 **What vegetable has the most money in it?**
Mint.

8 **What vegetable needs a plumber?**
Leek.

9 **What fruit is like a book?**
The strawberry, because it is read (red).

10 **What fruit is found on a penny?**
Date.

11 **Why do people preserve vegetables more than they used to?**
Because today they can.

WHAT'S THE GOOD WORD?

1   **What word of six letters contains six words besides itself, without transposing any of its letters?**

Herein—he, her, here, ere, rein, in.

2   **In what common word does the letter O sound like the letter I?**

Women.

3   **Can you name two words that begin with P, in which the P is silent?**

Psalms; pneumonia.

4   **Can you name three common words, each containing a B, in which the B is silent?**

Doubt, debt and subtle.

5   **Can you name a word containing the letter I, in which the I is silent?**

Plaid.

6 **What word, by changing the position of one letter, becomes its opposite?**

United—untied.

7 **What word is it from which the whole may be taken and yet some will be left?**

Wholesome.

8 **What word of five letters has only one left when two letters are subtracted from it?**

St(one).

9 **What word, when deprived of one of its letters, makes you sick?**

(M)usic.

10 **Is there a word in the English language that contains all the vowels?**

Unquestionably.

11 **In a certain word the letter L is in the middle, in the beginning, and at the end. There is only one L in the word. What is this peculiar word?**

The word is "inland." L is in the middle. In is the beginning. And is at the end.

12 **What word of five letters has six left after you take two away?**

Six-ty.

13 **What word of fifteen letters is there from which you can subtract twelve and leave ten?**

Pre-ten-tiousness.

14 Can you think of two eight-letter words, one of which has one syllable and the other five syllables?

Strength and ideality.

15 What word of five syllables is it that, if you take away one syllable, no syllable remains?

Monosyllable. Take away mo, and no-syllable remains.

16 Which word in the English language contains the greatest number of letters?

Antidisestablishmentarianism (28 letters).

17 There is a common word of three syllables from which, if you take away five letters, a male will remain. If you take away four letters, a female will remain. If you take away three, a great man will appear, and the whole word tells you what Joan of Arc was.

Heroine—He, her, hero, heroine.

18 What word of ten letters might be spelled with five?

Expediency—XPDNC.

19 What words can be pronounced quicker and shorter by adding another syllable to them?

The words "quick" and "short."

20 What word of eight letters is there from which you can subtract five and leave ten?

Ten-dency.

21 There are two words in the English language in which the five

179 ?

vowels follow each other in their regular order—A, E, I, O, U. Which words are they?

Facetious and abstemious.

22 **What word of four syllables represents Sin riding on a little animal?**

Synonymous (Sin on a mouse).

23 **What is the longest word in the English language?**

Smiles, because there is a mile between its first and last letter.

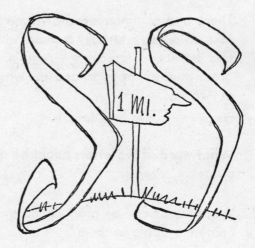

TURN-AROUND
RIDDLES

The answer to each of the following riddles is found by turning around the letters of the first word to form the second.

1 **Can you turn around a portion and get a snare?**

Part—trap.

2 **Can you turn around a short sleep and get a kitchen utensil?**

Nap—pan.

3 **Can you turn around a well-known kind of cheese and get a word meaning "fabricated"?**

Edam—made.

4 **Can you turn around a part of a ship and get a vegetable?**

Keel—leek.

?

5 **Can you turn around a part of a fence and get a prevaricator?**
Rail—liar.

6 **Can you turn around a small one-masted sailboat and get little lakes?**
Sloop—pools.

7 **Can you turn around fate and get a state of mind?**
Doom—mood.

8 **Can you turn around clever and get English trolley cars?**
Smart—trams.

9 **Can you turn around wicked and get wide-awake?**
Evil—live.

10 **Can you turn around a mouthful and get a stopper?**
Gulp—plug.

11 **Can you turn around a strong, sharp taste and get an insect?**
Tang—gnat.

FLOWER RIDDLES

1 **What flower tells what the teacher did when he sat on a tack?**
Rose.

2 **What flowers does everybody have?**
Tulips (two lips).

3 **What flower do unmarried men often lose?**
Bachelor's buttons.

4 **What flower is like a lot of birds?**
Phlox (flocks).

5 **What flower is like a pretty girl who has had a quarrel with her boy-friend?**
Bluebell.

6   **What flower represents what the walls of stage castles are made of?**
Sham-rock.

7   **What flower does every new mother want to listen to?**
Baby's breath.

8   **What flower do some penniless people hope to do?**
Marigold (Marry gold).

9   **What flower is an American pin-up girl?**
American Beauty.

10   **What flower is a wise and experienced person?**
Sage.

11   **What flower is an eyeful?**
Iris.

12   **What flower represents a landlord who shuts off the heat?**
Freesia (freeze you).

13   **What flower resembles a tattered bird?**
Ragged robin.

14   **What flower is just the thing for a girl to wear to a party?**
Lady's slipper.

15   **What flower reminds you of teatime?**
Four o'clock.

16 **What flower is a dressed-up wild animal?**
Dandelion (dandy lion).

17 **What flower is a church official?**
Elder.

18 **What flower resembles the rising sun?**
Morning glory.

19 **What flower is a dear boy?**
Sweet William.

20 **What flower is what pa did when he proposed to ma?**
Aster (asked her).

21 **What flower is most used by cooks?**
Buttercup.

22 **What flower is a parting remark to a friend?**
Forget-me-not.

23 **What flower is worn by the fishermen of Holland?**
Dutchman's breeches.

24 **What flower goes with the easy chair and the paper?**
Dutchman's pipe.

25 **What flower is both pleasant and distasteful at the same time?**
Bittersweet.

26 **What flower reminds you of winter weather?**
Snowdrop.

27 **What flower tells what George Washington was to his country?**
Poppy.

28 **What flower suggests neat lines?**
Primrose (prim rows).

29 **What flower suggests a feline bite?**
Cat-nip.

30 **What flower is a boy's delight in winter?**
Snowball.

31 **If a mercenary man were to ask a girl to marry him, what flower might he name?**
Anemone (any money)?

32 **What is it that is very queer about flowers?**
They shoot before they have pistols (pistils).

33 **What flower most resembles a bull's mouth?**
A cowslip (cow's lip).

34 **What flower, when deprived of one of its letters, is most often used by friends who are separated?**
(P)ink.

35 **What flower do television comedians often rely on?**
Cornflower.

SOME
HARD NUTS
TO CRACK

1 **What nut is found beside the sea?**
   Beechnut.

2 **What nut is a slow-burning nut?**
   Candlenut.

3 **What nut is the staff of life?**
   Breadnut.

4 **What nut is a hot drink?**
   Coconut.

5 **What nut is an uncooked-bread nut?**
   Doughnut.

6 **What nut is made from a product of cows?**
   Butternut.

7 What nut is a girl's name?

Hazelnut.

8 What nut is part of a room?

Walnut (wall nut).

9 What nut is a vegetable?

Peanut.

10 What nut is a box?

Chestnut.

11 What nut is a South American country?

Brazil nut.

12 What nut sounds like a sneeze?

Cashew nut.

13 Why are a walnut and a regiment of soldiers alike?

Because they both have a kernel (colonel).

14 Did you hear about the big accident down at the railroad station?

A train ran over a peanut, a shell exploded, and two kernels (colonels) were crushed.

15 What nut has neither shell nor kernel and does not grow on a tree?

Doughnut.

LET 'ER RIDE!

1 **What two letters express the words "not difficult"?**
EZ (easy).

2 **What two letters express the word "deteriorate"?**
DK (decay).

3 **What number and letter describe a popular outdoor game?**
10 S (tennis).

4 **What two letters describe that which exceeds the required amount?**
XS (excess).

5 **What three letters describe a foe?**
NME (enemy).

6 **What three letters give the name of a midwestern state?**
IOA (Iowa).

7 **What two letters and a number mean to turn aside?**
DV8 (deviate).

8 **What two letters name a climbing plant?**
IV (ivy).

9 **What three letters and a number mean relieve?**
LEV8 (alleviate).

10 **What two letters describe a wormlike fish?**
EL (eel).

11 **What three letters spell something that exists?**
NTT (entity).

12 **What two letters spell barren or bare?**
MT (empty).

13 **What one letter and a number describe a dog?**
K9 (canine).

14 **What two letters spell a word meaning jealousy?**
NV (envy).

15 **What two letters spell a number less than one hundred?**
AT (eighty).

16 **What three letters and a number describe a person who flies an airplane?**
AV8R (aviator).

?

17 **What two letters describe a kind of light gun?**
BB.

18 **What two letters spell a word that means "having to do with art"?**
RT (arty).

19 **What four letters spell a title given to high diplomatic officials?**
XLNC (Excellency).

20 **What one number and one letter spell a raid against the enemy?**
4A (foray).

21 **What two letters spell a girl's name?**
KT, LN and LC (Katie, Ellen and Elsie).

22 **What number and letter spell anticipate?**
4C (foresee).

23 **What are the most forcible three letters in the alphabet?**
NRG (energy).

24 **What two letters spell to do better?**
XL (excel).

25 **What letter and number spell conquered?**
B 10 (beaten).

26 **What letter and number spell having finished a meal?**
E 10 (eaten).

27 **What two letters spell a word meaning some?**
NE (any).

28 **What two letters spell a word meaning try to do?**
SA (essay).

29 **What letter and number mean ahead of or in front of?**
B 4 (before).

30 **What two letters and a number mean to flow forth?**
MN 8 (emanate).

31 **What two letters spell an attractive girl?**
QT (cutie).

32 **What two letters spell a cotton fabric?**
PK (pique).

33 **What two letters spell shabby or ragged?**
CD (seedy).

34 **What two letters spell a seat in church?**
PU (pew).

35 **What two letters spell chilly?**
IC (icy).

36 **What two letters spell an Indian tent?**
TP (tepee).

37 **What two letters spell results?**
FX (effects).

?

38 What three letters spell great happiness?
XTC (ecstasy).

39 What three letters spell a funeral poem?
LEG (elegy).

40 What letters spell not dumb?
Y's (wise).

41 What three letters spell a poet's place of simple pleasures?
RKD (arcady).

42 What letters spell comfort?
E's (ease).

43 What two letters and a number spell a drug?
OP8 (opiate).

44 What letters spell a great deal of water?
C's (seas).

45 What letters spell what bad boys do?
T's (tease).

46 What five letters spell advisability?
XPDNC (expediency).

47 What two letters are a hot condiment?
KN (cayenne).

48 What two letters spell an English county?
SX (Essex).

49 **Like which four letters of the alphabet is a honey-producing insect when he is not feeling too well?**

ACDB (a seedy bee).

50 **How would you say in two letters that you were twice as heavy as a friend?**

IW (I double you).

WATCH YOUR STEP!

1 **What part of a watch supports a flower?**
Stem.

2 **What part of a watch was used before by somebody else?**
Second hand.

3 **What does a watch mark that is read by the secretary at a meeting?**
Minutes.

4 **What part of a watch is something that a tight-rope walker is good at?**
Balance wheel.

5 **What part of a watch is used as tableware?**
Crystal.

6 **What part of a watch is what the palmist studies?**
Hands.

7 **What part of a watch do we use when we greet someone?**
Hour hand.

8 **What part of a watch do women love for ornaments?**
Jewels.

9 **What part of a watch will always give you a cool drink?**
Spring.

10 **What part of a watch sometimes, according to certain people, stops a clock?**
Face.

11 **Why is modesty the strongest characteristic of a watch?**
Because it always keeps its hands before its face and runs down its own works.

12 **Why is a watch like a river?**
Because it won't run long without winding.

13 **Why should a man always wear a watch when he travels in a desert?**
Because every watch has a spring in it.

14 **Why can't a thief steal a watch very easily?**
Because he must take it off its guard.

15 **Why are the hours from one to twelve like good policemen?**
Because they are always on the watch.

?

16 What is it that has a face, but no head; hands, but no feet; yet travels everywhere and is usually running?

A watch.

RIDDLES
IN
RHYME

1   Round as a biscuit, busy as a bee,
    Prettiest little thing you ever did see.

    A watch.

2   A houseful, a roomful,
    Can't catch a spoonful.

    Smoke.

3   What runs, but does not walk,
    Has a tongue, but can't talk?

    A wagon.

4   What is deep as a house.
    And round as a cup,
    And all the king's horses
    Can't draw it up?

    A well.

5   Four jolly men sat down to play,
    And played all night till break of day;
    They played for cash and not for fun,
    With separate scores for everyone,
    Yet when they came to square accounts,
    They all had made quite fair amounts.
    Can you this paradox explain?
    If no one lost, how could all gain?

The four players were musicians in a dance orchestra.

6   I'm the name of a country, and strange, you'll declare,
    If you cut off my head, why, I am still there.
    Take away my tail twice, but nought you will gain,
    For e'en though you do, I still will remain.
    What country am I?

Then, take away A and M, and I still remains.
Siam. Cut off its head—S—and "I am" is still there.

7   The mother of men was a lady whose name
    Read backward or forward, is always the same.

Eve.

8   Sometimes I am very sly,
    Other times a trade I ply;
    Over the billows swift I fly,
    Now, pray tell me, who am I?

Craft.

9   Thirty-two white horses on a red hill,
    Now they go, and now they stand still.

Your teeth.

10   What does a man love more than life?
      Hate more than death or mortal strife?
      That which contented men desire,
      The poor have, the rich require;
      The miser spends, the spendthrift saves,
      And all men carry to their graves?

Nothing.

11   As I was going to St. Ives,
      I chanced to meet nine old wives;
      Each wife had nine sacks,
      Each sack had nine cats,
      Each cat had nine kits.
      Kits, cats, sacks and wives,
      How many were going to St. Ives?

Only one. The old wives were going in the opposite direction.

12   Little Nanny Etticote, in a white petticoat,
      Holding up a bright red rose;
      The longer she stands, the shorter she grows.

A candle.

13   Behind the barn at early morn
      I heard a herald blow his horn.
      His beard was flesh, his mouth was horn,
      The like of him was never born.

A rooster. (Roosters are hatched, not born.)

14   'Tis true I have both face and hands,
      And move before your eye;

201

Yet when I go my body stands,
And when I stand, I lie.

A clock.

15 I claim no magic power,
Yet a fast I can make a feast.
I am never among the first,
But the last I can make the least.

The gust of the wildest storm
I can change to a welcome guest,
In the North or the South I'm unknown,
But am found in the East or the West.

The letter E.

16 I tell heat, and I tell cold,
And they in turn tell me
To go up and down as I am told
They tell me; I agree.

The mercury in a thermometer.

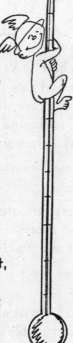

17 When walking through a field of wheat,
I picked up something good to eat,
'Twas neither fish, flesh, fowl nor bone;
I kept it till it ran alone.

An egg that hatched into a chicken.

18 I'm a feeling all persons detest,
Although I'm by everyone felt;
By two letters I'm fully expressed,
But by twice two I always am spelled.

NV—envy.

?

19 There's a word that's composed of three letters alone,
    Which reads backward and forward the same;
    It expresses the sentiments warm from the heart,
    And to beauty lays principal claim.

    Eye.

20 Part of a foot with judgment transpose,
    And the answer you'll find just under your nose.

    Inch—chin.

21 Legs I have, but seldom walk;
    I backbite all, yet never talk.

    A flea.

22 You saw me where I never was,
    And where I could not be;
    And yet within that very place,
    My face you often see.

    A reflection in the mirror.

23 There was a man who was not born,
    His father was not before him;
    He did not live, he did not die,
    His epitaph is not o'er him.
    Who could this have been?

    A man whose name was Nott.

24 Your initials begin with an A,
    You've an A at the end of your name.
    The whole of your name is an A,
    And it's backward and forward the same.

    Anna.

25   Old Mother Twitchhead had but one eye,
     And a long tail, which she let fly;
     Every time she went over a gap,
     She left a bit of her tail in a trap.

     A needle and thread.

26   Those who take me improve, be their task what it may,
     Those who have me are sorrowful through the long day;
     I am hated alike by the foolish and wise,
     Yet without me none ever to eminence rise.

     Pains.

27   Adam and Eve and Pinch Me
     Went down to the river to bathe;
     Adam and Eve were drowned,
     And who do you think was saved?

     Pinch Me! (When your friend answers "Pinch me," go
     right ahead and pinch him, since he asked for it.)

28   Up and down, up and down,
     Touching neither sky nor ground.

     A pump handle.

29   Instead of complaining when it may rain,
     We should do as they do in Spain.
     And what is that?

     Let it rain.

30   It wasn't my sister, nor my brother,
     But still was the child of my father and mother.
     Who was it?

     Myself.

31 We travel much, yet prisoners are,
    And close confined, to boot,
    We with the swiftest horse keep pace,
    Yet always go on foot.

    A pair of spurs.

32 I often murmur, but never weep;
    Lie in bed, but never sleep;
    My mouth is larger than my head,
    In spite of the fact I'm never fed;
    I have no feet, yet swiftly run;
    The more falls I get, move faster on.

    A river.

33 Unable to think, unable to speak,
    Yet I tell the truth to all who peek.

    A pair of scales.

34 Though I dance at a ball,
    I am nothing at all.

    A shadow.

35 Great numbers do our use despise,
    But yet, at last they find,
    Without our help in many things,
    They might as well be blind.

    A pair of spectacles.

36 If a well-known animal you behead,
    Another one you will have instead.

    F—ox.

37 Ever running on my race,
Never staying at one place,
Through the world I make my tour,
Everywhere at the same hour.
If you please to spell my name,
Backward and forward, it's the same.

Noon.

38 What is it that no man ever yet did see,
Which never was, but always is to be?

Tomorrow.

39 I can throw an egg against the wall
And it will neither break nor fall.
How is this?

The wall won't either break or fall.

40 I tremble at each breath of air,
And yet the heaviest burdens bear.

Water.

41 Three of us in six, and five of us in seven,
Four of us in nine, and six in eleven.

Letters.

42 It shoots you when you're looking,
It shoots you when you're not.
This candid instrument, indeed,
Can put you on the spot.

A camera.

43   No need for brush, no need for broom,
     I'm used a lot to tidy a room.

     A vacuum cleaner.

44   You can press your attire,
     When I contact a wire.

     An electric iron.

45   What is it you can touch,
     And also you can feel;
     It has neither size nor shape,
     But just the same, it's real.

     The air.

ADAM AND EVE AND THE APPLE

This is a famous but rather complicated riddle.

A group of friends were discussing the subject of how many apples Adam and Eve ate in the Garden of Eden. The first person to speak was very matter-of-fact and said that it could only have been one apple.

The second person asserted that Adam 8 and Eve ate 2, making a total of 10.

The third person said there was something wrong with that, because Eve 8 and Adam 8 also, making 16.

"But," said another person, "if Eve 8 and Adam 82, that would be a total of 90."

Still another person said: "According to history, Eve 81 and Adam 82. That would total 163."

"But," put in someone else, "don't you see that if Eve 81 and Adam 812, that would make a total of 893."

"According to my figuring," said a college professor, "if Eve 814 Adam and Adam 8124 Eve, that would total 8938."

At that point, they all gave up.

?

DICTIONARY CITIES

1 What is an odd city?

2 What is a weak city?

3 What is a measuring city?

4 What is a lighted city?

5 What is a savage city?

6 What is a very bad city?

7 What is a greedy city?

8 What is a very fast city?

9 What is a bold city?

10 What is a fast-developing city?

11 What is a happy city?

12 What is a quarrelsome city?

13 What is a truthful city?

14 **What is a resilient city?**

15 **What is a genuine city?**

16 **What is a discerning city?**

17 **What is a wise city?**

18 **What is a rural city?**

19 **What is a false city?**

20 **What is an advertiser's city?**

21 **What is a homey city?**

22 **What is a hypocritical city?**

1 Eccentricity   2 Incapacity   3 Capacity   4 Electricity
5 Ferocity   6 Atrocity   7 Rapacity   8 Velocity
9 Audacity   10 Precocity   11 Felicity   12 Pugnacity
13 Veracity   14 Elasticity   15 Authenticity
16 Perspicacity 17 Sagacity 18 Rusticity 19 Mendacity
20 Publicity   21 Domesticity   22 Duplicity

BIRD BAFFLERS

1   **What bird is a letter?**
    Jay.

2   **What bird is essential to eating?**
    Swallow.

3   **What bird is a high dignitary of the church?**
    Cardinal.

4   **What bird is a chessman?**
    Rook.

5   **What good bird deserves another?**
    Tern (turn).

6   **What two birds are foolish?**
    Loons and cuckoos.

7   What bird is a name?
    Robin.

8   What bird is getting run over all the time?
    Rail.

9   What bird can lift the heaviest weight?
    Crane.

10 What is the rudest bird?
    Mockingbird.

11 How do we know that nightingales are very gay birds?
    Because they have a high time after dark.

12 How do canary birds pay their debts?
    By giving their notes.

13 When is a pigeon like a drinking glass?
    When it's a tumbler.

14 Which bird is the lowest-spirited?
    Bluebird.

15 What bird is it that is found in Africa, and though it has wings, can't fly?
    A dead one.

ABBREVIATED STATES

1 **What state is a number?**
Tenn.

2 **What state is a doctor?**
Md.

3 **What state always seems to be in poor health?**
Ill.

4 **What state serves as a source of metal?**
Ore.

5 **What state is the cleanest?**
Wash.

6 **What state is as good as a mile?**
Miss.

7 **What state is to cut long grass?**
   Mo.

8 **What state never forgets itself?**
   Me.

9 **What state is Moslem?**
   Ala.

10 **What state saved Noah and his family?**
    Ark.

11 **What state is an exclamation?**
    O.

12 **What state is a grain?**
    R.I. (Rye).

13 **What state is a fond parent?**
    Pa.

14 **What state is to study carefully?**
    Conn. (Con).

15 **What state is the happiest?**
    Ga. (Gay).

TRANSPOSED TREES

The following words can be rearranged to spell the names of trees. What trees are they?

1	Mile	7	Cared
2	North	8	Cheap
3	Panes	9	Mug
4	Clouts	10	Reap
5	Ample	11	Melon
6	Has	12	Lamp
		13	Lump

1 Lime 2 Thorn 3 Aspen 4 Locust 5 Maple 6 Ash 7 Cedar
8 Peach 9 Gum 10 Pear 11 Lemon 12 Palm 13 Plum

A PENNY
FOR
YOUR
THOUGHTS

1   **What is on a penny that is part of a nail?**
Head.

2   **What is on a penny that is part of a hill?**
Brow.

3   **What is on a penny that Patrick Henry wanted?**
Liberty.

4   **What is on a penny that is slang for conversation?**
Chin.

5   **What is on a penny that is part of a needle?**
Eye.

6   **What is it on a penny that means in favor of, and to rasp?**
Pro–file.

7   What is on a penny that is a narrow piece of land?
    A neck.

8   What are on a penny that are found in post offices?
    Letters.

9   What is on a penny that is part of a river?
    Mouth.

10 What is on a penny that "fresh" people have?
    Cheek.

11 What is on a penny that understands?
    Nose (knows).

12 What is on a penny that is a messenger?
    One sent (cent).

13 What is on a penny that is an ancient weapon?
    Bow.

14 What is on a penny that is part of a book?
    Leaves.

15 What is on a penny that is a policeman?
    Copper.

16 What is on a penny that is a big industrial combination?
    Trust.

17 What is on a penny that is one-third of the world's land surface?
    America.

18 **What is on a penny that is like being married?**
United.

19 **What is on a penny that is a book of the Bible?**
Numbers.

KATE'S
A GOOD
SKATE

1 **What Kate talks and writes a lot?**
Communicate.

2 **What Kate makes things invisible?**
Eradicate.

3 **What Kate is twins?**
Duplicate.

4 **What Kate is always showing the way?**
Indicate.

5 **What Kate finds things for you?**
Locate.

6 **What Kate can't breathe?**
Suffocate.

7   **What Kate likes school?**
Educate.

8   **What Kate is in many newspapers?**
Syndicate.

9   **What Kate is full of advice?**
Advocate.

10 **What Kate is good at getting out of tight places?**
Extricate.

11 **What Kate keeps the machinery going smoothly?**
Lubricate.

12 **What Kate is inclined to be sickly?**
Delicate.

13 **What Kate is always chewing on something?**
Masticate.

14 **What Kate is clever at predicting things?**
Prognosticate.

15 **What Kate consecrates things?**
Dedicate.

16 **What Kate gives up the throne?**
Abdicate.

17 **What two Kates tell fibs?**
Fabricate and Prevaricate.

18 **What Kate is a good peacemaker?**
Placate.

19 **What Kate is always leaving places?**
Vacate.

20 **What Kate justifies people?**
Vindicate.

21 **What Kate is always disapproving?**
Deprecate.

22 **What Kate gets people in trouble?**
Implicate.

RIDDLES
WITH
DUMB
ENDINGS

1 **What is dumb but knowing?**
   Wisdom.

2 **What is dumb but liberty-loving?**
   Freedom.

3 **What is dumb and also tiresome?**
   Boredom.

4 **What is dumb and infrequent?**
   Seldom.

5 **What is dumb but full of high public officers?**
   Officialdom.

6 **What is dumb but sacrifices itself for ideals?**
Martyrdom.

7 **What is dumb and ruled by a powerful monarch?**
Kingdom.

JUST
DUCKY

1 **Why does a duck go in the water?**

For diverse (diver's) reasons.

2 **Why does he come out?**

For sundry (sun—dry) reasons.

3 **What does every duckling become when it first takes to the water?**

It becomes wet.

4 **Why does a duck who needs some money come out of the water?**

To make a run on the bank.

5 **When a farm woman was asked how many ducks she had, she replied: "As they all ran down the path, I saw there was a duck in front of two ducks, a duck behind two ducks, and a duck between two ducks." How many ducks were there?**

Three ducks, one after the other.

6 **What is the difference between a duck with one wing and one with two?**

Merely a difference of a pinion (opinion).

7 **What is the difference between a duck and a ballet dancer?**

One goes quack on its beautiful eggs, and the other goes quick on her beautiful legs.

8 **What is the difference between a man dodging boots that are being thrown at him and a man chasing a flock of ducks out of his pond?**

One ducks the shoes, and the other shoos the ducks.

DO
YOU KNOW
YOUR
AUNTS?

1   **What aunt is a traveling aunt?**
    Itinerant.

2   **What aunt is a sweet-smelling aunt?**
    Fragrant.

3   **What aunt is a despotic aunt?**
    Tyrant.

4   **What aunt is a vagabond aunt?**
    Vagrant.

5   **What aunt is a schoolteacher aunt?**
    Pedant.

6   **What aunt is a hard, unyielding aunt?**
    Adamant.

7 **What aunt is a zestful aunt?**
Piquant.

8 **What aunt is a conspicuous aunt?**
Flagrant.

9 **What aunt is a dangerous aunt?**
Malignant.

10 **What aunt is a bossy aunt?**
Dominant.

11 **What aunt is a calculating aunt?**
Accountant.

12 **What aunt is always put out about something?**
Indignant.

13 **What aunt is an uninformed aunt?**
Ignorant.

14 **What aunt is a beggar aunt?**
Mendicant.

15 **What aunt is a prevailing aunt?**
Predominant.

16 **What aunt is an inharmonious aunt?**
Discordant.

17 **What aunt is an impertinent aunt?**
Flippant.

18 **What aunt makes good jelly?**
Currant.

19 **What aunt is like a still pond?**
Stagnant.

20 **What are the biggest kind of aunts?**
Giants.

21 **What aunt provides a place for you to eat?**
Restaurant.

REAL CITIES

1 What city is a sofa?

2 What city is a very hard substance?

3 What city is found in the library?

4 What city is a kind of paper?

5 What city is an improvement on Noah's boat?

6 What city is a small stone?

7 What city is a good cigar?

8 What city is a briny body of water?

9 What city is a perfume?

10 What city is a famous President?

11 What city likes to wander about?

12 What city is a place on which to play a game?

1 Davenport 2 Flint 3 Reading 4 Manila 5 Newark
6 Little Rock 7 Havana 8 Salt Lake City 9 Cologne
10 Lincoln (or Washington) 11 Rome 12 Bowling Green

JACKS
OF ALL
TRADES

1 **What Jack is a woodsman?**
   Lumberjack.

2 **What Jack has a head but no body?**
   Jack-o-Lantern.

3 **What Jack paints people's windows?**
   Jack Frost.

4 **What Jack's name takes too long to say?**
   Jack Robinson.

5 **What Jacks do most of us wear?**
   Jackets.

6 **What Jack is performed in diving?**
   Jackknife.

7   What Jack helps to remove foot coverings?
    Bootjack.

8   What Jack flies on a British ship?
    Union Jack.

9   What Jack is a whiz?
    Crackerjack.

10 What Jack resembles a wolf?
    Jackal.

11 What Jack is a terrible disease?
    Yellowjack.

12 What Jack has no legs but jumps?
    Jack-in-the-box.

13 What Jack is always a sailor?
    Jack tar.

14 What Jack has strings?
    Jumping jack.

15 What Jack tastes good with syrup?
    Flapjack.

16 What Jack has long ears and a white tail?
    Jackrabbit.

17 What Jack do we seldom hit?
    Jackpot.

? 238

TRICKS
OF THE
TRADES

1 **What trade does the sun follow?**
   Tanner.

2 **What trade does the President follow?**
   Cabinet-maker.

3 **Of what trade is a man whose best works are always trampled on?**
   Shoemaker.

4 **Of what trade can it be said that all its members are men of letters?**
   Printing trade.

5 **What trade is best qualified to cook a rabbit?**
   Hairdressers (hare dressers).

6 What trade is noted among the authors of English literature?

Goldsmith.

7 Of what trade is the preacher at a wedding?

Joiner.

THE BISHOP'S RIDDLE

A famous old riddle is said to have been made up by the English Bishop Wilberforce. Here is his riddle:

I am a wonderful trunk, which contains the following articles: 1 A box. 2 Two lids. 3 Two musical instruments. 4 A number of articles that are indispensable to a carpenter. 5 Two tropical trees. 6 Two good fish. 7 A number of shellfish. 8 A fine stag. 9 A number of small animals, swift and shy. 10 Two playful animals. 11 Weapons of warfare. 12 Steps of a hotel. 13 Some whips without handles. 14 Two learners. 15 The upper edge of a hill. 16 A number of weathercocks. 17 Two established measures. 18 Two sides of a vote. 19 Fine flowers. 20 A fruit. 21 Two places of worship. 22 A possible remark of Nebuchadnezzar when eating grass. 23 Ten Spanish noblemen. 24 A desert place. 25 Part of a bell. 26 A garden vegetable. 27 An isthmus.

The trunk is the human body. It contains: 1 Chest.
2 Eyelids. 3 Eardrums. 4 Nails. 5 Palms. 6 Soles.

7 Muscles (mussels). 8 Heart (hart). 9 Hairs (hares).
10 Calves. 11 Arms. 12 Insteps (inn steps). 13 Lashes.
14 Pupils. 15 Brow. 16 Veins (vanes). 17 Feet and hands.
18 Eyes and nose (ayes and noes). 19 Two lips (tulips).
20 Adam's apple. 21 Temples. 22 Eyebrows (I browse).
23 Tendons (ten dons). 24 Waist (waste). 25 Tongue.
26 Pulse. 27 Neck (of land).

FOR BIGGER, BETTER OR WORSE

1 **A man named Bigger got married. How did he compare in size with his wife?**

He was larger, for he always had been Bigger.

2 **Mrs. Bigger had a baby. Now who was bigger?**

The baby, because he was a little Bigger.

3 **Mr. Bigger died. Then who was bigger?**

Mrs. Bigger, for she was Bigger still.

4 **What is better than to give credit where credit is due?**

Give cash.

5 **What is better than presence of mind in a railroad accident?**

Absence of body.

243 ?

6 **What is worse than raining cats and dogs?**

Hailing buses.

7 **What is worse than a giraffe with a sore throat?**

A centipede with sore feet.